HYMNS OLD & NEW

New Century Edition

Compiled by
Kevin Mayhew

Music Editor
Joanne Clarke

Text Editor
Jo Donlevy

Kevin Mayhew

Every effort has been made to trace the owners of copyright material, and we hope that no copyright has been infringed. Pardon is sought and apology made if the contrary be the case, and a correction will be made in any reprint of this book.

By the same token we would remind the users of this book that many of the songs in this collection are copyright: further reproduction of any kind without the express permission of the copyright owner is both illegal and immoral. Copyright owners are clearly indicated in the Acknowledgement section.

Compilation © Kevin Mayhew Ltd
1977, 1979, 1983, 1984, 1989, 1994

First published in Great Britain in 1994 by
KEVIN MAYHEW LTD,
Rattlesden,
Bury St Edmunds,
Suffolk IP30 0SZ

The following editions are available

People's copy (Standard cover)	ISBN	0 86209 532 8
	Catalogue No	1405143
People's copy (Plastic cover)	ISBN	0 86209 533 6
	Catalogue No	1405144
Large Print (Standard cover)	ISBN	0 86209 534 4
	Catalogue No	1405145
Melody/Guitar (Hardback)	ISBN	0 86209 535 2
	Catalogue No	1405146
Organ/Choir (Hardback)	ISBN	0 86209 536 0
	Catalogue No	1405147

Front cover design by Graham Johnstone
Printed and bound in Great Britain

Foreword

This is the fourth revision of *Hymns Old & New* since it was first published in 1977. The original book contained just 163 hymns, each subsequent edition being added to, until by the 1986 edition there were 812 hymns. If the book was to be further revised the time had come for a radical review: *Hymns Old & New: New Century Edition* is the result.

Much of what was found in previous editions is still here, but a process of thorough consultation has highlighted those hymns which are no longer used and these have been omitted. Newer hymns and further borrowings from other Christian traditions have been added as well as the work of the remarkable writer Michael Forster. His labour of love in writing texts which reflect the themes of the Lectionary readings ensures that each week there is at least one hymn tailor-made for the liturgy.

As an editor and publisher I have been responsible for many of the Catholic hymn books of the second half of the twentieth century. Besides *Hymns Old & New* it has been my privilege to bring to birth *The Parish Hymnal, Praise the Lord, Twentieth Century Folk Hymnal, Celebration Hymnal* and *Songs of the Spirit*. I have never considered it a responsibility of editorship to impose my own taste on a hymn book. My purpose is to provide people with a tool to aid worship. Just as I do not expect another to criticise my own way of praying, so I do not wish to exclude tried and tested material which other people find helpful. For this reason *Hymns Old & New* is an eclectic collection of old favourites,

standard hymns and newer compositions. Such diversity is to be welcomed. A Church that can, on the one hand, provide fine, formal liturgy incorporating great music, or sit on bean bags and sing 'Kum ba yah', on the other, is taking care to provide food and drink at each resting place on the spiritual journey.

From time to time it is necessary to examine texts for changes in meaning and emphasis – most of us can quote a line which sounded well when first written but would now be greeted with incredulity.

Another concern of many people has been the over-emphasis to modern ears of the masculine pronoun in hymnody. Where a minor amendment can eliminate this problem I have not hesitated to make it. Where this has been done it is attested by the indication, alt. Living authors whom I approached on this matter have been willing without exception to revise their texts. It is my earnest hope that those who use *Hymns Old & New* will feel that these small emendations have been done with skill and sensitivity, and that their inclusion will further affirm the position of Catholic women.

The singing of hymns and psalms in worship pre-dates Christianity. It is something that Jesus himself would have been familiar with in the temple, and he certainly sang at the Last Supper – 'After psalms had been sung they left for the Mount of Olives', writes Matthew in his account of the institution of the Eucharist. What a wonderful tradition we share!

KEVIN MAYHEW

1

*A new commandment
I give unto you:
that you love one another
as I have loved you,
that you love one another
as I have loved you.*

1. By this shall mankind
   know you are my disciples
   if you have love one for another.
   By this shall mankind
   know you are my disciples
   if you have love one for another.

2. You are my friends
   if you do what I command you.
   Without my help you can do nothing.
   You are my friends
   if you do what I command you.
   Without my help you can do nothing.

3. I am the true vine,
   my Father is the gard'ner.
   Abide in me: I will be with you.
   I am the true vine,
   my Father is the gard'ner.
   Abide in me: I will be with you.

4. True love is patient,
   not arrogant nor boastful;
   love bears all things, love is eternal.
   True love is patient,
   not arrogant nor boastful;
   love bears all things, love is eternal.

*Unknown, based on John 13:34-35,
John 15 and 1 Cor 13*

2

*Abba, Abba, Father.
You are the potter,
we are the clay,
the work of your hands.*

1. Mould us, mould us and fashion us
   into the image of Jesus, your Son,
   of Jesus, your Son.

2. Father, may we be one in you,
   as he is in you and you are in him,
   and you are in him.

3. Glory, glory and praise to you,
   glory and praise to you for ever, amen,
   for ever, amen.

Carey Landry
© 1977 North American Liturgy Resources

3

*Abba, Father, let me be
yours and yours alone.
May my will for ever be
evermore your own.
Never let my heart grow cold,
never let me go.
Abba, Father, let me be
yours and yours alone.*

Dave Bilbrough
© 1977 Kingsway's Thankyou Music

4

1. Abba, Father, send your Spirit.
   Glory, Jesus Christ.
   Abba, Father, send your Spirit.
   Glory, Jesus Christ.

   *Glory, hallelujah, glory, Jesus Christ!
   Glory, hallelujah, glory, Jesus Christ!*

2. I will give you living water.

3. If you seek me you will find me.

4. If you listen you will hear me.

Continued overleaf

5. Come, my children, I will teach you.

Glory, hallelujah, glory, Jesus Christ!
Glory, hallelujah, glory, Jesus Christ!

6. I'm your shepherd, I will lead you.

7. Peace I leave you, peace I give you.

8. I'm your life and resurrection.

9. Glory, Father, glory, Spirit.

Other words from Scripture may be substituted
according to the occasion or the season.
For example, in Advent:

10. Come, Lord Jesus, Light of nations.

11. Come, Lord Jesus, born of Mary.

12. Come, and show the Father's glory.

Verses 1-9: Sister Virginia Vissing
Verses 10-12: Damian Lundy (b. 1944)

5

1. Abide with me,
   fast falls the eventide;
   the darkness deepens,
   Lord, with me abide!
   When other helpers fail,
   and comforts flee,
   help of the helpless,
   O abide with me.

2. Swift to its close
   ebbs out life's little day;
   earth's joys grow dim,
   its glories pass away;
   change and decay
   in all around I see;
   O thou who changest not,
   abide with me.

3. I need thy presence
   every passing hour;
   what but thy grace can foil
   the tempter's power?
   Who like thyself my guide
   and stay can be?
   Through cloud and sunshine,
   O abide with me.

4. I fear no foe
   with thee at hand to bless;
   ills have no weight,
   and tears no bitterness.
   Where is death's sting?
   Where, grave, thy victory?
   I triumph still,
   if thou abide with me.

5. Hold thou thy cross
   before my closing eyes;
   shine through the gloom,
   and point me to the skies;
   heaven's morning breaks,
   and earth's vain shadows flee;
   in life, in death, O Lord,
   abide with me!

Henry Francis Lyte (1793-1847)

6

1. Accept, O Father, in thy love,
   these humble gifts of bread and wine,
   that with ourselves we offer thee,
   returning gifts already thine.

2. Behold this host and chalice, Lord,
   to thee in heaven the gifts we raise;
   through them may we our homage pay,
   our adoration and our praise.

3. No earthly claim to grace is ours,
   save what thy sacrifice has won;
   grant then thy grace, fulfil our needs,
   and may thy will in ours be done.

J. Clifford Evers

7

1. Adeste fideles,
   læti triumphantes;
   venite, venite in Bethlehem;
   natum videte regem angelorum:

   Venite adoremus,
   venite adoremus,
   venite adoremus Dominum.

2. Deum de Deo,
   lumen de lumine,
   gestant puellæ viscera:
   Deum verum, genitum, non factum:

3. Cantet nunc Io!
   Chorus angelorum:
   cantet nunc aula cælestium;
   Gloria in excelsis Deo!

4. Ergo qui natus
   die hodierna,
   Jesu tibi sit gloria:
   Patris æterni Verbum caro factum!
   John Wade (1711-1786)

8

Adoramus te, Domine.

1. With the angels and archangels:

2. With the patriarchs and prophets:

3. With the virgin Mary, mother of God:

4. With the apostles and evangelists:

5. With all the martyrs of Christ:

6. With all who witness to the Gospel
   of the Lord:

7. With all your people of the church
   throughout the world:
   Taizé Community

9

Alabaré, alabaré, alabaré a mi Señor.
Alabaré, alabaré, alabaré a mi Señor.

1. John saw the number
   of all those redeemed,
   and all were singing praises to the Lord.
   Thousands were praying,
   ten thousand rejoicing,
   and all were singing praises to the Lord.

2. There is no god as great
   as you, O Lord,
   there is none, there is none.
   There is no god as great
   as you, O Lord,
   there is none, there is none.
   There is no god who does the
   mighty wonders that the
   Lord our God has done.
   There is no god who does the
   mighty wonders that the
   Lord our God has done.
   Neither with an army,
   nor with their weapons,
   but by the Holy Spirit's power.
   Neither with an army,
   nor with their weapons,
   but by the Holy Spirit's power.
   And even mountains shall be moved,
   and even mountains shall be moved,
   and even mountains shall be moved
   by the Holy Spirit's power.

3. And even England* shall be saved,
   and even England shall be saved,
   and even England shall be saved
   by the Holy Spirit's power.

*or Scotland, Ireland, Wales, or wherever you
live. (The Spanish phrase 'Alabaré a mi Señor'
translates as 'I will praise my Lord')*

Unknown

10

1. All creation, bless the Lord.
   Earth and heaven, bless the Lord.
   Spirits, powers, bless the Lord.
   Praise him for ever.
   Sun and moon, bless the Lord.
   Stars and planets, bless the Lord.
   Dews and showers, bless the Lord.
   Praise him for ever.

2. Winds and breezes, bless the Lord.
   Spring and autumn, bless the Lord.
   Winter, summer, bless the Lord.
   Praise him for ever.
   Fire and heat, bless the Lord.
   Frost and cold, bless the Lord.
   Ice and snow, bless the Lord.
   Praise him for ever.

3. Night and daytime, bless the Lord.
   Light and darkness, bless the Lord.
   Clouds and lightning, bless the Lord.
   Praise him for ever.
   All the earth, bless the Lord.
   Hills and mountains, bless the Lord.
   Trees and flowers, bless the Lord.
   Praise him for ever.

4. Springs and rivers, bless the Lord.
   Seas and oceans, bless the Lord.
   Whales and fishes, bless the Lord.
   Praise him for ever.
   Birds and insects, bless the Lord.
   Beasts and cattle, bless the Lord.
   Let all creatures bless the Lord.
   Praise him for ever.

5. Let God's people bless the Lord.
   Men and women, bless the Lord.
   All creation, bless the Lord.
   Praise him for ever.
   Let God's people bless the Lord.
   Men and women, bless the Lord.
   All creation, bless the Lord.
   Praise him for ever.

Hayward Osborne

11

1. All creatures of our God and King,
   lift up your voice and with us sing
   alleluia, alleluia!
   Thou burning sun with golden beam,
   thou silver moon with softer gleam:

   O praise him, O praise him,
   alleluia, alleluia, alleluia.

2. Thou rushing wind that art so strong,
   ye clouds that sail in heav'n along,
   O praise him, alleluia!
   Thou rising morn, in praise rejoice,
   ye lights of evening, find a voice:

3. Thou flowing water, pure and clear,
   make music for thy Lord to hear,
   alleluia, alleluia!
   Thou fire so masterful and bright,
   that givest us both warmth and light:

4. Dear mother earth, who day by day
   unfoldest blessings on our way,
   O praise him, alleluia!
   The flowers and fruits that in thee grow
   let them his glory also show.

5. All you with mercy in your heart,
   forgiving others, take your part,
   O sing ye, alleluia!
   Ye who long pain and sorrow bear,
   praise God and on him cast your care:

6. And thou, most kind and gentle death,
   waiting to hush our latest breath,
   O praise him, alleluia!
   Thou leadest home the child of God,
   and Christ our Lord the way hath trod:

7. Let all things their Creator bless,
   and worship him in humbleness,
   O praise him, alleluia!
   Praise, praise the Father,
   praise the Son,
   and praise the Spirit, Three in One.

   William Henry Draper (1855-1933) alt.,
   based on the 'Cantico Di Frate Sole'
   of St Francis of Assisi (1182-1226)

12

All glory, laud and honour,
to thee, Redeemer King,
to whom the lips of children
made sweet hosannas ring.

1. Thou art the King of Israel,
   thou David's royal Son,
   who in the Lord's name comest,
   the king and blessèd one.

2. The company of angels
   are praising thee on high,
   and mortals, joined with all things
   created, make reply.

3. The people of the Hebrews
   with palms before thee went:
   our praise and prayer and anthems
   before thee we present.

4. To thee before thy passion
   they sang their hymns of praise:
   to thee now high exalted
   our melody we raise.

5. Thou didst accept their praises,
   accept the prayers we bring,
   who in all good delightest,
   thou good and gracious king.

   St Theodulph of Orleans (d. 821)
   tr. John Mason Neale (1818-1866) alt.

13

All glory to you, Redeemer and Lord,
Son of the Father.

1. Lord Jesus Christ, to you be glory,
   alleluia.
   For you reign with your Father,
   alleluia.

2. Lord Jesus Christ, to you be glory,
   alleluia.
   You were born of the virgin,
   alleluia.

3. Lord Jesus Christ, to you be glory,
   alleluia.
   You fought evil and conquered,
   alleluia.

4. Lord Jesus Christ, to you be glory,
   alleluia.
   Risen Lord, we acclaim you,
   alleluia.

5. Lord Jesus Christ, to you be glory,
   alleluia.
   You have ransomed God's people,
   alleluia.

6. Lord Jesus Christ, to you be glory,
   alleluia.
   You have made us God's children,
   alleluia.

7. Lord Jesus Christ, to you be glory,
   alleluia.
   Lead us all to your kingdom,
   alleluia.

   Damian Lundy (b. 1944)

14

1. All God's people, come together,
   worship the King!
   For his love will last for ever,
   worship the King!
   Through life's struggles he'll be with us,
   he'll be guiding, watching o'er us.
   We rejoice, sing hallelujah,
   worship the King!

2. All God's people, pray together,
   peace to the world,
   loving brother, loving sister,
   peace to the world!
   God is love and God is kindness,
   he will guide us through the darkness.
   We rejoice, sing hallelujah,
   peace to the world!

3. All God's people, love each other,
   glory to God!
   Though we die we live for ever,
   glory to God!
   We will enter life eternal,
   chosen, blessed, for ever praising.
   We rejoice, sing hallelujah,
   glory to God!

Peter Watcyn-Jones (b. 1944)

15

1. All hail the pow'r of Jesus' name;
   let angels prostrate fall;
   bring forth the royal diadem
   to crown him, crown him,
   crown him, crown him Lord of all.

2. Crown him, ye martyrs of your God,
   who from his altar call;
   praise him whose way of pain ye trod,
   and crown him Lord of all.

3. Ye prophets who our freedom won,
   ye searchers, great and small,
   by whom the work of truth is done,
   now crown him Lord of all.

4. Sinners, whose love can ne'er forget
   the wormwood and the gall,
   go spread your trophies at his feet,
   and crown him Lord of all.

5. Bless him, each poor oppressèd race
   that Christ did upward call;
   his hand in each achievement trace,
   and crown him Lord of all.

6. Let every tribe and every tongue
   to him their hearts enthral:
   lift high the universal song,
   and crown him Lord of all.

Edward Perronet (1726-1792)

16

1. All my hope on God is founded;
   he doth still my trust renew.
   Me through change and chance
     he guideth,
   only good and only true.
   God unknown, he alone
   calls my heart to be his own.

2. Pride of man and earthly glory,
   sword and crown betray God's trust;
   what with lavish care man buildeth,
   tower and temple, fall to dust.
   But God's power, hour by hour,
   is my temple and my tower.

3. God's great goodness ay endureth,
   deep his wisdom, passing thought:
   splendour, light and life attend him,
   beauty springeth out of nought.
   Evermore, from his store,
   new-born worlds rise and adore.

4. Still from earth to God eternal
   sacrifice of praise be done,
   high above all praises praising
   for the gift of Christ his Son.
   Christ doth call one and all:
   ye who follow shall not fall.

   Robert Bridges (1844-1930) based on the German
   of Joachim Neander (1650-1680)

17

1. All over the world
   the Spirit is moving,
   all over the world,
   as the prophets said it would be.
   All over the world
   there's a mighty revelation
   of the glory of the Lord,
   as the waters cover the sea.

2. All over this land.

3. All over the church.

4. All over us all.

5. Deep down in my heart.

   Roy Turner (b. 1940)
   © 1984 Kingsway's Thankyou Music

18

1. All people that on earth do dwell,
   sing to the Lord with cheerful voice;
   him serve with fear, his praise forth tell,
   come ye before him and rejoice.

2. The Lord, ye know, is God indeed,
   without our aid he did us make;
   we are his folk, he doth us feed
   and for his sheep he doth us take.

3. O enter then his gates with praise,
   approach with joy his courts unto;
   praise, laud and bless his name always,
   for it is seemly so to do.

4. For why, the Lord our God is good:
   his mercy is for ever sure;
   his truth at all times firmly stood,
   and shall from age to age endure.

5. To Father, Son and Holy Ghost,
   the God whom heaven and earth adore,
   from us and from the angel-host
   be praise and glory evermore.

   William Kethe (d. 1594),
   from 'Day's Psalter' (1560) alt.

19

1. All that I am, all that I do,
   all that I'll ever have I offer now to you.
   Take and sanctify these gifts
   for your honour, Lord.
   Knowing that I love and serve you
   is enough reward.
   All that I am, all that I do,
   all that I'll ever have I offer now to you.

2. All that I dream, all that I pray,
   all that I'll ever make I give to you today.
   Take and sanctify these gifts
   for your honour, Lord.
   Knowing that I love and serve you
   is enough reward.
   All that I am, all that I do,
   all that I'll ever have I offer now to you.

   Sebastian Temple (b. 1928)

20

All the earth proclaim the Lord,
sing your praise to God.

1. Serve you the Lord, heart filled
    with gladness.
    Come into his presence, singing for joy.

2. Know that the Lord is our creator.
    Yes, he is our Father, we are his own.

3. We are the sheep of his green pasture,
    for we are his people; he is our God.

4. Enter his gates bringing thanksgiving,
    O enter his courts while singing
        his praise.

5. Our Lord is good, his love enduring,
    his Word is abiding now with us all.

6. Honour and praise be to the Father,
    the Son, and the Spirit, world
        without end.

Lucien Deiss (b. 1921), based on Psalm 100, alt.

21

All the ends of the earth,
all you creatures of the sea,
lift up your eyes
to the wonders of the Lord.
For the Lord of the earth,
the Master of the sea,
has come with justice for the world.

1. Break into song at the deeds
        of the Lord,
    the wonders he has done in ev'ry age.

2. Heaven and earth shall rejoice in
        his might;
    ev'ry heart, ev'ry nation call him Lord.

3. The Lord has made his salvation known,
    faithful to his promises of old.
    Let the sea of the earth,
    let the sea and all it holds
    make music before our King!

Bob Dufford based on Psalm 98
© Copyright 1981 New Dawn Music

22

All the nations of the earth,
praise the Lord who brings to birth
the greatest star, the smallest flower.
Alleluia.

1. Let the heavens praise the Lord,
    alleluia.
    Moon and stars, praise the Lord,
    alleluia.

2. Snow-capped mountains, praise the
        Lord,
    alleluia.
    Rolling hills, praise the Lord,
    alleluia.

3. Deep sea water, praise the Lord,
    alleluia.
    Gentle rain, praise the Lord,
    alleluia.

4. Roaring lion, praise the Lord,
    alleluia.
    Singing birds, praise the Lord,
    alleluia.

5. Kings and princes, praise the Lord,
    alleluia.
    Young and old, praise the Lord,
    alleluia.

Michael Cockett (b. 1938)

23

All things bright and beautiful,
all creatures great and small,
all things wise and wonderful,
the Lord God made them all.

1. Each little flow'r that opens,
   each little bird that sings,
   he made their glowing colours,
   he made their tiny wings.

2. The purple-headed mountain,
   the river running by,
   the sunset and the morning,
   that brightens up the sky.

3. The cold wind in the winter,
   the pleasant summer sun,
   the ripe fruits in the garden,
   he made them ev'ry one.

4. The tall trees in the greenwood,
   the meadows for our play,
   the rushes by the water,
   to gather ev'ry day.

5. He gave us eyes to see them,
   and lips that we may tell
   how great is God Almighty,
   who has made all things well.

   Cecil Frances Alexander (1818-1895)

24

1. All ye who seek a comfort sure
   in trouble and distress,
   whatever sorrow vex the mind,
   or guilt the soul oppress:

2. Jesus, who gave himself for you
   upon the cross to die,
   opens to you his sacred heart;
   O, to that heart draw nigh.

3. Ye hear how kindly he invites;
   ye hear his words so blest:
   'All ye that labour, come to me,
   and I will give you rest.'

4. What meeker than the
       Saviour's heart?
   As on the cross he lay,
   it did his murderers forgive,
   and for their pardon pray.

5. O heart, thou joy of saints on high,
   thou hope of sinners here,
   attracted by those loving words
   to thee I lift my prayer.

6. Wash thou my wounds in that
       dear blood
   which forth from thee doth flow;
   new grace, new hope inspire, a new
   and better heart bestow.

   18th century Latin tr. Edward Caswall (1814-1878)

25

All you nations,
sing out your joy to the Lord;
alleluia, alleluia.

1. Joyfully shout, all you on earth,
   give praise to the glory of God;
   and with a hymn
   sing out his glorious praise;
   alleluia!

Continued overleaf

2. Lift up your hearts; sing to your God;
   tremendous his deeds on the earth!
   Vanquished your foes,
   struck down by power and might;
   alleluia!

   All you nations,
   sing out your joy to the Lord;
   alleluia, alleluia.

3. Let all the earth kneel in his sight,
   extolling his marvellous fame;
   honour his name,
   in highest heaven give praise;
   alleluia!

4. Come forth and see all the great works
   that God has brought forth by his might;
   fall on your knees
   before his glorious throne;
   alleluia!

5. Parting the seas with might and power,
   he rescued his people from shame;
   let us give thanks
   for all his merciful deeds;
   alleluia!

6. His eyes keep watch on all the earth,
   his strength is forever renewed;
   and let no-one
   rebel against his commands;
   alleluia!

7. Tested are we by God the Lord,
   as silver is tested by fire;
   burdened with pain,
   we fall ensnared in our sins;
   alleluia!

8. Over our heads wicked ones rode;
   we passed through the fire and
      the flood;
   then, Lord, you brought
   your people into your peace;
   alleluia!

9. Glory and thanks be to the Father;
   honour and praise to the Son;
   and to the Spirit,
   source of life and of love;
   alleluia!

Lucien Deiss (b. 1921), based on Psalm 66, alt.

26

Alleluia, alleluia,
give thanks to the risen Lord,
alleluia, alleluia,
give praise to his name.

1. Jesus is Lord of all the earth.
   He is the King of creation.

2. Spread the good news o'er all the earth.
   Jesus has died and is risen.

3. We have been crucified with Christ.
   Now we shall live for ever.

4. God has proclaimed the just reward:
   life eternal for all who believe.

5. Come, let us praise the living God,
   joyfully sing to our Saviour.

Donald Fishel (b. 1950) alt.

27

1. Alleluia, sing to Jesus,
   his the sceptre, his the throne;
   alleluia, his the triumph,
   his the victory alone:
   hark the songs of peaceful Sion
   thunder like a mighty flood:
   Jesus, out of ev'ry nation,
   hath redeemed us by his blood.

2. Alleluia, not as orphans
   are we left in sorrow now;
   alleluia, he is near us,
   faith believes, nor questions how;
   though the cloud from sight
     received him
   when the forty days were o'er,
   shall our hearts forget his promise,
   'I am with you evermore'?

3. Alleluia, Bread of Angels,
   thou on earth our food, our stay;
   alleluia, here the sinful
   flee to thee from day to day;
   intercessor, friend of sinners,
   earth's Redeemer, plead for me,
   where the songs of all the sinless
   sweep across the crystal sea.

4. Alleluia, King eternal,
   thee the Lord of lords we own;
   alleluia, born of Mary,
   earth thy footstool, heaven thy throne;
   thou within the veil hast entered
   robed in flesh, our great High Priest;
   thou on earth both priest and victim
   in the Eucharistic Feast.

   William Chatterton Dix (1837-1898)

28

Alma redemptoris mater,
quæ pervia cæli porta manes,
et stella maris, succurre cadenti,
surgere qui curat populo:
tu quæ genuisti, natura mirante,
tuum sanctum genitorem:
virgo prius ac posterius,
Gabrielis ab ore sumens illud ave,
peccatorum miserere.

Hermann the Lame (d. 1054)

29

1. Almighty Father, Lord most high,
   who madest all, who fillest all,
   thy name we praise and magnify,
   for all our needs on thee we call.

2. We offer to thee of thine own,
   ourselves and all that we can bring,
   in bread and cup before thee shown,
   our universal offering.

3. All that we have we bring to thee,
   yet all is naught when all is done,
   save that in it thy love can see
   the sacrifice of thy dear Son.

4. By this command in bread and cup,
   his body and his blood we plead;
   what on the cross he offered up
   is here our sacrifice indeed.

5. For all thy gifts of life and grace,
   here we thy servants humbly pray
   that thou wouldst look upon the face
   of thine anointed Son today.

   Vincent Stuckey Stratton Coles (1845-1929)

30

1. Almighty Father, take this bread
   thy people offer thee;
   where sins divide us, take instead
   one fold and family.

2. The wine we offer soon will be
   Christ's blood, redemption's price;
   receive it, Holy Trinity,
   this holy sacrifice.

3. O God, by angels' choirs adored,
   thy name be praised on earth;
   on all may be that peace outpoured
   once promised at his birth.

   Unknown, alt.

31

1. Amazing grace! How sweet the sound
   that saved a wretch like me.
   I once was lost, but now I'm found;
   was blind, but now I see.

2. 'Twas grace that taught my heart
      to fear,
   and grace my fears relieved.
   How precious did that grace appear
   the hour I first believed.

3. Through many dangers, toils and snares
   I have already come.
   'Tis grace hath brought me safe
      thus far,
   and grace will lead me home.

4. The Lord has promised good to me,
   his word my hope secures.
   He will my shield and portion be
   as long as life endures.

   John Newton (1725-1807)

32

1. And can it be that I should gain
   an int'rest in the Saviour's blood?
   Died he for me, who caused his pain?
   For me, who him to death pursued?
   Amazing love! How can it be
   that thou, my God, shouldst die for me?

   Amazing love! How can it be
   that thou, my God, shouldst die for me?

2. 'Tis myst'ry all! The Immortal dies:
   who can explore his strange design?
   In vain the first-born seraph tries
   to sound the depths of love divine!
   'Tis mercy all! Let earth adore,
   let angel minds inquire no more.

3. He left his Father's throne above
   so free, so infinite his grace;
   emptied himself of all but love,
   and bled for Adam's helpless race;
   'tis mercy all, immense and free;
   for, O my God, it found out me.

4. Long my imprisoned spirit lay
   fast bound in sin and nature's night;
   thine eye diffused a quickening ray,
   I woke, the dungeon flamed with light;
   my chains fell off, my heart was free;
   I rose, went forth, and followed thee.

5. No condemnation now I dread;
   Jesus, and all in him, is mine!
   Alive in him, my living Head,
   and clothed in righteousness divine,
   bold I approach the eternal throne,
   and claim the crown, through
      Christ my own.

   Charles Wesley (1707-1788)

33

1. And did those feet in ancient time
   walk upon England's mountains green?
   And was the holy Lamb of God
   on England's pleasant pastures seen?
   And did the countenance divine
   shine forth upon our clouded hills?
   And was Jerusalem builded here
   among those dark satanic mills?

2. Bring me my bow of burning gold!
   Bring me my arrows of desire!
   Bring me my spear! O clouds, unfold!
   Bring me my chariot of fire!
   I will not cease from mental fight,
   nor shall my sword sleep in my hand,
   till we have built Jerusalem
   in England's green and pleasant land.

   William Blake (1757-1827)

34

1. Angel voices ever singing
   round thy throne of light,
   angel harps for ever ringing,
   rest not day or night;
   thousands only live to bless thee,
   and confess thee
   Lord of might.

2. Thou who art beyond the farthest
   mortal eye can scan,
   can it be that thou regardest
   songs of sinful man?
   Can we know that thou art near us
   and wilt hear us?
   Yes, we can.

3. Yes, we know that thou rejoicest
   o'er each work of thine;
   thou didst ears and hands and voices
   for thy praise design;
   craftsmen's art and music's measure
   for thy pleasure
   all combine.

4. In thy house, great God, we offer
   of thine own to thee;
   and for thine acceptance proffer
   all unworthily,
   hearts and minds
     and hands and voices
   in our choicest
   psalmody.

5. Honour, glory, might and merit,
   thine shall ever be,
   Father, Son and Holy Spirit,
   blessèd Trinity.
   Of the best that thou hast given
   earth and heaven
   render thee.

Francis Pott (1832-1909)

35

1. Angels we have heard in heaven
   sweetly singing o'er our plains;
   and the mountain tops in answer
   echoing their joyous strains.

   Gloria in excelsis Deo.
   Gloria in excelsis Deo.

2. Shepherds, why this exultation?
   Why your rapturous strain prolong?
   Tell us of the gladsome tidings
   which inspire your joyous song.

3. Come to Bethlehem, and see him
   o'er whose birth the angels sing:
   come, adore, devoutly kneeling,
   Christ the Lord, the new-born King.

4. See him in a manger lying
   whom the choir of angels praise!
   Mary, Joseph, come to aid us
   while our hearts in love we raise.

James Chadwick (1813-1882)

36

1. Angels we have heard on high
   sweetly singing o'er our plains,
   and the mountains in reply
   echo still their joyous strains.

   Gloria in excelsis Deo.
   Gloria in excelsis Deo.

2. Shepherds, why this jubilee?
   Why your rapturous strain prolong?
   Say, what may your tidings be,
   which inspire your heavenly song.

Continued overleaf

3. Come to Bethlehem and see
him whose birth the angels sing:
come, adore on bended knee
the infant Christ, the new-born King.

Gloria in excelsis Deo.
Gloria in excelsis Deo.

4. See within a manger laid,
Jesus, Lord of heaven and earth!
Mary, Joseph, lend your aid
to celebrate our Saviour's birth.

James Chadwick (1813-1882)

37

Arise, come to your God,
sing him your songs of rejoicing!

1. Cry out with **joy** to the **Lord**,
all the **earth.**
Serve the Lord with **glad**ness.
Come be**fore** him, **sing**ing for **joy.**

2. Know that **he**, the **Lord**, is **God.**
He **made** us, we be**long** to **him**,
we are his **peo**ple,
the **sheep** of his **flock.**

3. **Go** within his **gates**, giving **thanks.**
Enter his **courts** with **songs** of **praise.**
Give **thanks** to him
and **bless** his **name.**

4. In**deed**, how **good** is the **Lord**,
e**ter**nal his **mer**ciful **love;**
he is **faith**ful from **age** to **age.**

5. Give **glo**ry to the **Father** Al**migh**ty,
to his **Son**, Jesus **Christ**, the **Lord**,
to the **Spirit** who **dwells** in our **hearts.**

Psalm 99, Grail translation

38

1. As earth that is dry
and parched in the sun
lies waiting for rain,
my soul is a desert,
arid and waste;
it longs for your word, O Lord.

Come to the waters,
all you who thirst,
come, now, and eat my bread.

2. Though you have no money,
come, buy my corn
and drink my red wine.
Why spend precious gold
on what will not last?
Hear me, and your soul will live.

3. As one on a journey
strays from the road
and falls in the dark,
my mind is a wand'rer,
choosing wrong paths
and longing to find a star.

4. The Lord is your light,
the Lord is your strength,
turn back to him now,
for his ways are not
the ways you would choose,
and his thoughts are always new.

5. As rain from the mountains
falls on the land
and brings forth the seed,
the word of the Lord
sinks deep in our hearts,
creating the flow'r of truth.

Anne Conway (b. 1940)
based on Isaiah 55

39

1. As I kneel before you,
   as I bow my head in prayer,
   take this day, make it yours
   and fill me with your love.

   Ave, Maria, gratia plena,
   Dominus tecum, benedicta tu.

2. All I have I give you,
   ev'ry dream and wish are yours;
   mother of Christ, mother of mine,
   present them to my Lord.

3. As I kneel before you,
   and I see your smiling face,
   ev'ry thought, ev'ry word
   is lost in your embrace.

   Maria Parkinson (b. 1956)

40

1. As the deer pants for the water,
   so my soul longs after you.
   You alone are my heart's desire
   and I long to worship you.

   You alone are my strength, my shield,
   to you alone may my spirit yield.
   You alone are my heart's desire
   and I long to worship you.

2. I want you more than gold or silver,
   only you can satisfy.
   You alone are the real joy-giver
   and the apple of my eye.

3. You're my friend and you are
   my brother,
   even though you are a King.
   I love you more than any other,
   so much more than anything.

   Martin Nystrom based on Psalm 42:1-2
   © 1983 Restoration Music/Sovereign Lifestyle Music Ltd.

41

1. As with gladness men of old
   did the guiding star behold,
   as with joy they hailed its light,
   leading onward, beaming bright,
   so, most gracious God, may we
   evermore be led to thee.

2. As with joyful steps they sped,
   to that lowly manger-bed,
   there to bend the knee before
   him whom heaven and earth adore,
   so may we with willing feet
   ever seek thy mercy-seat.

3. As they offered gifts most rare,
   at that manger rude and bare,
   so may we with holy joy,
   pure, and free from sin's alloy,
   all our costliest treasures bring,
   Christ, to thee our heav'nly King.

4. Holy Jesu, every day
   keep us in the narrow way;
   and, when earthly things are past,
   bring our ransomed souls at last
   where they need no star to guide,
   where no clouds thy glory hide.

5. In the heav'nly country bright
   need they no created light,
   thou its light, its joy, its crown,
   thou its sun which goes not down;
   there for ever may we sing
   alleluias to our King.

   William Chatterton Dix (1837-1898)

42

1. At the cross her station keeping,
   stood the mournful mother weeping,
   close to Jesus to the last.

2. Through her heart, his sorrow sharing,
   all his bitter anguish bearing,
   now at length the sword has passed.

3. O, how sad and sore distressed
   was that mother highly blest,
   of the sole-begotten One.

4. Christ above in torment hangs;
   she beneath beholds the pangs
   of her dying glorious Son.

5. Is there one who would not weep,
   whelmed in miseries so deep,
   Christ's dear mother to behold?

6. Can the human heart refrain
   from partaking in her pain,
   in that mother's pain untold?

7. Bruised, derided, cursed, defiled,
   she beheld her tender child,
   all with bloody scourges rent.

8. For the sins of his own nation,
   saw him hang in desolation,
   till his spirit forth he sent.

9. O thou mother! Fount of love!
   Touch my spirit from above,
   make my heart with thine accord.

10. Make me feel as thou hast felt;
    make my soul to glow and melt
    with the love of Christ my Lord.

11. Holy Mother, pierce me through,
    in my heart each wound renew
    of my Saviour crucified.

12. Let me share with thee his pain
    who for all my sins was slain,
    who for me in torments died.

13. Let me mingle tears with thee,
    mourning him who mourned for me,
    all the days that I may live.

14. By the cross with thee to stay,
    there with thee to weep and pray,
    this I ask of thee to give.

Ascribed to Jacopone da Todi (d. 1306)
tr. Edward Caswall (1814-1878)

43

1. At the name of Jesus
   ev'ry knee shall bow,
   ev'ry tongue confess him
   King of glory now;
   'tis the Father's pleasure
   we should call him Lord,
   who from the beginning,
   was the mighty Word.

2. At his voice creation
   sprang at once to sight,
   all the angels' faces,
   all the hosts of light,
   thrones and dominations,
   stars upon their way,
   all the heavenly orders
   in their great array.

3. Humbled for a season,
   to receive a name
   from the lips of sinners
   unto whom he came,
   faithfully he bore it,
   spotless to the last,
   brought it back victorious
   when from death he passed.

4. Bore it up triumphant,
   with its human light,
   through all ranks of creatures
   to the central height,
   to the throne of Godhead,
   to the Father's breast,
   filled it with the glory
   of that perfect rest.

5. Name him, Christians, name him,
   with love as strong as death;
   but with awe and wonder,
   and with bated breath.
   He is God the Saviour,
   he is Christ the Lord,
   ever to be worshipped,
   trusted and adored.

6. In your hearts enthrone him;
   there let him subdue
   all that is not holy,
   all that is not true;
   crown him as your captain;
   in temptation's hour
   let his will enfold you
   in its light and power.

7. Christians, this Lord Jesus
   shall return again,
   with his Father's glory,
   with his angel train;
   for all wreaths of empire
   meet upon his brow,
   and our hearts confess him
   King of glory now.

   Caroline Maria Noel (1817-1877), alt.

44

1. Ave Maria, O maiden, O mother,
   fondly thy children are calling on thee;
   thine are the graces
   unclaimed by another,
   sinless and beautiful star of the sea.

Mater amabilis, ora pro nobis,
pray for thy children who call upon thee,
ave sanctissima, ave purissima,
sinless and beautiful star of the sea.

2. Ave Maria, the night shades are falling,
   softly, our voices arise unto thee;
   earth's lonely exiles
   for succour are calling
   sinless and beautiful star of the sea.

3. Ave Maria, thy children are kneeling,
   words of endearment
   are murmured to thee;
   softly thy spirit upon us is stealing,
   sinless and beautiful star of the sea.

   'Sister M'

45

Ave, Regina cælorum!
Ave, Domina angelorum!
Salve radix, salve porta,
ex qua mundo lux est orta.
Gaude Virgo gloriosa,
super omnes speciosa:
vale, o valde decora,
et pro nobis Christum exora.

Unknown, 12th century

46

1. Awake, awake and greet the new morn,
   for angels herald its dawning,
   sing out your joy, for now he is born,
   behold, the child of our longing.
   Come as a baby weak and poor,
   to bring all hearts together,
   he opens wide the heav'nly door
   and lives now inside us for ever.

Continued overleaf

2. To us, to all in sorrow and fear,
   Emmanuel comes a-singing,
   his humble song is quiet and near,
   yet fills the earth with its ringing;
   music to heal the broken soul
   and hymns of loving kindness,
   the thunder of his anthems roll
   to shatter all hatred and blindness.

3. In darkest night his coming shall be,
   when all the world is despairing,
   as morning light so quiet and free,
   so warm and gentle and caring.
   Then shall the mute break forth in song,
   the lame shall leap in wonder,
   the weak be raised above the strong,
   and weapons be broken asunder.

4. Rejoice, rejoice, take heart in the night,
   though dark the winter and cheerless,
   the rising sun shall crown you with light,
   be strong and loving and fearless;
   love be our song and love our prayer,
   and love our endless story,
   may God fill ev'ry day we share,
   and bring us at last into glory.

   Marty Haugen (b. 1950)

47

1. Away in a manger,
   no crib for a bed,
   the little Lord Jesus
   laid down his sweet head.
   The stars in the bright sky
   looked down where he lay,
   the little Lord Jesus,
   asleep on the hay.

2. The cattle are lowing,
   the baby awakes,
   but little Lord Jesus
   no crying he makes.
   I love thee, Lord Jesus!
   Look down from the sky,
   and stay by my side
   until morning is nigh.

3. Be near me, Lord Jesus;
   I ask thee to stay
   close by me for ever,
   and love me, I pray.
   Bless all the dear children
   in thy tender care,
   and fit us for heaven,
   to live with thee there.

   William James Kirkpatrick (1838-1921)

48

1. Battle is o'er, hell's armies flee:
   raise we the cry of victory
   with abounding joy resounding,
   alleluia, alleluia.

2. Christ who endured the shameful tree,
   o'er death triumphant welcome we,
   our adoring praise outpouring,
   alleluia, alleluia.

3. On the third morn from death rose he,
   clothed with what light in heaven
      shall be,
   our unswerving faith deserving,
   alleluia, alleluia.

4. Hell's gloomy gates yield up their key,
   paradise door thrown wide we see;
   never-tiring be our choiring,
   alleluia, alleluia.

5. Lord, by the stripes men laid on thee,
   grant us to live from death set free,
   this our greeting still repeating,
   alleluia, alleluia.

   'Simphonia Sirenum' (1695)
   tr. Ronald Arbuthnott Knox (1888-1957)

49

1. Be still and know I am with you,
   be still, I am the Lord.
   I will not leave you orphans.
   I leave with you my world. Be one.

2. You fear the light may be fading,
   you fear to lose your way.
   Be still, and know I am near you.
   I'll lead you to the day and the sun.

3. Be glad the day you have sorrow,
   be glad, for then you live.
   The stars shine only in darkness,
   and in your need I give my peace.

   Anne Conway (b. 1940)

50

1. Be still and know that I am God.
   Be still and know that I am God.
   Be still and know that I am God.

2. I am the Lord that healeth thee.
   I am the Lord that healeth thee.
   I am the Lord that healeth thee.

3. In thee, O Lord, I put my trust.
   In thee, O Lord, I put my trust.
   In thee, O Lord, I put my trust.

   Unknown, based on Psalm 46

51

1. Be still, for the presence of the Lord,
   the Holy One, is here;
   come, bow before him now,
   with reverence and fear.
   In him no sin is found,
   we stand on holy ground.
   Be still, for the presence of the Lord,
   the Holy One, is here.

2. Be still, for the glory of the Lord
   is shining all around;
   he burns with holy fire,
   with splendour he is crowned.
   How awesome is the sight,
   our radiant King of light!
   Be still, for the glory of the Lord
   is shining all around.

3. Be still, for the power of the Lord
   is moving in this place,
   he comes to cleanse and heal,
   to minister his grace.
   No work too hard for him,
   in faith receive from him;
   be still, for the power of the Lord
   is moving in this place.

   Dave Evans (b. 1957)
   © 1986 Kingsway's Thankyou Music

52

1. Be still, my soul:
   the Lord is on your side;
   bear patiently the cross
   of grief and pain;
   leave to your God
   to order and provide;
   in ev'ry change
   he faithful will remain.
   Be still, my soul:
   your best, your heav'nly friend,
   through thorny ways,
   leads to a joyful end.

Continued overleaf

2. Be still, my soul:
   your God will undertake
   to guide the future
   as he has the past.
   Your hope, your confidence
   let nothing shake,
   all now mysterious
   shall be clear at last.
   Be still, my soul:
   the tempests still obey
   his voice, who ruled them
   once on Galilee.

3. Be still, my soul:
   the hour is hastening on
   when we shall be for ever
   with the Lord,
   when disappointment,
   grief and fear are gone,
   sorrow forgotten,
   love's pure joy restored.
   Be still, my soul:
   when change and tears are past,
   all safe and blessèd
   we shall meet at last.

Katharina Von Schlegal (b. 1697)
tr. J.L. Barthwick

53

1. Be thou my vision,
   O Lord of my heart,
   naught be all else to me
   save that thou art;
   thou my best thought
   in the day and the night,
   waking or sleeping,
   thy presence my light.

2. Be thou my wisdom,
   be thou my true word,
   I ever with thee
   and thou with me, Lord;
   thou my great Father,
   and I thy true heir;
   thou in me dwelling,
   and I in thy care.

3. Be thou my breast-plate,
   my sword for the fight,
   be thou my armour,
   and be thou my might,
   thou my soul's shelter,
   and thou my high tower,
   raise thou me heavenward,
   O Power of my power.

4. Riches I need not,
   nor all the world's praise,
   thou mine inheritance
   through all my days;
   thou, and thou only,
   the first in my heart,
   high King of heaven,
   my treasure thou art!

5. High King of heaven
   when battle is done,
   grant heaven's joy to me,
   O bright heav'n's sun;
   Christ of my own heart,
   whatever befall,
   still be my vision,
   O Ruler of all.

Irish (c. 8th century)
tr. Mary Byrne (1880- 1931)
and Eleanor Hull (1860-1935), alt.

54

1. Because the Lord is my shepherd,
   I have ev'rything I need.
   He lets me rest in the meadow
   and leads me
   to the quiet streams.
   He restores my soul and he leads me
   in the paths that are right:

   Lord, you are my shepherd,
   you are my friend.
   I want to follow you always,
   just to follow my friend.

2. And when the road leads to darkness,
   I shall walk there unafraid.
   Even when death is close
   I have courage,
   for your help is there.
   You are close beside me with comfort,
   you are guiding my way:

3. In love you make me a banquet
   for my enemies to see.
   You make me welcome,
   pouring down honour
   from your mighty hand;
   and this joy fills me with gladness,
   it is too much to bear:

4. Your goodness always is with me
   and your mercy I know.
   Your loving kindness
   strengthens me always
   as I go through life.
   I shall dwell in your presence forever,
   giving praise to your name:

   Christopher Walker (b. 1947)
   based on Psalm 22 (23)
   © 1985 OCP Publications

55

1. Before the light of evening fades
   we pray, O Lord of all,
   that by your love we may be saved
   from ev'ry grievous fall.

2. Repel the terrors of the night
   and Satan's power of guile,
   impose a calm and restful sleep
   that nothing may defile.

3. Most holy Father, grant our prayer
   through Christ your only Son,
   that in your Spirit we may live
   and praise you ever one.

   'Te Lucis ante terminum'
   tr. Dom Ralph Wright (b. 1938)

56

Benedictus qui venit in nomine Domini.
Benedictus qui venit in nomine Domini.
Hosanna, hosanna, hosanna in excelsis.

   From the Roman Missal

57

1. Bethlehem, of noblest cities
   none can once with thee compare;
   thou alone the Lord from heaven
   didst for us incarnate bear.

2. Fairer than the sun at morning
   was the star that told his birth,
   to the lands their God announcing,
   hid beneath a form of earth.

Continued overleaf

3. By its lambent beauty guided,
   see the eastern kings appear;
   see them bend, their gifts to offer,
   gifts of incense, gold and myrrh.

4. Solemn things of mystic meaning!
   Incense doth the God disclose;
   gold a royal child proclaimeth;
   myrrh a future tomb foreshows.

5. Holy Jesu, in thy brightness
   to the gentile world displayed,
   with the Father and the Spirit,
   endless praise to thee be paid.

   Aurelius Clemens Prudentius (348-413)
   tr. Edward Caswall (1814-1878)

58

Bind us together, Lord,
bind us together with cords
that cannot be broken.
Bind us together, Lord,
bind us together, Lord,
bind us together in love.

1. There is only one God,
   there is only one King.
   There is only one Body,
   that is why we sing:

2. Fit for the glory of God,
   purchased by his precious Blood,
   born with the right to be free:
   Jesus the vict'ry has won.

3. We are the fam'ly of God,
   we are his promise divine,
   we are his chosen desire,
   we are the glorious new wine.

   Bob Gillman
   © 1977 Kingsway's Thankyou Music

59

Bless the Lord, my soul,
and bless his holy name.
Bless the Lord, my soul,
he rescues me from death.

Taizé Comunity, from Psalm 103

60

1. Bless the Lord, O my soul,
   bless the Lord, O my soul,
   and all that is within me,
   bless his holy name.

2. Praise the Lord, O my soul,
   praise the Lord, O my soul,
   and all that is within me,
   praise his holy name.

3. Love the Lord, O my soul,
   love the Lord, O my soul,
   and all that is within me,
   love his holy name.

   Unknown

61

1. Blessed are my people, says the Lord.
   Blessed are my people, says the Lord.

   Come to me, friends of mine,
   come share my life divine,
   come to the banquet of the Lord.

2. Blessed are the lonely, says the Lord.
   Blessed are the lonely, says the Lord.

3. Blessed are the humble, says the Lord.
   Blessed are the humble, says the Lord.

4. Blessed are the downcast, says the Lord.
   Blessed are the downcast, says the Lord.

5. Blessed are the gentle, says the Lord.
   Blessed are the gentle, says the Lord.

6. Blessed are the hungry, says the Lord.
   Blessed are the hungry, says the Lord.

Kevin Mayhew (b. 1942) based on The Beatitudes

62

1. Blest are the pure in heart,
   for they shall see our God;
   the secret of the Lord is theirs,
   their soul is Christ's abode.

2. The Lord who left the heavens
   our life and peace to bring,
   to dwell in lowliness with us,
   our pattern and our King.

3. Still to the lowly soul
   he doth himself impart,
   and for his dwelling and his throne
   chooseth the pure in heart.

4. Lord, we thy presence seek;
   may ours this blessing be:
   give us a pure and lowly heart,
   a temple meet for thee.

Vs 1, 3: John Keble (1792-1866),
Vs 2, 4: W. J. Hall's 'Psalms and Hymns' (1836), alt.

63

1. Blest are you, Lord, God of all creation,
   thanks to your goodness
   this bread we offer:
   fruit of the earth, work of our hands,
   it will become the bread of life.

Blessed be God! Blessed be God!
Blessed be God forever! Amen!
Blessed be God! Blessed be God!
Blessed be God forever! Amen!

2. Blest are you, Lord, God of all creation,
   thanks to your goodness
   this wine we offer:
   fruit of the earth, work of our hands,
   it will become the cup of life.

Aniceto Nazareth
based on the Roman Missal

64

Blest are you, O poor in spirit;
here is wealth beyond all telling.
Blest are you that faint with hunger;
here is food all want dispelling.
Blest are you that weep for sorrow;
endless gladness here is given.
Blest are you when all shall hate you;
I will be your joy in heaven.

James Quinn (b. 1919)
based on The Beatitudes

65

Blest be the Lord; blest be the Lord,
the God of mercy, the God who saves.
I shall not fear the dark of night,
nor the arrow that flies by day.

1. He will release me
   from the nets of all my foes.
   He will protect me
   from their wicked hands.
   Beneath the shadow of his wings
   I will rejoice
   to find a dwelling place secure.

Continued overleaf

2. I need not shrink
   before the terrors of the night,
   nor stand alone
   before the light of day.
   No harm shall come to me,
   no arrow strike me down,
   no evil settle in my soul.

   Blest be the Lord; blest be the Lord,
   the God of mercy, the God who saves.
   I shall not fear the dark of night,
   nor the arrow that flies by day.

3. Although a thousand strong
   have fallen at my side,
   I'll not be shaken
   with the Lord at hand.
   His faithful love is all
   the armour that I need
   to wage my battle with the foe.

   Dan Schutte based on Psalm 91
   © 1976 New Dawn Music

66

Bread we bring to the God of love,
as an offering at his table laid,
bread of the earth, work of our hands.
Wine we bring to the God of love,
as an offering at his table laid,
fruit of the vine, work of our hands.

1. Lord, we bring you our doubt:
   for not trusting you,
   for not hearing you,
   in your mercy forgive.
   When we've gone astray
   from your gentle way,
   in your mercy forgive.

2. Lord, we bring you our strength:
   in the work we do
   may we follow you
   to the praise of your name.
   Father, make us strong,
   though the work be long,
   to the praise of your name.

3. Lord, we bring you our faith:
   through the gift of prayer
   may we learn to share
   in the love you have given;
   make us steadfast
   till we come, at last,
   to your kingdom in heaven.

   Christopher Walker (b. 1947)
   © 1985 OCP Publications

67

1. Breathe on me, breath of God,
   fill me with life anew,
   that I may love what thou dost love,
   and do what thou wouldst do.

2. Breathe on me, breath of God,
   until my heart is pure:
   until with thee I have one will
   to do and to endure.

3. Breathe on me, breath of God,
   till I am wholly thine,
   until this earthly part of me
   glows with thy fire divine.

4. Breathe on me, breath of God,
   so shall I never die,
   but live with thee the perfect life
   of thine eternity.

   Edwin Hatch (1835-1889)

68

1. Bring, all ye dear-bought nations, bring,
   your richest praises to your King,
   alleluia, alleluia,
   that spotless Lamb, who more than due,
   paid for his sheep, and those sheep you.

   Alleluia, alleluia, alleluia,
   alleluia, alleluia!

2. That guiltless Son, who bought
      your peace,
   and made his Father's anger cease,
   alleluia, alleluia,
   then, life and death together fought,
   each to a strange extreme
      were brought.

3. Life died, but soon revived again,
   and even death by it was slain,
   alleluia, alleluia.
   Say, happy Magdalen, O say,
   what didst thou see there by the way?

4. 'I saw the tomb of my dear Lord,
   I saw himself, and him adored,
   alleluia, alleluia,
   I saw the napkin and the sheet,
   that bound his head and wrapped
      his feet.'

5. 'I heard the angels witness bear,
   Jesus is ris'n; he is not here,
   alleluia, alleluia;
   go, tell his followers they shall see
   thine and their hope in Galilee.'

6. We, Lord, with faithful hearts
      and voice,
   on this thy rising day rejoice,
   alleluia, alleluia.
   O thou, whose power o'ercame
      the grave,
   by grace and love us sinners save.

   Wipo 11th century
   tr. Walter Kirkham Blount (d. 1717)

69

1. Bring flow'rs of the rarest,
   bring blossoms the fairest,
   from garden and woodland
   and hillside and dale;
   our full hearts are swelling,
   our glad voices telling
   the praise of the loveliest
   flow'r of the vale.

   O Mary, we crown thee
   with blossoms today,
   Queen of the angels
   and Queen of the May.
   O Mary, we crown thee
   with blossoms today,
   Queen of the angels
   and Queen of the May.

2. Their lady they name thee,
   their mistress proclaim thee.
   O, grant that thy children
   on earth be as true,
   as long as the bowers
   are radiant with flowers
   as long as the azure
   shall keep its bright hue.

3. Sing gaily in chorus,
   the bright angels o'er us
   re-echo the strains
   we begin upon earth;
   their harps are repeating
   the notes of our greeting,
   for Mary herself is
   the cause of our mirth.

   A Sister of Notre Dame

70

1. By the blood that flowed from thee
   in thy grievous agony;
   by the traitor's guileful kiss,
   filling up thy bitterness;

   Jesus, Saviour, hear our cry;
   thou wert suff'ring once as we:
   now enthroned in majesty
   countless angels sing to thee.

2. By the cords that, round thee cast,
   bound thee to the pillar fast,
   by the scourge so meekly borne,
   by the purple robe of scorn.

3. By the thorns that crowned thy head;
   by the sceptre of a reed;
   by thy foes on bending knee,
   mocking at thy royalty.

4. By the people's cruel jeers;
   by the holy women's tears;
   by thy footsteps, faint and slow,
   weighed beneath thy cross of woe.

5. By thy weeping mother's woe;
   by the sword that pierced her through,
   when in anguish standing by,
   on the cross she saw thee die.

   Frederick William Faber (1814-1863)

71

1. By the waters,
   the waters of Babylon,
   we sat down and wept,
   and wept for thee, Zion;
   we remember thee,
   remember thee,
   remember thee, Zion.

2. On the willows,
   the willows of Babylon,
   we hung up our harps,
   our harps, for thee, Zion;
   how can we sing,
   how can we sing,
   can we sing of thee, Zion?

3. There our captors,
   our captors from Babylon,
   tried to make us sing,
   to sing of thee, Zion;
   but we could not sing,
   we could not sing,
   we could not sing, Zion.

   Based on Psalm 137

72

By your steadfast love
I will enter your house;
I will worship you
in your holy temple,
and revere your name
as I bow before you,
exalt in you,
my Lord, my shield.

Alleluia, alleluia,
alleluia, alleluia,
alleluia, alleluia,
alleluia, alleluia.

   Frank Docherty (b. 1944)

73

1. Child in the manger, infant of Mary;
   outcast and stranger, Lord of all;
   child who inherits all our transgressions,
   all our demerits on him fall.

2. Once the most holy child of salvation
   gently and lowly lived below;
   now as our glorious mighty Redeemer,
   see him victorious o'er each foe.

3. Prophets foretold him,
      infant of wonder;
   angels behold him on his throne;
   worthy our Saviour of all their praises;
   happy for ever are his own.

   Mary MacDonald (1817-1890)
   tr. Lachlan MacBean (1853-1931)

74

1. Christ be beside me,
   Christ be before me,
   Christ be behind me,
   King of my heart.
   Christ be within me,
   Christ be below me,
   Christ be above me,
   never to part.

2. Christ on my right hand,
   Christ on my left hand,
   Christ all around me,
   shield in the strife.
   Christ in my sleeping,
   Christ in my sitting,
   Christ in my rising,
   light of my life.

3. Christ be in all hearts
   thinking about me.
   Christ be in all tongues
   telling of me.
   Christ be the vision
   in eyes that see me,
   in ears that hear me,
   Christ ever be.

   Adapted from 'St Patrick's Breastplate'
   by James Quinn (b. 1919)

75

1. Christ is King of earth and heaven!
   Let his subjects all proclaim,
   in the splendour of his temple,
   honour to his holy name.

2. Christ is King! No soul created
   can refuse to bend the knee
   to the God made man who reigneth,
   as 'twas promised, from the tree.

3. Christ is King! Let humble sorrow
   for our past neglect atone,
   for the lack of faithful service
   to the Master whom we own.

4. Christ is King! Let joy and gladness
   greet him; let his courts resound
   with the praise of faithful subjects
   to his love in honour bound.

5. Christ is King! In health and sickness,
   till we breathe our latest breath,
   till we greet in highest heaven,
   Christ the victor over death.

   Ivor J. E. Daniel (1883-1967)

76

1. Christ is made the sure foundation,
   Christ the head and corner-stone,
   chosen of the Lord and precious,
   binding all the Church as one,
   holy Sion's help for ever,
   and her confidence alone.

2. To this temple, where we call you,
   come, O Lord of hosts, today;
   you have promised loving kindness,
   hear your servants as we pray,
   bless your people now before you,
   turn our darkness into day.

Continued overleaf

3. Hear the cry of all your people,
   what they ask and hope to gain;
   what they gain from you, for ever
   with your chosen to retain,
   and hereafter in your glory
   ever more with you to reign.

4. Praise and honour to the Father,
   praise and honour to the Son,
   praise and honour to the Spirit,
   ever Three and ever One,
   One in might and One in glory
   while unending ages run.

   'Urbs beata Jerusalem' (c. 7th century)
   tr. John Mason Neale (1818-1866)

77

Christ is our King,
let the whole world rejoice!
May all the nations
sing out with one voice!
Light of the world,
you have helped us to see
that we are one people
and one day we all shall be free.

1. He came to open
   the eyes of the blind,
   letting the sunlight
   pour into their minds.
   Vision is waiting
   for those who have hope.
   He is the light of the world.

2. He came to speak
   tender words to the poor,
   he is the gateway
   and he is the door.
   Riches are waiting
   for all those who hope.
   He is the light of the world.

3. He came to open
   the doors of the jail,
   he came to help
   the downtrodden and frail.
   Freedom is waiting
   for all those who hope.
   He is the light of the world.

4. He came to open
   the lips of the mute,
   letting them speak out
   with courage and truth.
   His words are uttered
   by all those who hope.
   He is the light of the world.

5. He came to heal
   all the crippled and lame,
   sickness took flight
   at the sound of his name.
   Vigour is waiting
   for all those who hope.
   He is the light of the world.

6. He came to love
   ev'ryone on this earth
   and through his Spirit
   he promised rebirth.
   New life is waiting
   for all those who hope.
   He is the light of the world.

   Estelle White (b. 1925)

78

1. Christ the Lord is ris'n today!
   Christians, haste your vows to pay,
   offer ye your praises meet
   at the paschal victim's feet;
   for the sheep the Lamb hath bled,
   sinless in the sinner's stead.
   Christ the Lord is ris'n on high;
   now he lives, no more to die.

2. Christ, the victim undefiled,
God and sinners reconciled
when in strange and awful strife
met together death and life;
Christians, on this happy day,
haste with joy your vows to pay.
Christ the Lord is ris'n on high;
now he lives, no more to die.

3. Say, O wond'ring Mary, say,
what thou sawest on thy way.
'I beheld, where Christ had lain,
empty tomb and angels twain,
I beheld the glory bright
of the rising Lord of light;
Christ my hope is ris'n again;
now he lives, and lives to reign.'

4. Christ, who once for sinners bled,
now the first-born from the dead,
throned in endless might and power,
lives and reigns for ever more.
Hail, eternal hope on high!
Hail, thou King of victory!
Hail, thou Prince of life adored!
Help and save us, gracious Lord.

Wipo (11th century)
tr. Jane Elizabeth Leeson (1809-1881), alt.

79

1. Colours of day dawn into the mind,
the sun has come up,
the night is behind.
Go down in the city, into the street,
and let's give the message
to the people we meet.

So light up the fire
and let the flame burn,
open the door, let Jesus return,
take seeds of his Spirit,
let the fruit grow,
tell the people of Jesus,
let his love show.

2. Go through the park, on into the town;
the sun still shines on;
it never goes down.
The light of the world is risen again;
the people of darkness
are needing our friend.

3. Open your eyes, look into the sky,
the darkness has come,
the sun came to die.
The evening draws on,
the sun disappears,
but Jesus is living,
and his Spirit is near.

Sue McClellan (b. 1951), John Paculabo (b 1946)
and Keith Ryecroft, (b. 1949)
© 1974 Kingsway's Thankyou Music

80

Come and be filled
as you sit at my table,
quenching your thirst
as you drink of my wine;
bringing the mem'ry
of my dying and rising
into your blood-stream
which is mingled with mine.

1. This is the bread
that has come down from heaven.
This is my blood
for the life of the world.

2. He leads us out
   of the power of darkness
   and brings us safe
   to his kingdom of life.

   Come and be filled
   as you sit at my table,
   quenching your thirst
   as you drink of my wine;
   bringing the mem'ry
   of my dying and rising
   into your blood-stream
   which is mingled with mine.

3. No longer I,
   but now Christ lives within me.
   I live by faith
   in the Son of our God.

4. For those in Christ
   there is no condemnation.
   He sets them free
   through the Spirit he sends.

5. Thus shall the world
   know you are my disciples,
   if you can love,
   and if you can forgive.

   Aniceto Nazareth, based on Scripture

81

1. Come and bless, come and praise,
   come and praise the living God.
   Allelu, allelu, alleluia, Jesus Christ.

   Allelu, allelu, alleluia, Jesus Christ.
   Allelu, allelu, alleluia, Jesus Christ.

2. Come and seek, come and find,
   come and find the living God.
   Allelu, allelu, alleluia, Jesus Christ.

3. Come and hear, come and know,
   come and know the living God.
   Allelu, allelu, alleluia, Jesus Christ.

4. Come and bless, come and praise,
   come and praise the Word of God.
   Word of God, Word made flesh,
   alleluia, Jesus Christ.

Optional verses for Christmas.

5. Come behold, come and see,
   come and see the new-born babe.
   Allelu, allelu, alleluia, Jesus Christ.

6. Angel choirs sing above,
   'Glory to the Son of God.'
   Shepherd folk sing below,
   'Allelu, Emmanuel.'

   Mimi Farra (b. 1938)
   © 1971 Celebration/Kingsway's Thankyou Music

82

1. Come and go with me
   to my Father's house,
   to my Father's house,
   to my Father's house.
   Come and go with me
   to my Father's house
   where there's joy, joy, joy.

2. It's not very far
   to my Father's house,
   to my Father's house,
   to my Father's house.
   It's not very far
   to my Father's house
   where there's joy, joy, joy.

3. There is room for all
   in my Father's house,
   in my Father's house,
   in my Father's house.
   There is room for all
   in my Father's house
   where there's joy, joy, joy.

4. Ev'rything is free
   in my Father's house,
   in my Father's house,
   in my Father's house.
   Ev'rything is free
   in my Father's house
   where there's joy, joy, joy.

5. Jesus is the way
   to my Father's house,
   to my Father's house,
   to my Father's house.
   Jesus is the way
   to my Father's house
   where there's joy, joy, joy.

6. Jesus is the light
   in my Father's house,
   in my Father's house,
   in my Father's house.
   Jesus is the light
   in my Father's house
   where there's joy, joy, joy.

*Other verses may be added spontaneously,
such as:*

We will clap our hands

There is liberty

We will praise the Lord, etc.

Unknown

83

*Come and join the celebration.
It's a very special day.
Come and share our jubilation;
there's a new King born today!*

1. See the shepherds
   hurry down to Bethlehem,
   gaze in wonder
   at the Son of God
   who lay before them.

2. Wise men journey,
   led to worship by a star,
   kneel in homage,
   bringing precious gifts
   from lands afar. So,

3. 'God is with us,'
   round the world the message bring.
   He is with us.
   'Welcome,' all the bells
   on earth are pealing.

Valerie Collison

84

Come and praise him,
   royal priesthood.
Come and worship, holy nation.
Worship Jesus, our Redeemer.
He is risen, King of glory.

Andy Carter (b. 1951)
© 1977 Kingway's Thankyou Music

85

1. Come and praise the Lord our King,
   alleluia,
   come and praise the Lord our King,
   alleluia!

Continued overleaf

2. Christ was born in Bethlehem, alleluia,
   Son of God and Son of Man, alleluia.

3. He grew up an earthly child, alleluia,
   in the world, but undefiled, alleluia.

4. He who died at Calvary, alleluia,
   rose again triumphantly, alleluia.

5. He will cleanse us from our sin, alleluia,
   if we live by faith in him, alleluia.

   Unknown

86

1. Come back to me with all your heart.
   Don't let fear keep us apart.
   Trees do bend,
   though straight and tall;
   so must we to others' call.

   Long have I waited
   for your coming home to me
   and living deeply our new life.

2. The wilderness will lead you
   to your heart where I will speak.
   Integrity and justice
   with tenderness you shall know.

3. You shall sleep secure with peace;
   faithfulness will be your joy.

4. Come back to me with all your heart.
   Don't let fear keep us apart.
   Trees do bend,
   though straight and tall;
   so must we to others' call.

   Gregory Norbert
   based on Hosea

87

Come, come, come to the manger,
children, come to the children's King;
sing, sing, chorus of angels,
star of morning o'er Bethlehem sing.

1. He lies 'mid the beasts of the stall,
   who is Maker and Lord of us all;
   the wintry wind blows cold and dreary,
   see, he weeps, the world is weary;
   Lord, have pity and mercy on me!

2. He leaves all his glory behind,
   to be born and to die for mankind,
   with grateful beasts his cradle chooses,
   thankless world his love refuses;
   Lord, have pity and mercy on me!

3. To the manger of Bethlehem come,
   to the Saviour Emmanuel's home;
   the heav'nly hosts above are singing,
   set the Christmas bells a-ringing;
   Lord, have pity and mercy on me!

   Unknown, alt.

88

1. Come down, O Love divine,
   seek thou this soul of mine,
   and visit it with
   thine own ardour glowing;
   O Comforter, draw near,
   within my heart appear,
   and kindle it,
   thy holy flame bestowing.

2. O let it freely burn,
   till earthly passions turn
   to dust and ashes
   in its heat consuming;
   and let thy glorious light
   shine ever on my sight,
   and clothe me round,
   the while my path illuming.

3. Let holy charity
mine outward vesture be,
and lowliness become
mine inner clothing;
true lowliness of heart,
which takes the humbler part,
and o'er its own shortcomings
weeps with loathing.

4. And so the yearning strong,
with which the soul will long,
shall far outpass
the pow'r of human telling;
for none can guess its grace,
till he become the place
wherein the Holy Spirit
makes his dwelling.

Bianco da Siena (d. 1434)
tr. Richard F. Littledale (1833-1890)

89

1. Come from the north, giver of life,
breathe on us now, Spirit of Christ.
Give us your strength, our faith renew
that we may hold to what is true.

2. Come from the south, like a caress,
Spirit of love and tenderness.
Help us to be patient and kind,
opening our hearts to all mankind.

3. Come from the east, wisdom's
own breath,
that we may know our inner selves.
Teach us to pray deep in the heart,
and perfect peace to us impart.

4. Come from the west, as the light fades,
Spirit who guides through
darkest shades.
And when our time on earth is done,
on wings of joy, then bear us home.

Estelle White (b. 1925)

90

1. Come, Holy Ghost, Creator, come
from thy bright heav'nly throne,
come, take possession of our souls,
and make them all thine own.

2. Thou who art called the Paraclete,
best gift of God above,
the living spring, the living fire,
sweet unction and true love.

3. Thou who art sev'nfold in thy grace,
finger of God's right hand;
his promise, teaching little ones
to speak and understand.

4. O guide our minds with thy blest light,
with love our hearts inflame;
and with thy strength,
which ne'er decays,
confirm our mortal frame.

5. Far from us drive our deadly foe;
true peace unto us bring;
and through all perils lead us safe
beneath thy sacred wing.

6. Through thee may we
the Father know,
through thee th'eternal Son,
and thee the Spirit of them both,
thrice-blessèd Three in One.

Continued overleaf

7. All glory to the Father be,
with his co-equal Son:
the same to thee, great Paraclete,
while endless ages run.
Ascribed to Rabanus Maurus (776-856), tr. unknown

91

1. Come, Holy Spirit, come!
Inflame our souls with love,
transforming ev'ry heart and home
with wisdom from above.
O let us not despise
the humble path Christ trod,
but choose, to shame the worldly-wise,
the foolishness of God.

2. All knowing Spirit, prove
the poverty of pride,
by knowledge of the Father's love
in Jesus crucified;
and grant us faith to know
the glory of that sign,
and in our very lives to show
the marks of love divine.

3. Come with the gift to heal
the wounds of guilt and fear,
and to oppression's face reveal
the kingdom drawing near.
Where chaos longs to reign,
descend, O holy dove,
and free us all to work again
the miracles of love.

4. Spirit of truth, arise;
inspire the prophet's voice:
expose to scorn the tyrant's lies,
and bid the poor rejoice.
O Spirit, clear our sight,
all prejudice remove,
and help us to discern the right,
and covet only love.

5. Give us the tongues to speak,
in ev'ry time and place,
to rich and poor, to strong and weak,
the word of love and grace.
Enable us to hear
the words that others bring,
interpreting with open ear
the special song they sing.

6. Come, Holy Spirit, dance
within our hearts today,
our earth-bound spirits to entrance,
our mortal fears allay;
and teach us to desire,
all other things above,
that self-consuming holy fire,
the perfect gift of love!
Michael Forster (b. 1946)

92

1. Come into his presence singing:
alleluia,
alleluia,
alleluia.

2. Come into his presence singing:
Jesus is Lord,
Jesus is Lord,
Jesus is Lord.

3. Come into his presence singing:
worthy the Lamb,
worthy the Lamb,
worthy the Lamb.

4. Come into his presence singing:
glory to God,
glory to God,
glory to God.

5. Come into his presence singing:
   peace to the world,
   peace to the world,
   peace to the world.

v. 1 Unknown,
additional vv John Ballantine (b. 1945)

93

Come, let us go up to the Lord,
to the temple of our God,
so that he may teach us his ways
and we may walk in his paths.

1. In the days that are to come,
   the mountain of the house of the Lord
   shall be raised as the highest,
   and nations will come and say:

2. He will gather all the peoples
   and settle their disputes in peace,
   swords and spears will be taken
   and made into tools for the land.

3. Wars will cease between the nations,
   and all in peace will live
   among their fig trees and vineyards,
   and no-one will make them afraid.

Maria Parkinson

94

Come, let us raise a joyful song
to the Lord, a shout of triumph!
Come, let us raise a joyful song
to the Lord, and give him thanks!

1. The furthest places on the earth
   are in his hands.
   He made them, and we sing his praise.

2. The seas and waters on the earth
   are in his hands.
   He made them, and we sing his praise.

3. The hills and valleys on the earth
   are in his hands.
   He made them, and we sing his praise.

4. All living creatures on the earth
   are in his hands.
   He made them, and we sing his praise.

5. And we his people on the earth
   are in his hands.
   He saved us, and we sing his praise.

Mike Anderson (b. 1956), based on Psalm 95

95

1. Come, Lord Jesus, come.
   Come, take my hands,
   take them for your work.
   Take them for your service, Lord.
   Take them for your glory, Lord.
   Come, Lord Jesus, come.
   Come, Lord Jesus, take my hands.

2. Come, Lord Jesus, come.
   Come, take my eyes,
   may they shine with joy.
   Take them for your service, Lord.
   Take them for your glory, Lord.
   Come, Lord Jesus, come.
   Come, Lord Jesus, take my eyes.

3. Come, Lord Jesus, come.
   Come, take my lips,
   may they speak your truth.
   Take them for your service, Lord.
   Take them for your glory, Lord.
   Come, Lord Jesus, come.
   Come, Lord Jesus, take my lips.

Continued overleaf

4. Come, Lord Jesus, come.
   Come, take my feet,
   may they walk your path.
   Take them for your service, Lord.
   Take them for your glory, Lord.
   Come, Lord Jesus, come.
   Come, Lord Jesus, take my feet.

5. Come, Lord Jesus, come.
   Come, take my heart,
   fill it with your love.
   Take it for your service, Lord.
   Take it for your glory, Lord.
   Come, Lord Jesus, come.
   Come, Lord Jesus, take my heart.

6. Come, Lord Jesus, come.
   Come, take my life,
   take it for your own.
   Take it for your service, Lord.
   Take it for your glory, Lord.
   Come, Lord Jesus, come.
   Come, Lord Jesus, take my life.

Kevin Mayhew (b. 1942)

96

1. Come, praise the Lord, the almighty,
   the King of all nations!
   Tell forth his fame, O ye peoples,
   with loud acclamations!
   His love is sure;
   faithful his word shall endure,
   steadfast through all generations!

2. Praise to the Father most gracious,
   the Lord of creation!
   Praise to his Son, the Redeemer,
   who wrought our salvation!
   O heav'nly Dove,
   praise to thee, fruit of their love,
   giver of all consolation!

James Quinn (b. 1919), based on Psalm 117

97

1. Come, thou long-expected Jesus,
   born to set thy people free;
   from our fears and sins release us;
   let us find our rest in thee.

2. Israel's strength and consolation,
   hope of all the earth thou art;
   dear desire of ev'ry nation,
   joy of ev'ry longing heart.

3. Born thy people to deliver;
   born a child and yet a king;
   born to reign in us for ever;
   now thy gracious kingdom bring.

4. By thy own eternal Spirit,
   rule in all our hearts alone:
   by thy all-sufficient merit,
   raise us to thy glorious throne.

Charles Wesley (1707-1788)

98

1. Come to us, Lord of light,
   come in your strength and might,
   and with your searing flame
   burn in our hearts your name.
   All of our fears remove
   that we may choose what's good.
   Ev'ry sin consume,
   come, Holy Spirit, come!

2. Come to the hearts that grieve,
   anguish of mind relieve.
   Give to those who bear sorrow
   courage to face tomorrow.
   Breath of the King of kings,
   guard us beneath your wings,
   hope of the soul oppressed,
   come, Holy Spirit, blest.

3. Come with your words that heal,
   come to us and reveal
   God's loving tenderness
   we can ourselves possess.
   O ever faithful guide
   be always at our side,
   and when our days are done,
   Comforter, lead us home.

   Estelle White (b. 1925)

4. Then, thou Church triumphant, come,
   raise the song of harvest-home;
   all be safely gathered in,
   free from sorrow, free from sin,
   there for ever purified
   in God's garner to abide:
   come, ten thousand angels, come,
   raise the glorious harvest-home!

   Henry Alford (1810-1871)

99

1. Come, ye thankful people, come,
   raise the song of harvest-home!
   All be safely gathered in,
   ere the winter storms begin;
   God, our maker, doth provide
   for our wants to be supplied;
   come to God's own temple, come;
   raise the song of harvest-home!

2. We ourselves are God's own field,
   fruit unto his praise to yield;
   wheat and tares together sown,
   unto joy or sorrow grown;
   first the blade and then the ear,
   then the full corn shall appear:
   grant, O harvest Lord, that we
   wholesome grain and pure may be.

3. For the Lord our God shall come,
   and shall take his harvest home,
   from his field shall purge away
   all that doth offend, that day,
   give his angels charge at last
   in the fire the tares to cast,
   but the fruitful ears to store
   in his garner ever more.

100

'Comfort, comfort my people,'
says the Lord, your God.
'Cry out loud to Jerusalem,
God has pardoned you!'

1. Ev'ry valley shall be filled,
   ev'ry mount and hill made low.

2. In the desert make a path
   for the Lord Emmanuel.

3. For the glory of the Lord
   soon shall be revealed to me.

   Anthony D'Souza (b. 1950)
   based on Isaiah 40

101

1. Crown him with many crowns,
   the Lamb upon his throne;
   hark, how the heav'nly anthem drowns
   all music but its own:
   awake, my soul, and sing
   of him who died for thee,
   and hail him as thy matchless King
   through all eternity.

Continued overleaf

2. Crown him the virgin's Son,
   the God incarnate born,
   whose arm those crimson trophies won
   which now his brow adorn;
   fruit of the mystic rose,
   as of that rose the stem,
   the root, whence mercy ever flows,
   the babe of Bethlehem.

3. Crown him the Lord of love;
   behold his hands and side,
   rich wounds, yet visible above,
   in beauty glorified:
   no angel in the sky
   can fully bear that sight,
   but downward bends his burning eye
   at mysteries so bright.

4. Crown him the Lord of peace,
   whose pow'r a sceptre sways
   from pole to pole,
   that wars may cease,
   absorbed in prayer and praise:
   his reign shall know no end,
   and round his piercèd feet
   fair flowers of paradise extend
   their fragrance ever sweet.

5. Crown him the Lord of heaven,
   one with the Father known,
   and the blest Spirit through him given
   from yonder triune throne:
   all hail, Redeemer, hail,
   for thou hast died for me;
   thy praise shall never, never fail
   throughout eternity.

Matthew Bridges (1800-1894)

102

1. Daily, daily, sing to Mary,
   sing, my soul, her praises due;
   all her feasts, her actions worship,
   with her heart's devotion true.
   Lost in wond'ring contemplation
   be her majesty confessed:
   call her mother, call her virgin,
   happy mother, virgin blest.

2. She is mighty to deliver;
   call her, trust her lovingly.
   When the tempest rages round thee,
   she will calm the troubled sea.
   Gifts of heaven she has given,
   noble lady, to our race:
   she, the queen, who decks her subjects,
   with the light of God's own grace.

3. Sing, my tongue, the virgin's trophies,
   who for us her Maker bore;
   for the curse of old inflicted,
   peace and blessings to restore.
   Sing in songs of praise unending,
   sing the world's majestic queen;
   weary not nor faint in telling
   all the gifts she gives to men.

4. All my senses, heart, affections,
   strive to sound her glory forth;
   spread abroad, the sweet memorials,
   of the virgin's priceless worth.
   Where the voice of music thrilling,
   where the tongues of eloquence,
   that can utter hymns beseeming
   all her matchless excellence?

5. All our joys do flow from Mary,
   all then join her praise to sing;
   trembling, sing the virgin mother,
   mother of our Lord and King,
   while we sing her awful glory,
   far above our fancy's reach,
   let our hearts be quick to offer
   love the heart alone can teach.

   Ascribed to St Bernard of Cluny (12th century)
   tr. Henry Bittleston (1818-1886)

103

1. Day is done, but love unfailing
   dwells ever here;
   shadows fall, but hope prevailing
   calms ev'ry fear.
   Loving Father, none forsaking,
   take our hearts, of love's own making,
   watch our sleeping, guard our waking,
   be always near!

2. Dark descends, but light unending
   shines through our night;
   you are with us, ever lending
   new strength to sight;
   one in love, your truth confessing,
   one in hope of heaven's blessing,
   may we see, in love's possessing,
   love's endless light!

3. Eyes will close, but you, unsleeping,
   watch by our side;
   death may come: in love's safe keeping
   still we abide.
   God of love, all evil quelling,
   sin forgiving, fear dispelling,
   stay with us, our hearts indwelling,
   this eventide!

   James Quinn (b. 1919)

104

1. Dear Lord and Father of mankind,
   forgive our foolish ways!
   Re-clothe us in our rightful mind,
   in purer lives thy service find,
   in deeper rev'rence praise,
   in deeper rev'rence praise.

2. In simple trust like theirs who heard,
   beside the Syrian sea,
   the gracious calling of the Lord,
   let us, like them, without a word,
   rise up and follow thee,
   rise up and follow thee.

3. O Sabbath rest by Galilee!
   O calm of hills above,
   where Jesus knelt to share with thee
   the silence of eternity,
   interpreted by love!
   interpreted by love!

4. Drop thy still dews of quietness,
   till all our strivings cease;
   take from our souls
      the strain and stress,
   and let our ordered lives confess
   the beauty of thy peace,
   the beauty of thy peace.

5. Breathe through the heats
      of our desire
   thy coolness and thy balm;
   let sense be dumb, let flesh retire;
   speak through the earthquake,
      wind and fire,
   O still small voice of calm!
   O still small voice of calm!

   John Greenleaf Whittier (1807-1892)

105

1. Dear maker of the stars of night,
   thy people's everlasting light,
   O Jesu, Saviour of us all,
   regard thy servants when they call.

2. Thou, sorrowing at the helpless cry
   of all creation doomed to die,
   didst come to save our fallen race
   by healing gifts of heavenly grace.

3. At thy great name, exalted now,
   all knees in lowly homage bow;
   all things in heaven and earth adore,
   and own thee King for evermore.

4. To thee, O Holy One, we pray,
   our judge in that tremendous day,
   ward off, while yet we dwell below,
   the weapons of our crafty foe.

5. To God the Father, God the Son,
   and God the Spirit, Three in One,
   praise, honour, might, and glory be
   from age to age eternally.

7th century,
tr. Edward Caswall (1814-1878)

106

1. Dear Saint Joseph, pure and gentle,
   guardian of the Saviour child,
   treading with the virgin mother,
   Egypt's deserts rough and wild.

   Hail, Saint Joseph, spouse of Mary,
   blessed above all saints on high,
   when the death-shades round us gather,
   teach, O teach us, how to die,
   teach, O teach us, how to die.

2. He who rested on thy bosom
   is by countless saints adored;
   prostrate angels in his presence
   sing hosannas to their Lord.

3. Now to thee no gift refusing,
   Jesus stoops to hear thy prayer;
   then, dear saint, from thy fair dwelling,
   give to us a father's care.

4. Dear Saint Joseph, kind and loving,
   stretch to us a helping hand;
   guide us through life's toils and sorrows,
   safely to the distant land.

Unknown

107

Deep peace of the running wave to you,
deep peace of the flowing air to you,
deep peace of the quiet earth to you,
deep peace of the shining stars to you,
deep peace of the Son of peace to you.

Fiona MacLeod (1855-1905)

108

1. Ding dong, merrily on high!
   In heav'n the bells are ringing;
   ding dong, verily the sky
   is riv'n with angels singing.

   Gloria, hosanna in excelsis!
   Gloria, hosanna in excelsis!

2. E'en so here below, below,
   let steeple bells be swungen,
   and io, io, io,
   by priest and people sungen.

3. Pray you, dutifully prime
   your matin chime, ye ringers;
   may you beautifully rhyme
   your evetime song, ye singers.

George Ratcliffe Woodward (1848-1934)

109

Do not be afraid,
for I have redeemed you.
I have called you by your name;
you are mine.

1. When you walk through the waters,
   I'll be with you.
   You will never sink beneath the waves.

2. When the fire is burning
   all around you,
   you will never be consumed by
      the flames.

3. When the fear of loneliness
   is looming,
   then remember I am at your side.

4. When you dwell in the exile
   of the stranger,
   remember you are precious in my eyes.

5. You are mine, O my child;
   I am your Father,
   and I love you with a perfect love.

Gerard Markland, based on Isaiah 43:1-4

110

Eat this bread, drink this cup,
come to me and never be hungry.
Eat this bread, drink this cup,
trust in me and you will not thirst.

1. I am the Bread of Life,
   the true bread sent from the Father.

2. Your ancestors ate manna in the desert,
   but this is the bread come down
      from heaven.

3. Eat my flesh, and drink my blood,
   and I will raise you up on the last day.

4. Anyone who eats this bread
   will live for ever.

5. If you believe and eat this bread
   you will have eternal life.

Taizé Community, based on Scripture

111

1. Eternal Father, strong to save,
   whose arm doth bind the restless wave,
   who bidd'st the mighty ocean deep
   its own appointed limits keep:
   O hear us when we cry to thee
   for those in peril on the sea.

2. O Saviour, whose almighty word
   the winds and waves submissive heard,
   who walkedst on the foaming deep
   and calm, amid its rage, didst sleep:
   O hear us when we cry to thee
   for those in peril on the sea.

3. O sacred Spirit, who didst brood
   upon the waters dark and rude,
   and bid their angry tumult cease,
   and give, for wild confusion, peace:
   O hear us when we cry to thee
   for those in peril on the sea.

4. O Trinity of love and power,
   our brethren shield in danger's hour.
   From rock and tempest, fire and foe,
   protect them whereso'er they go,
   and ever let there rise to thee
   glad hymns of praise from land and sea.

William Whiting (1825-1878)

112

1. Faith of our fathers, living still
   in spite of dungeon, fire and sword;
   O, how our hearts beat high with joy
   whene'er we hear that glorious word!

   Faith of our fathers! Holy Faith!
   We will be true to thee till death,
   we will be true to thee till death.

2. Our fathers, chained in prisons dark,
   were still in heart and conscience free;
   how sweet would be their children's fate,
   if they, like them, could die for thee!

3. Faith of our fathers, Mary's prayers
   shall win our country back to thee;
   and through the truth that comes
      from God
   England shall then indeed be free.

4. Faith of our fathers, we will love
   both friend and foe in all our strife,
   and preach thee too, as love knows how,
   by kindly words and virtuous life.

   Frederick William Faber (1814-1863)

2. Wine and bread the symbols,
   love and life convey,
   offered by your people,
   work and joy portray.
   All we own consigning,
   nothing is retained;
   tokens of our service,
   gifts and song contain.

3. Transformation wondrous,
   water into wine;
   mingled in the Godhead
   we are made divine.
   Birth into his body
   brought us life anew,
   total consecration,
   fruit from grafting true.

4. Christ, the head, and members
   living now as one,
   offered to the Father
   by his holy Son;
   and our adoration
   purified we find,
   through the Holy Spirit
   breathing in mankind.

   A. J. Newman

113

1. Father and life-giver,
   grace of Christ impart;
   he, the Word incarnate,
   food for mind and heart.
   Children of the promise,
   homage now we pay;
   sacrificial banquet
   cheers the desert way.

114

1. Father, I place into your hands
   the things that I can't do.
   Father, I place into your hands
   the times that I've been through.
   Father, I place into your hands
   the way that I should go,
   for I know I always can trust you.

2. Father, I place into your hands
   my friends and family.
   Father, I place into your hands
   the things that trouble me.
   Father, I place into your hands
   the person I would be,
   for I know I always can trust you.

3. Father, we love to seek your face,
   we love to hear your voice.
   Father, we love to sing your praise,
   and in your name rejoice.
   Father, we love to walk with you
   and in your presence rest,
   for we know we always can trust you.

4. Father, I want to be with you
   and do the things you do.
   Father, I want to speak the words
   that you are speaking too.
   Father, I want to love the ones
   that you will draw to you,
   for I know that I am one with you.

Jenny Hewer (b. 1945)
© 1975 Kingsway's Thankyou Music

115

1. Father, in my life I see
   you are God who walks with me.
   You hold my life in your hands:
   close beside you I will stand.
   I give all my life to you:
   help me, Father, to be true.

2. Jesus, in my life I see
   you are God who walks with me.
   You hold my life in your hands:
   close beside you I will stand.
   I give all my life to you:
   help me, Jesus, to be true.

3. Spirit, in my life I see
   you are God who walks with me.
   You hold my life in your hands:
   close beside you I will stand.
   I give all my life to you:
   help me, Spirit, to be true.

Frank Anderson

116

1. Father, we adore you,
   lay our lives before you.
   How we love you.

2. Jesus, we adore you,
   lay our lives before you.
   How we love you.

3. Spirit, we adore you,
   lay our lives before you.
   How we love you.

Terrye Coelho (b. 1952)
© 1972 Maranatha! Music/CopyCare Ltd

117

1. Father, we love you,
   we praise you, we adore you.
   Glorify your name in all the earth.
   Glorify your name, glorify your name,
   glorify your name in all the earth.

2. Jesus, we love you,
   we praise you, we adore you.
   Glorify your name in all the earth.
   Glorify your name, glorify your name,
   glorify your name in all the earth.

3. Spirit, we love you,
   we praise you, we adore you.
   Glorify your name in all the earth.
   Glorify your name, glorify your name,
   glorify your name in all the earth.

Donna Adkins (b. 1940)
© 1976 Maranatha! Music/CopyCare Ltd

118

Father welcomes all his children
to his fam'ly through his Son.
Father giving his salvation,
life for ever has been won.

1. Little children come to me,
   for my kingdom is of these.
   Love and new life have I to give,
   pardon for your sin.

2. In the water, in the Word,
   in his promise, be assured:
   all who believe and are baptised
   shall be born again.

3. Let us daily die to sin;
   let us daily rise with him –
   walk in the love of Christ our Lord,
   live in the peace of God.

   Robin Mann (b. 1949)

119

Feed us now, O Son of God,
as you fed them long ago.

1. The people came to hear you,
   the poor, the lame, the blind.
   They asked for food to save them,
   you fed them body and mind.

2. The ones who didn't listen,
   the rich, the safe, the sure,
   they didn't think they needed
   the off'ring of a cure.

3. It's hard for us to listen,
   things haven't changed at all.
   We've got the things we wanted;
   we don't want to hear your call.

4. Yet millions still have hunger,
   disease, no homes, and fear.
   We offer them so little,
   and it costs them very dear.

5. So help us see the writing,
   written clear upon the wall:
   he who doesn't feed his neighbour
   will get no food at all.

   Peter Allen (b. 1935)

120

1. Fill your hearts with joy and gladness,
   sing and praise your God and mine!
   Great the Lord in love and wisdom,
   might and majesty divine!
   He who framed the starry heavens
   knows and names them as they shine.
   Fill your hearts with joy and gladness,
   sing and praise your God and mine!

2. Praise the Lord, his people, praise him!
   Wounded souls his comfort know.
   Those who fear him find his mercies,
   peace for pain and joy for woe;
   humble hearts are high exalted,
   human pride and pow'r laid low.
   Praise the Lord, his people, praise him!
   Wounded souls his comfort know.

3. Praise the Lord for times and seasons,
   cloud and sunshine, wind and rain;
   spring to melt the snows of winter
   till the waters flow again;
   grass upon the mountain pastures,
   golden valleys thick with grain.
   Praise the Lord for times and seasons,
   cloud and sunshine, wind and rain.

4. Fill your hearts with joy and gladness,
   peace and plenty crown your days!
   Love his laws, declare his judgements,
   walk in all his words and ways,
   he the Lord and we his children;
   praise the Lord, all people, praise!
   Fill your hearts with joy and gladness,
   peace and plenty crown your days!

Timothy Dudley-Smith (b. 1926)

121

1. Firmly I believe and truly
   God is three, and God is one,
   and I next acknowledge duly
   manhood taken by the Son.

2. And I trust and hope most fully
   in that manhood crucified;
   and each thought and deed unruly
   do to death, as he has died.

3. Simply to his grace and wholly
   light and life and strength belong;
   and I love supremely, solely,
   him the holy, him the strong.

4. And I hold in veneration,
   for the love of him alone,
   Holy Church, as his creation,
   and her teachings, as his own.

5. Adoration aye be given,
   with and through th'angelic host,
   to the God of earth and heaven,
   Father, Son and Holy Ghost.

John Henry Newman (1801-1890)

122

Follow me, follow me,
leave your home and family,
leave your fishing nets and boats
upon the shore.
Leave the seed that you have sown,
leave the crops that you've grown,
leave the people you have known
and follow me.

1. The foxes have their holes
   and the swallows have their nests,
   but the Son of Man
   has no place to lie down.
   I do not offer comfort,
   I do not offer wealth,
   but in me will all happiness be found.

2. If you would follow me,
   you must leave old ways behind.
   You must take my cross
   and follow on my path.
   You may be far from loved ones,
   you may be far from home,
   but my Father will welcome you at last.

3. Although I go away
   you will never be alone,
   for the Spirit will
   be there to comfort you.
   Though all of you may scatter,
   each follow his own path,
   still the Spirit of love will lead you home.

Michael Cockett (b. 1938)

123

1. For all the saints
   who from their labours rest,
   who thee by faith
   before the world confessed,
   thy name, O Jesus,
   be for ever blest.

Alleluia, alleluia!

Continued overleaf

2. Thou wast their rock,
   their fortress and their might;
   thou, Lord, their captain
   in the well-fought fight;
   thou in the darkness drear
   their one true light.

   Alleluia, alleluia!

3. O may thy soldiers,
   faithful, true and bold,
   fight as the saints
   who nobly fought of old,
   and win, with them,
   the victor's crown of gold.

4. O blest communion!
   Fellowship divine!
   We feebly struggle,
   they in glory shine;
   yet all are one in thee,
   for all are thine.

5. And when the strife is fierce,
   the warfare long,
   steals on the ear
   the distant triumph-song,
   and hearts are brave again,
   and arms are strong.

6. The golden evening
   brightens in the west;
   soon, soon to faithful
   warriors cometh rest:
   sweet is the calm of
   paradise the blest.

7. But lo! There breaks
   a yet more glorious day;
   the saints triumphant
   rise in bright array:
   the King of glory
   passes on his way.

8. From earth's wide bounds,
   from ocean's farthest coast,
   through gates of pearl
   streams in the countless host,
   singing to Father,
   Son and Holy Ghost.

   William Walsham How (1823-1897)

124

For I'm building a people of power
and I'm making a people of praise,
that will move through this land
by my Spirit,
and will glorify my precious name.
Build your church, Lord,
make us strong, Lord,
join our hearts, Lord, through your Son.
Make us one, Lord, in your body,
in the kingdom of your Son.

Dave Richards (b. 1947), based on Eph. 2:21,22
© 1977 Kingsway's Thankyou Music

125

1. For the healing of the nations,
   Lord, we pray with one accord;
   for a just and equal sharing
   of the things that earth affords.
   To a life of love in action
   help us rise and pledge our word.

2. Lead us, Father, into freedom,
   from despair your world release;
   that, redeemed from war and hatred,
   all may come and go in peace.
   Show us how, through care
     and goodness,
   fear will die and hope increase.

3. All that kills abundant living
   let it from the earth be banned;
   pride of status, race or schooling,
   dogmas that obscure your plan.
   In our common quest for justice
   may we hallow life's brief span.

4. You, Creator-God, have written
   your great name on all mankind;
   for our growing in your likeness
   brings the life of Christ to mind,
   that by our response and service
   earth its destiny may find.

Fred Kaan (b. 1929) alt.

126

For you are my God,
you alone are my joy.
Defend me, O Lord.

1. You give marvellous comrades to me:
   the faithful who dwell in your land.
   Those who choose alien gods
   have chosen an alien band.

2. You are my portion and cup;
   it is you that I claim for my prize.
   Your heritage is my delight,
   the lot you have given to me.

3. Glad are my heart and my soul;
   securely my body shall rest.
   For you will not leave me for dead,
   nor lead your beloved astray.

4. You show me the path for my life;
   in your presence the fullness of joy.
   To be at your right hand for ever
   for me would be happiness always.

John Foley
© 1970 New Dawn Music

127

1. Forth in the peace of Christ we go;
   Christ to the world with joy we bring;
   Christ in our minds, Christ on our lips,
   Christ in our hearts,
   the world's true King.

2. King of our hearts, Christ makes
   us kings;
   kingship with him his servants gain;
   with Christ, the Servant-Lord of all,
   Christ's world we serve
   to share Christ's reign.

3. Priests of the world, Christ sends
   us forth
   the world of time to consecrate,
   the world of sin by grace to heal,
   Christ's world in Christ
   to re-create.

4. Christ's are our lips, his words we speak;
   prophets are we whose deeds proclaim
   Christ's truth in love that we may be
   Christ in the world,
   to spread Christ's name.

5. We are the Church; Christ bids us show
   that in his Church all nations find
   their hearth and home where
       Christ restores
   true peace, true love,
   to all mankind.

James Quinn (b. 1919)

128

1. Forth in thy name, O Lord, I go,
   my daily labour to pursue;
   thee, only thee, resolved to know,
   in all I think or speak or do.

Continued overleaf

2. The task thy wisdom hath assigned
O let me cheerfully fulfil;
in all my works thy presence find,
and prove thy good and perfect will.

3. Thee may I set at my right hand,
whose eyes my inmost substance see,
and labour on at thy command,
and offer all my works to thee.

4. Give me to bear thy easy yoke,
and ev'ry moment watch and pray,
and still to things eternal look,
and hasten to thy glorious day.

5. For thee delightfully employ
whate'er thy bounteous grace
    hath given,
and run my course with even joy,
and closely walk with thee to heaven.

Charles Wesley (1707-1788)

129

1. Forty days and forty nights
thou wast fasting in the wild;
forty days and forty nights
tempted still, yet unbeguiled.

2. Sunbeams scorching all the day,
chilly dew-drops nightly shed,
prowling beasts about thy way,
stones thy pillow, earth thy bed.

3. Let us thy endurance share
and from earthly greed abstain,
with thee watching unto prayer,
with thee strong to suffer pain.

4. Then if evil on us press,
flesh or spirit to assail,
victor in the wilderness,
help us not to swerve or fail!

5. So shall peace divine be ours;
holier gladness ours shall be;
come to us angelic powers,
such as ministered to thee.

6. Keep, O keep us, Saviour dear,
ever constant by thy side,
that with thee we may appear
at th'eternal Eastertide.

George Hunt Smyttan (1822-1870) and others

130

1. From heav'n you came, helpless babe,
entered our world, your glory veiled;
not to be served but to serve,
and give your life that we might live.

*This is our God, the Servant King,
he calls us now to follow him,
to bring our lives as a daily offering
of worship to the Servant King.*

2. There in the garden of tears,
my heavy load he chose to bear;
his heart with sorrow was torn,
'Yet not my will but yours,' he said.

3. Come see his hands and his feet,
the scars that speak of sacrifice,
hands that flung stars into space
to cruel nails surrendered.

4. So let us learn how to serve,
and in our lives enthrone him;
each other's needs to prefer,
for it is Christ we're serving.

Graham Kendrick (b. 1950)
© 1983 Kingsway's Thankyou Music

131

1. From many grains, once scattered
     far and wide,
   each one alone, to grow as best it may,
   now safely gathered in and unified,
   one single loaf we offer here today.
   So may your church, in ev'ry time
     and place,
   be in this meal united by your grace.

2. From many grapes, once living on
     the vine,
   now crushed and broken under
     human feet,
   we offer here this single cup of wine:
   the sign of love,
     unbroken and complete.
   So may we stand among the crucified,
   and live the risen life of him who died.

3. From many places gathered,
     we are here,
   each with a gift that we alone
     can bring.
   O Spirit of the living God, draw near,
   make whole by grace
     our broken offering.
   O crush the pride that bids us
     stand alone;
   let flow the love that makes our
     spirits one.

   Michael Forster (b. 1946)

132

1. From the very depths of darkness
     springs a bright and living light;
   out of falsehood and deceit
   a greater truth is brought to sight;
   in the halls of death, defiant,
   life is dancing with delight!
   The Lord is risen indeed!

Christ is risen! Hallelujah!
Christ is risen! Hallelujah!
Christ is risen! Hallelujah!
The Lord is risen indeed!

2. Jesus meets us at the dawning
   of the resurrection day;
   speaks our name with love, and gently
   says that here we may not stay:
   'Do not cling to me, but go to all
   the fearful ones and say,
   "The Lord is risen indeed!" '

3. So proclaim it in the high rise,
   in the hostel let it ring;
   make it known in Cardboard City,
   let the homeless rise and sing:
   'He is Lord of life abundant,
   and he changes everything;
   the Lord is risen indeed!'

4. In the heartlands of oppression,
   sound the cry of liberty:
   where the poor are crucified,
   behold the Lord of Calvary;
   from the fear of death and dying,
   Christ has set his people free;
   the Lord is risen indeed!

5. To the tyrant, tell the gospel
   of a love he's never known
   in his guarded palace tomb,
   condemned to live and die alone:
   'Take the risk of love and freedom;
   Christ has rolled away the stone!
   The Lord is risen indeed!'

6. When our spirits are entombed
   in mortal prejudice and pride;
   when the gates of hell itself
   are firmly bolted from inside;
   at the bidding of his Spirit,
   we may fling them open wide;
   the Lord is risen indeed!

   Michael Forster (b. 1946)

133

Gather around, for the table is spread,
welcome the food and rest!
Wide is our circle, with Christ at the head,
he is the honoured guest.
Learn of his love, grow in his grace,
pray for the peace he gives;
here at this meal, here in this place,
know that his spirit lives!
Once he was known
in the breaking of bread,
shared with a chosen few;
multitudes gathered and
by him were fed,
so will he feed us too.

Jean Holloway (b. 1939)

134

1. Gifts of bread and wine,
   gifts we've offered,
   fruits of labour, fruits of love;
   taken, offered, sanctified,
   blessed and broken;
   words of one who died:

   'Take my body, take my saving blood.'
   Gifts of bread and wine:
   Christ our Lord.

2. Christ our Saviour,
   living presence here,
   as he promised while on earth:
   'I am with you for all time,
   I am with you
   in this bread and wine.'

3. Through the Father,
   with the Spirit,
   one in union with the Son,
   for God's people, joined in prayer,
   faith is strengthened
   by the food we share.

   Christine McCann (b. 1951)

135

1. Give me joy in my heart,
   keep me praising,
   give me joy in my heart, I pray.
   Give me joy in my heart,
   keep me praising,
   keep me praising till the end of day.

   Sing hosanna! Sing hosanna!
   Sing hosanna to the King of kings!
   Sing hosanna! Sing hosanna!
   Sing hosanna to the King!

2. Give me peace in my heart,
   keep me resting,
   give me peace in my heart, I pray.
   Give me peace in my heart,
   keep me resting,
   keep me resting till the end of day.

3. Give me love in my heart,
   keep me serving,
   give me love in my heart, I pray.
   Give me love in my heart,
   keep me serving,
   keep me serving till the end of day.

4. Give me oil in my lamp,
   keep me burning,
   give me oil in my lamp, I pray.
   Give me oil in my lamp,
   keep me burning,
   keep me burning till the end of day.

   Traditional

136

Glory and praise to our God,
who alone gives light to our days.
Many are the blessings he bears
to those who trust in his ways.

1. We, the daughters and sons of him
   who built the valleys and plains,
   praise the wonders our God has done
   in ev'ry heart that sings.

2. In his wisdom he strengthens us,
   like gold that's tested in fire.
   Though the power of sin prevails,
   our God is there to save.

3. Ev'ry moment of ev'ry day
   our God is waiting to save,
   always ready to seek the lost,
   to answer those who pray.

4. God has watered our barren land
   and sent his merciful rain.
   Now the rivers of life run full
   for anyone to drink.

   Dan Schutte, based on Psalm 65, 66
   © 1976 New Dawn Music

137

1. Glory be to Jesus
   who, in bitter pains,
   poured for me the life-blood
   from his sacred veins.

2. Grace and life eternal
   in that blood I find:
   blest be his compassion,
   infinitely kind.

3. Blest, through endless ages,
   be the precious stream
   which, from endless torment,
   doth the world redeem.

4. There the fainting spirit
   drinks of life her fill;
   there, as in a fountain,
   laves herself at will.

5. Abel's blood for vengeance
   pleaded to the skies,
   but the blood of Jesus
   for our pardon cries.

6. Oft as it is sprinkled
   on our guilty hearts
   Satan in confusion
   terror-struck departs.

7. Oft as earth exulting
   wafts its praise on high
   hell with horror trembles;
   heav'n is filled with joy.

8. Lift ye, then, your voices;
   swell the mighty flood;
   louder still and louder,
   praise the precious blood.

   18th century, tr. Edward Caswall (1814-1878)

138

1. Glory to God, glory to God,
   glory to the Father.
   Glory to God, glory to God,
   glory to the Father.
   To him be glory for ever.
   To him be glory for ever.
   Alleluia, amen.
   Alleluia, amen,
   alleluia, amen,
   alleluia, amen.

Continued overleaf

2. Glory to God, glory to God,
Son of the Father.
**Glory to God, glory to God,
Son of the Father.**
To him be glory for ever.
To him be glory for ever.
Alleluia, amen.
**Alleluia, amen,
alleluia, amen,
alleluia, amen.**

3. Glory to God, glory to God,
glory to the Spirit.
**Glory to God, glory to God,
glory to the Spirit.**
To him be glory for ever.
To him be glory for ever.
Alleluia, amen.
**Alleluia, amen,
alleluia, amen,
alleluia, amen.**

*Traditional Peruvian,
collected by John Ballantine (b. 1945)*

139

1. Glory to thee, Lord God!
In faith and hope we sing.
Through this completed sacrifice
our love and praise we bring.
We give thee for our sins
a price beyond all worth,
which none could ever fitly pay
but this thy Son on earth.

2. Here is the Lord of all,
to thee in glory slain;
of worthless givers, worthy gift,
a victim without stain.
Through him we give thee thanks,
with him we bend the knee,
in him be all our life, who is
our one true way to thee.

3. So may this sacrifice
we offer here this day,
be joined with our poor lives in all
we think and do and say.
By living true to grace,
for thee and thee alone,
our sorrows, labours, and our joys
will be his very own.

John Greally

140

1. Glory to thee, my God, this night,
for all the blessings of the light;
keep me, O keep me, King of kings,
beneath thine own almighty wings.

2. Forgive me, Lord, for thy dear Son,
the ill that I this day have done,
that with the world, myself and thee,
I, ere I sleep, at peace may be.

3. Teach me to live, that I may dread
the grave as little as my bed;
teach me to die, that so I may
rise glorious at the awful day.

4. O may my soul on thee repose,
and with sweet sleep mine eyelids close;
sleep that may me more vig'rous make
to serve my God when I awake.

5. Praise God, from whom all
blessings flow;
praise him, all creatures here below;
praise him above, ye heavenly host;
praise Father, Son and Holy Ghost.

Thomas Ken (1637-1710)

141

Go, tell it on the mountain,
over the hills and ev'rywhere,
go, tell it on the mountain
that Jesus Christ is born.

1. While shepherds kept their watching
   o'er wand'ring flocks by night,
   behold, from out of heaven,
   there shone a holy light.

2. And lo, when they had seen it,
   they all bowed down and prayed;
   they travelled on together
   to where the babe was laid.

3. When I was a seeker,
   I sought both night and day:
   I asked my Lord to help me
   and he showed me the way.

4. He made me a watchman
   upon the city wall,
   and, if I am a Christian,
   I am the least of all.
   Traditional

142

1. Go, the Mass is ended,
   children of the Lord.
   Take his Word to others
   as you've heard it spoken to you.
   Go, the Mass is ended,
   go and tell the world
   the Lord is good, the Lord is kind,
   and he loves ev'ryone.

2. Go, the Mass is ended,
   take his love to all.
   Gladden all who meet you,
   fill their hearts with hope and courage.
   Go, the Mass is ended,
   fill the world with love,
   and give to all what you've received
   – the peace and joy of Christ.

3. Go, the Mass is ended,
   strengthened in the Lord,
   lighten ev'ry burden,
   spread the joy of Christ around you.
   Go, the Mass is ended,
   take his peace to all.
   This day is yours to change the world
   – to make God known and loved.
   Marie Lydia Pereira (b. 1920)

143

God be in my head,
and in my understanding;
God be in mine eyes,
and in my looking;
God be in my mouth,
and in my speaking;
God be in my heart,
and in my thinking;
God be at mine end,
and at my departing.
'Book of Hours' (1514)

144

God fills me with joy, alleluia.
His holy presence is my robe, alleluia.

1. My soul, now glorify the Lord
   who is my Saviour.
   Rejoice, for who am I,
   that God has shown me favour.

Continued overleaf

2. The world shall call me blest
   and ponder on my story.
   In me is manifest
   God's greatness and his glory.

   God fills me with joy, alleluia.
   His holy presence is my robe, alleluia.

3. For those who are his friends,
   and keep his laws as holy,
   his mercy never ends,
   and he exalts the lowly.

4. But by his power the great,
   the proud, the self-conceited,
   the kings who sit in state,
   are humbled and defeated.

5. He feeds the starving poor,
   he guards his holy nation,
   fulfilling what he swore
   long since in revelation.

6. Then glorify with me
   the Lord who is my Saviour:
   one holy Trinity
   for ever and for ever.

   Jean-Paul Lécot (b. 1947)
   based on Luke 1:46-55, tr. Michael Hodgetts

145

1. God forgave my sin in Jesus' name.
   I've been born again in Jesus' name.
   And in Jesus' name I come to you
   to share his love as he told me to.

   He said: 'Freely, freely you have received;
   freely, freely give.
   Go in my name, and because you believe,
   others will know that I live.'

2. All pow'r is giv'n in Jesus' name,
   in earth and heav'n in Jesus' name.
   And in Jesus' name I come to you
   to share his pow'r as he told me to.

3. God gives us life in Jesus' name,
   he lives in us in Jesus' name.
   And in Jesus' name I come to you
   to share his peace as he told me to.

   Carol Owens
   © 1972 Bud John Songs Inc/CopyCare Ltd

146

God has filled me with endless joy,
alleluia!
He has vested me with holiness,
alleluia!

1. My soul praises
   the glory of the Lord,
   and my spirit exults
   in God my Saviour.

2. He has looked on his
   handmaid's lowliness;
   from now on ev'ryone
   shall call me blessèd.

3. The Almighty has done
   great things for me,
   and his mercy is shown
   to all who fear him.

4. He has put down the mighty
   from their thrones,
   and has raised up on high
   the poor and lowly.

5. He has filled those who hunger
   with good things,
   but the rich he has sent
   away quite empty.

6. He protected his
   servant Israel,
   as he promised to
   Abraham for ever.

7. God the Father,
   the Son and Spirit praise,
   as it was, and is now,
   and ever shall be.

   Jean-Paul Lécot (b. 1947),
   based on Luke 1:46-55, tr. W. R. Lawrence

147

1. God is love,
   and the one who lives in love
   lives in God, and God lives in him.
   God is love,
   and the one who lives in love
   lives in God, and God lives in him.
   And we have come to know
   and have believed
   the love which God has for us.
   God is love,
   and the one who lives in love
   lives in God, and God lives in him.

2. God is hope,
   and the one who lives in hope
   lives in God, and God lives in her.
   God is hope,
   and the one who lives in hope
   lives in God, and God lives in her.
   And we have come to know
   and have believed
   the love which God has for us.
   God is hope,
   and the one who lives in hope
   lives in God, and God lives in her.

3. God is peace,
   and the one who lives in peace
   lives in God, and God lives in him.
   God is peace,
   and the one who lives in peace
   lives in God, and God lives in him.
   And we have come to know
   and have believed
   the love which God has for us.
   God is peace,
   and the one who lives in peace
   lives in God, and God lives in him.

4. God is joy,
   and the one who lives in joy
   lives in God, and God lives in her.
   God is joy,
   and the one who lives in joy
   lives in God, and God lives in her.
   And we have come to know
   and have believed
   the love which God has for us.
   God is joy,
   and the one who lives in joy
   lives in God, and God lives in her.

   Traditional

148

1. God is love: his the care,
   tending each, ev'rywhere.
   God is love, all is there!
   Jesus came to show him,
   that mankind might know him!

   Sing aloud, loud, loud!
   Sing aloud, loud, loud!
   God is good! God is truth!
   God is beauty! Praise him!

Continued overleaf

2. None can see God above;
   we can share life and love;
   thus may we Godward move,
   seek him in creation,
   holding ev'ry nation.

   Sing aloud, loud, loud!
   Sing aloud, loud, loud!
   God is good! God is truth!
   God is beauty! Praise him!

3. Jesus lived on the earth,
   life and hope brought to birth
   and affirmed human worth,
   for he came to save us
   by the truth he gave us.

4. To our Lord praise we sing,
   light and life, friend and king,
   coming down, love to bring,
   pattern for our duty,
   showing God in beauty.

   Percy Dearmer (1867-1936), alt.

149

1. God of mercy and compassion,
   look with pity upon me;
   Father, let me call thee Father,
   'tis thy child returns to thee.

   Jesus, Lord, I ask for mercy,
   knowing it is not in vain:
   all my sins I now detest them,
   help me not to sin again.

2. Only by thy grace and mercy
   may I hope for heav'n above,
   where the saints rejoice for ever
   in a sea of boundless love.

3. See our Saviour, bleeding, dying
   on the cross of Calvary;
   to that cross my sins have nailed him,
   yet he bleeds and dies for me.

   Edmund Vaughan (1827-1908), alt.

150

God rest you merry, gentlemen,
let nothing you dismay,
for Jesus Christ our Saviour
was born on Christmas day,
to save us all from Satan's power
when we were gone astray:

O tidings of comfort and joy,
comfort and joy,
O tidings of comfort and joy.

2. In Bethlehem, in Jewry,
   this blessèd babe was born,
   and laid within a manger,
   upon this blessèd morn;
   the which his mother Mary
   did nothing take in scorn.

3. From God, our heav'nly Father,
   a blessèd angel came,
   and unto certain shepherds
   brought tidings of the same,
   how that in Bethlehem was born
   the Son of God by name.

4. 'Fear not,' then said the angel,
   'let nothing you affright,
   this day is born a Saviour,
   of virtue, pow'r and might;
   so frequently to vanquish all
   the friends of Satan quite.'

5. The shepherds at those tidings
   rejoicèd much in mind,
   and left their flocks a-feeding,
   in tempest, storm and wind,
   and went to Bethlehem straightway
   this blessèd babe to find.

6. But when to Bethlehem they came,
   whereat this infant lay,
   they found him in a manger,
   where oxen feed on hay;
   his mother Mary kneeling,
   unto the Lord did pray.

7. Now to the Lord sing praises,
all you within this place,
and with true love and fellowship
each other now embrace;
this holy tide of Christmas
all others doth deface.

Traditional English

151

1. Godhead here in hiding,
whom I do adore,
masked by these bare shadows,
shape and nothing more,
see, Lord, at thy service
low lies here a heart
lost, all lost in wonder
at the God thou art.

2. Seeing, touching, tasting
are in thee deceived;
how says trusty hearing,
that shall be believed?
What God's Son hath told me,
take for truth I do;
truth himself speaks truly,
or there's nothing true.

3. On the cross thy Godhead
made no sign to men;
here thy very manhood
steals from human ken;
both are my confession,
both are my belief;
and I pray the prayer
of the dying thief.

4. I am not like Thomas,
wounds I cannot see,
but can plainly call thee
Lord and God as he;
this faith each day deeper
be my holding of,
daily make me harder
hope and dearer love.

5. O thou our reminder
of Christ crucified,
living Bread, the life of
us for whom he died,
lend this life to me then;
feed and feast my mind,
there be thou the sweetness
man was meant to find.

6. Jesu, whom I look at
shrouded here below,
I beseech thee send me
what I long for so,
some day to gaze on thee
face to face in light
and be blest for ever
with thy glory's sight.

Ascribed to St Thomas Aquinas (1227-1274)
tr. Gerard Manley Hopkins (1844-1889)

152

1. God's Spirit is in my heart.
He has called me and set me apart.
This is what I have to do,
what I have to do.

He sent me to give
the Good News to the poor,
tell pris'ners that
they are pris'ners no more,
tell blind people that they can see,
and set the downtrodden free,
and go tell ev'ryone
the news that
the kingdom of God has come,
and go tell ev'ryone
the news that God's kingdom has come.

Continued overleaf

2. Just as the Father sent me,
   so I'm sending you out to be
   my witnesses throughout the world,
   the whole of the world.

   He sent me to give
   the Good News to the poor,
   tell pris'ners that
   they are pris'ners no more,
   tell blind people that they can see,
   and set the downtrodden free,
   and go tell ev'ryone
   the news that
   the kingdom of God has come,
   and go tell ev'ryone
   the news that God's kingdom has come.

3. Don't carry a load in your pack,
   you don't need two shirts on your back.
   A workman can earn his own keep,
   can earn his own keep.

4. Don't worry what you have to say,
   don't worry because on that day
   God's Spirit will speak in your heart,
   will speak in your heart.

   Alan Dale and Hubert J. Richards (b. 1921)

153

1. Going home, going home,
   I'm a-going home.
   Quiet like, some still day,
   I'm just going home.
   It's not far, just close by,
   through an open door.
   Work all done, care laid by,
   going to fear no more.
   Mother's there expecting me,
   father's waiting too.
   Lots of folk gathered there,
   all the friends I knew,
   all the friends I knew.

2. Morning star lights the way,
   restless dreams all done.
   Shadows gone, break of day,
   real life just begun.
   There's no break, there's no end,
   just a living on,
   wide awake with a smile,
   going on and on.
   Going home, going home.
   I'm just going home.
   It's not far, just close by,
   through an open door.
   I'm just going home.

   William Arms Fisher

154

1. Good King Wenceslas looked out
   on the feast of Stephen,
   when the snow lay round about,
   deep, and crisp, and even:
   brightly shone the moon that night,
   though the frost was cruel,
   when a poor man came in sight,
   gath'ring winter fuel.

2. 'Hither, page, and stand by me,
   if thou know'st it, telling,
   yonder peasant, who is he,
   where and what his dwelling?'
   'Sire, he lives a good league hence,
   underneath the mountain,
   right against the forest fence,
   by Saint Agnes' fountain.'

3. 'Bring me flesh, and bring me wine,
   bring me pine logs hither:
   thou and I will see him dine,
   when we bring them thither.'
   Page and monarch, forth they went,
   forth they went together;
   through the rude wind's wild lament,
   and the bitter weather.

4. 'Sire, the night is darker now,
   and the wind blows stronger;
   fails my heart, I know not how;
   I can go no longer.'
   'Mark my footsteps good, my page;
   tread thou in them boldly:
   thou shalt find the winter's rage
   freeze thy blood less coldly.'

5. In his master's steps he trod,
   where the snow lay dinted;
   heat was in the very sod
   which the Saint had printed.
   Therefore, Christians all, be sure,
   wealth or rank possessing,
   ye who now will bless the poor,
   shall yourselves find blessing.

   John Mason Neale (1818-1866), alt.

155

1. Great is thy faithfulness,
   O God my Father,
   there is no shadow
   of turning with thee;
   thou changest not,
   thy compassions, they fail not;
   as thou hast been
   thou forever wilt be.

   Great is thy faithfulness!
   Great is thy faithfulness!
   Morning by morning
   new mercies I see;
   all I have needed
   thy hand hath provided,
   great is thy faithfulness,
   Lord, unto me!

2. Summer and winter,
   and springtime and harvest,
   sun, moon and stars
   in their courses above,
   join with all nature
   in manifold witness
   to thy great faithfulness,
   mercy and love.

3. Pardon for sin and
   a peace that endureth,
   thine own dear presence
   to cheer and to guide;
   strength for today
   and bright hope for tomorrow,
   blessings all mine,
   with ten thousand beside!

   Thomas O. Chisholm (1866-1960)

156

1. Guide me, O thou great Redeemer,
   pilgrim through this barren land;
   I am weak, but thou art mighty,
   hold me with thy pow'rful hand:
   Bread of Heaven, Bread of Heaven,
   feed me till I want no more,
   feed me till I want no more.

2. Open now the crystal fountain,
   whence the healing stream doth flow;
   let the fire and cloudy pillar
   lead me all my journey through;
   strong deliverer, strong deliverer,
   be thou still my strength and shield,
   be thou still my strength and shield.

3. When I tread the verge of Jordan,
   bid my anxious fears subside,
   death of death, and hell's destruction,
   land me safe on Canaan's side;
   songs of praises, songs of praises,
   I will ever give to thee,
   I will ever give to thee.

   William Williams (1717-1791),
   tr. Peter Williams (1727-1796) and others

157

1. Hail, glorious Saint Patrick,
   dear saint of our isle,
   on us thy poor children
   bestow a sweet smile;
   and now thou art high
   in the mansions above,
   on Erin's green valleys
   look down in thy love.

   On Erin's green valleys,
   on Erin's green valleys,
   on Erin's green valleys
   look down in thy love.

2. Hail, glorious Saint Patrick,
   thy words were once strong
   against Satan's wiles and
   an infidel throng;
   not less is thy might
   where in heaven thou art;
   O, come to our aid,
   in our battle take part.

3. In the war against sin,
   in the fight for the faith,
   dear saint, may thy children
   resist unto death;
   may their strength be in meekness,
   in penance, in prayer,
   their banner the Cross
   which they glory to bear.

4. Thy people, now exiles
   on many a shore,
   shall love and revere thee
   till time be no more;
   and the fire thou hast kindled
   shall ever burn bright;
   its warmth undiminished,
   undying its light.

5. Ever bless and defend
   the sweet land of our birth,
   where the shamrock still blooms
   as when thou wert on earth,
   and our hearts shall yet burn,
   wheresoever we roam,
   for God and Saint Patrick,
   and our native home.

   Sister Agnes

158

1. Hail, Queen of heav'n, the ocean star,
   guide of the wand'rer here below;
   thrown on life's surge, we claim thy care;
   save us from peril and from woe.
   Mother of Christ, star of the sea,
   pray for the wand'rer, pray for me.

2. O gentle, chaste and spotless maid,
   we sinners make our prayers
      through thee;
   remind thy Son that he has paid
   the price of our iniquity.
   Virgin most pure, star of the sea,
   pray for the sinner, pray for me.

3. Sojourners in this vale of tears,
   to thee, blest advocate, we cry;
   pity our sorrows, calm our fears,
   and soothe with hope our misery.
   Refuge in grief, star of the sea,
   pray for the mourner, pray for me.

4. And while to him who reigns above,
   in Godhead One, in persons Three,
   the source of life, of grace, of love,
   homage we pay on bended knee,
   do thou, bright Queen, star of the sea,
   pray for thy children, pray for me.

   John Lingard (1771-1851)

159

1. Hail, Redeemer, King divine!
   Priest and Lamb, the throne is thine,
   King, whose reign shall never cease,
   Prince of everlasting peace.

   Angels, saints and nations sing:
   'Praised be Jesus Christ, our King,
   Lord of life, earth, sky and sea,
   King of love on Calvary.'

2. King whose name creation thrills,
   rule our minds, our hearts, our wills,
   till in peace each nation rings
   with thy praises, King of kings.

3. King most holy, King of truth,
   guide the lowly, guide the youth;
   Christ thou King of glory bright,
   be to us eternal light.

4. Shepherd-King, o'er mountains steep,
   homeward bring the wand'ring sheep,
   shelter in one royal fold
   states and kingdoms, new and old.

   Patrick Brennan (1877-1952)

160

1. Hail the day that sees him rise,
   alleluia!
   to his throne above the skies,
   alleluia!
   Christ, the Lamb for sinners giv'n,
   alleluia!
   enters now the highest heav'n,
   alleluia!

2. There for him high triumph waits;
   lift your heads eternal gates!
   He hath conquered death and sin;
   take the King of glory in!

3. Circled round with angel-powers,
   their triumphant Lord and ours;
   wide unfold the radiant scene,
   take the King of glory in!

4. Lo, the heav'n its Lord receives,
   yet he loves the earth he leaves;
   though returning to his throne,
   still he calls mankind his own.

5. See, he lifts his hands above,
   see, he shows the prints of love;
   hark, his gracious lips bestow
   blessings on his Church below.

6. Still for us he intercedes,
   his prevailing death he pleads;
   near himself prepares our place,
   he the first-fruits of our race.

7. Lord, though parted from our sight,
   far above the starry height,
   grant our hearts may thither rise,
   seeking thee above the skies.

8. Ever upward let us move,
   wafted on the wings of love;
   looking when our Lord shall come,
   longing, sighing after home.

   Charles Wesley (1707-1788),
   Thomas Cotterill (1779-1823) and others

161

1. Hail, thou star of ocean,
   portal of the sky,
   ever virgin mother
   of the Lord most high.
   O, by Gabriel's Ave,
   uttered long ago,
   Eva's name reversing,
   'stablish peace below.

Continued overleaf

2. Break the captive's fetters,
   light on blindness pour,
   all our ills expelling,
   ev'ry bliss implore.
   Show thyself a mother;
   offer him our sighs,
   who for us incarnate
   did not thee despise.

3. Virgin of all virgins,
   to thy shelter take us;
   gentlest of the gentle,
   chaste and gentle make us.
   Still, as on we journey,
   help our weak endeavour;
   till with thee and Jesus
   we rejoice for ever.

4. Through the highest heaven,
   to th'almighty Three,
   Father, Son and Spirit,
   One same glory be.

   9th century, tr. Edward Caswall (1814-1878)

162

1. Hail to the Lord's anointed!
   Great David's greater son;
   hail, in the time appointed,
   his reign on earth begun!
   He comes to break oppression,
   to set the captive free;
   to take away transgression,
   and rule in equity.

2. He shall come down like showers
   upon the fruitful earth,
   and love, joy, hope, like flowers,
   spring in his path to birth:
   before him on the mountains
   shall peace the herald go;
   and righteousness in fountains
   from hill to valley flow.

3. Kings shall fall down before him,
   and gold and incense bring;
   all nations shall adore him,
   his praise all people sing;
   to him shall prayer unceasing
   and daily vows ascend;
   his kingdom still increasing,
   a kingdom without end.

4. O'er ev'ry foe victorious,
   he on his throne shall rest,
   from age to age more glorious,
   all-blessing and all-blest;
   the tide of time shall never
   his covenant remove;
   his name shall stand for ever;
   that name to us is love.

   James Montgomery (1771-1854)

163

Hallelujah, my Father,
for giving us your Son;
sending him into the world
to be given up for all,
knowing we would bruise him
and smite him from the earth!
Hallelujah, my Father,
in his death is my birth.
Hallelujah, my Father,
in his life is my life.

Tim Cullen, alt.
© 1975 Celebration/Kingsway's Thankyou Music

164

1. Hark, a herald voice is calling:
   'Christ is nigh!' it seems to say;
   'Cast away the dreams of darkness,
   O ye children of the day!'

2. Startled at the solemn warning,
   let the earth-bound soul arise;
   Christ, her sun, all sloth dispelling,
   shines upon the morning skies.

3. Lo, the Lamb, so long expected,
comes with pardon down from heaven;
let us haste, with tears of sorrow,
one and all to be forgiven.

4. So when next he comes with glory,
wrapping all the earth in fear,
may he then, as our defender,
on the clouds of heav'n appear.

5. Honour, glory, virtue, merit,
to the Father and the Son,
with the co-eternal Spirit,
while unending ages run.

6th century,
tr. Edward Caswall (1814-1878)

165

1. Hark, the herald angels sing,
glory to the new-born King;
peace on earth and mercy mild,
God and sinners reconciled:
joyful all ye nations rise,
join the triumph of the skies,
with th'angelic host proclaim,
Christ is born in Bethlehem.

Hark, the herald angels sing,
glory to the new-born King.

2. Christ, by highest heav'n adored,
Christ, the everlasting Lord,
late in time behold him come,
offspring of a virgin's womb!
Veiled in flesh the Godhead see,
hail th'incarnate Deity!
Pleased as man with us to dwell,
Jesus, our Emmanuel.

3. Hail the heav'n-born Prince of peace!
Hail the Sun of righteousness!
Light and life to all he brings,
ris'n with healing in his wings;
mild he lays his glory by,
born that we no more may die,
born to raise us from the earth,
born to give us second birth.

Charles Wesley (1707-1788),
George Whitefield (1714-1770),
Martin Madan (1726-1790) and others, alt.

166

1. He brings us into his banqueting table,
his banner over me is love;
he brings us into his banqueting table,
his banner over me is love;
he brings us into his banqueting table,
his banner over me is love;
his banner over me is love.

2. The one way to peace
is the power of the cross,
his banner over me is love,
the one way to peace
is the power of the cross,
his banner over me is love;
the one way to peace
is the power of the cross,
his banner over me is love,
his banner over me is love.

3. He builds his Church
on a firm foundation,
his banner over me is love;
he builds his Church
on a firm foundation,
his banner over me is love;
he builds his Church
on a firm foundation,
his banner over me is love,
his banner over me is love.

Continued overleaf

4. In him we find a new creation,
   his banner over me is love;
   in him we find a new creation,
   his banner over me is love;
   in him we find a new creation,
   his banner over me is love,
   his banner over me is love.

5. He lifts us up to heavenly places,
   his banner over me is love;
   he lifts us up to heavenly places,
   his banner over me is love;
   he lifts us up to heavenly places,
   his banner over me is love,
   his banner over me is love.

   Traditional

167

1. He is Lord, he is Lord.
   He is risen from the dead
   and he is Lord.
   Ev'ry knee shall bow,
   ev'ry tongue confess
   that Jesus Christ is Lord.

2. He is King, he is King.
   He is risen from the dead
   and he is King.
   Ev'ry knee shall bow,
   ev'ry tongue confess
   that Jesus Christ is King.

3. He is love, he is love.
   He is risen from the dead
   and he is love.
   Ev'ry knee shall bow,
   ev'ry tongue confess
   that Jesus Christ is love.

   Unknown

168

1. He is risen, tell the story
   to the nations of the night;
   from their sin and from their blindness,
   let them walk in Easter light.
   Now begins a new creation,
   now has come our true salvation,
   Jesus Christ, the Son of God!

2. Mary goes to tell the others
   of the wonders she has seen;
   John and Peter come a-running
   – what can all this truly mean?
   O Rabboni, Master holy,
   to appear to one so lowly!
   Jesus Christ, the Son of God!

3. He has cut down death and evil,
   he has conquered all despair;
   he has lifted from our shoulders
   all the weight of anxious care.
   Risen Brother, now before you,
   we will worship and adore you,
   Jesus Christ, the Son of God!

4. Now get busy, bring the message,
   so that all may come to know
   there is hope for saint and sinner,
   for our God has loved us so.
   Ev'ry church bell is a-ringing,
   ev'ry Christian now is singing,
   Jesus Christ, the Son of God!

   Willard F. Jabusch (b. 1930)

169

1. He who would valiant be
   'gainst all disaster,
   let him in constancy
   follow the Master.
   There's no discouragement
   shall make him once relent
   his first avowed intent
   to be a pilgrim.

2. Who so beset him round
   with dismal stories,
   do but themselves confound:
   his strength the more is.
   No foes shall stay his might
   though he with giants fight:
   he will make good the right
   to be a pilgrim.

3. Since, Lord, thou dost defend
   us with thy Spirit,
   we know we at the end
   shall life inherit.
   Then fancies flee away!
   I'll fear not what men say,
   I'll labour night and day
   to be a pilgrim.

   Percy Dearmer (1867-1936)
   after John Bunyan (1628-1688)

170

1. Here in this place,
   new light is streaming,
   now is the darkness
   vanished away;
   see in this space,
   our fears and our dreamings,
   brought here to you
   in the light of this day.
   Gather us in, the lost and forsaken,
   gather us in, the blind and the lame;
   call to us now, and we shall awaken,
   we shall arise at the sound of
       your name.

2. We are the young,
   our lives are a myst'ry,
   we are the old
   who yearn for your face;
   we have been sung
   throughout all of hist'ry,
   called to be light
   to the whole human race.
   Gather us in, the rich and the haughty,
   gather us in, the proud and the strong;
   give us a heart so meek and so lowly,
   give us the courage to enter the song.

3. Here we will take
   the wine and the water,
   here we will take
   the bread of new birth;
   here you shall call
   your sons and your daughters,
   call us anew
   to be salt for the earth.
   Give us to drink the wine
       of compassion,
   give us to eat the bread that is you;
   nourish us well, and teach us
       to fashion
   lives that are holy and hearts that
       are true.

4. Not in the dark
   of buildings confining,
   not in some heaven,
   light years away,
   but here in this place
   the new light is shining,
   now is the kingdom,
   now is the day.
   Gather us in and hold us forever,
   gather us in and make us your own;
   gather us in, all peoples together,
   fire of love in our flesh and our bone.

   Marty Haugen (b. 1950)

171

1. He's got the whole world in his hand.
   He's got the whole world in his hand.
   He's got the whole world in his hand.
   He's got the whole world in his hand.

2. He's got you and me, brother,
      in his hand.
   He's got you and me, brother,
      in his hand.
   He's got you and me, brother,
      in his hand.
   He's got the whole world in his hand.

3. He's got you and me, sister,
      in his hand.
   He's got you and me, sister,
      in his hand.
   He's got you and me, sister,
      in his hand.
   He's got the whole world in his hand.

4. He's got the little tiny baby in his hand.
   He's got the little tiny baby in his hand.
   He's got the little tiny baby in his hand.
   He's got the whole world in his hand.

5. He's got ev'rybody here in his hand.
   He's got ev'rybody here in his hand.
   He's got ev'rybody here in his hand.
   He's got the whole world in his hand.

Traditional

172

1. Hevenu shalom aleikhem,
   hevenu shalom aleikhem,
   hevenu shalom aleikhem,
   hevenu shalom, shalom,
   shalom aleikhem.

2. We bring you peace and rejoicing,
   we bring you peace and rejoicing,
   we bring you peace and rejoicing,
   we bring you peace in God's name,
   peace. We sing shalom.

3. Hevenu shalom aleikhem,
   hevenu shalom aleikhem,
   hevenu shalom aleikhem,
   hevenu shalom, shalom,
   shalom aleikhem.

Traditional Israeli

173

1. His name is higher than any other.
   His name is Jesus; his name is Lord.
   His name is higher than any other.
   His name is Jesus; his name is Lord.

2. His name is Wonderful;
      his name is Counsellor.
   His name is Prince of Peace,
      the mighty God.
   His name is Wonderful;
      his name is Counsellor.
   His name is Prince of Peace,
      the mighty God.

3. His name is higher than any other.
   His name is Jesus; his name is Lord.
   His name is higher than any other.
   His name is Jesus; his name is Lord.

From Isaiah 9:6

174

1. Holy God, we praise thy name;
   Lord of all, we bow before thee.
   All on earth thy sceptre own,
   all in heaven above adore thee.
   Infinite thy vast domain,
   everlasting is thy reign.

2. Hark, the loud celestial hymn,
   angel choirs above are raising;
   cherubim and seraphim,
   in unceasing chorus praising,
   fill the heavens with sweet accord,
   holy, holy, holy Lord.

3. Holy Father, Holy Son,
   Holy Spirit, three we name thee,
   while in essence only one
   undivided God we claim thee;
   and adoring bend the knee,
   while we own the mystery.

4. Spare thy people, Lord, we pray,
   by a thousand snares surrounded;
   keep us without sin today;
   never let us be confounded.
   Lo, I put my trust in thee,
   never, Lord, abandon me.

   Ascribed to Ignaz Franz (1719-1790),
   tr. Clarence Walworth (1820-1900)

175

1. Holy, holy, holy, holy.
   Holy, holy, holy Lord
   God almighty;
   and we lift our hearts before you
   as a token of our love,
   holy, holy, holy, holy.

2. Gracious Father, gracious Father,
   we are glad to be your children,
   gracious Father;
   and we lift our heads before you
   as a token of our love,
   gracious Father, gracious Father.

3. Risen Jesus, risen Jesus,
   we are glad you have redeemed us,
   risen Jesus;
   and we lift our hands before you
   as a token of our love,
   risen Jesus, risen Jesus.

4. Holy Spirit, Holy Spirit,
   come and fill our hearts anew,
   Holy Spirit;
   and we lift our voice before you
   as a token of our love,
   Holy Spirit, Holy Spirit.

5. Hallelujah, hallelujah,
   hallelujah, hallelujah,
   hallelujah;
   and we lift our hearts before you
   as a token of our love,
   hallelujah, hallelujah.

   Jimmy Owens
   © 1972 Bud John Songs Inc/CopyCare Ltd

176

1. Holy, holy, holy is the Lord,
   holy is the Lord God almighty.
   Holy, holy, holy is the Lord,
   holy is the Lord God almighty:
   who was, and is, and is to come;
   holy, holy, holy is the Lord.

2. Jesus, Jesus, Jesus is the Lord,
   Jesus is the Lord God almighty.
   Jesus, Jesus, Jesus is the Lord,
   Jesus is the Lord God almighty:
   who was, and is, and is to come;
   Jesus, Jesus, Jesus is the Lord.

3. Worthy, worthy, worthy is the Lord,
   worthy is the Lord God almighty.
   Worthy, worthy, worthy is the Lord,
   worthy is the Lord God almighty:
   who was, and is, and is to come;
   worthy, worthy, worthy is the Lord.

Continued overleaf

4. Glory, glory, glory to the Lord,
glory to the Lord God almighty.
Glory, glory, glory to the Lord,
glory to the Lord God almighty:
who was, and is, and is to come;
glory, glory, glory is the Lord.

For liturgical version (Sanctus)
see hymn no 677

Unknown

177

1. Holy, holy, holy!
Lord God almighty!
Early in the morning
our song shall rise to thee;
holy, holy, holy!
Merciful and mighty!
God in three persons,
blessed Trinity!

2. Holy, holy, holy!
All the saints adore thee,
casting down their golden crowns
around the glassy sea;
cherubim and seraphim
falling down before thee,
which wert, and art, ·
and ever more shall be.

3. Holy, holy, holy!
Though the darkness hide thee,
though the eye made blind by sin
thy glory may not see,
only thou art holy,
there is none beside thee,
perfect in pow'r,
in love, and purity.

4. Holy, holy, holy!
Lord God almighty!
All thy works shall praise thy name,
in earth, and sky and sea;
holy, holy, holy!
Merciful and mighty!
God in three persons,
blessèd Trinity!

Reginald Heber (1783-1826)

178

1. Holy Spirit, come, confirm us
in the truth that Christ makes known;
we have faith and understanding
through your promised light alone.

2. Holy Spirit, come, console us,
come as Advocate to plead;
loving Spirit from the Father,
grant in Christ the help we need.

3. Holy Spirit, come renew us,
come yourself to make us live;
holy through your loving presence,
holy through the gifts you give.

4. Holy Spirit, come, possess us,
you the love of Three in One,
Holy Spirit of the Father,
Holy Spirit of the Son.

Brian Foley (b. 1919)

179

1. Holy Spirit, Lord of light,
from the clear celestial height,
thy pure beaming radiance give;
come, thou Father of the poor,
come with treasures which endure;
come, thou light of all that live!

2. Thou, of all consolers best,
   thou, the soul's delightsome guest,
   dost refreshing peace bestow:
   thou in toil art comfort sweet;
   pleasant coolness in the heat;
   solace in the midst of woe.

3. Light immortal, light divine,
   visit thou these hearts of thine,
   and our inmost being fill:
   if thou take thy grace away,
   nothing pure in us will stay;
   all his good is turned to ill.

4. Heal our wounds, our strength renew;
   on our dryness pour thy dew;
   wash the stains of guilt away;
   bend the stubborn heart and will;
   melt the frozen, warm the chill;
   guide the steps that go astray.

5. Thou, on those who ever more
   thee confess and thee adore,
   in thy sev'nfold gifts descend:
   give them comfort when they die;
   give them life with thee on high;
   give them joys that never end.

   Ascribed to Stephen Langton (d. 1228)
   tr. Edward Caswall (1814-1878), alt.

180

1. Holy virgin, by God's decree,
   you were called eternally;
   that he could give his Son to our race.
   Mary, we praise you, hail, full of grace.

   Ave, ave, ave, Maria.

2. By your faith and loving accord,
   as the handmaid of the Lord,
   you undertook God's plan to embrace.
   Mary, we thank you, hail, full of grace.

3. Joy to God you gave and expressed,
   of all women none more blessed,
   when in mankind your Son took
     his place.
   Mary, we love you, hail, full of grace.

4. Refuge for your children so weak,
   sure protection all can seek.
   Problems of life you help us to face.
   Mary, we trust you, hail, full of grace.

5. To our needy world of today
   love and beauty you portray,
   showing the path to Christ we
     must trace.
   Mary, our mother, hail, full of grace.

   Jean-Paul Lécot (b. 1947),
   tr. W. R. Lawrence (b. 1925)

181

How great is our God,
how great is his name!
How great is our God,
for ever the same!

1. He rolled back the waters
   of the mighty Red Sea,
   and he said: 'I'll never leave you.
   Put your trust in me.'

2. He sent his Son, Jesus,
   to set us all free,
   and he said: 'I'll never leave you.
   Put your trust in me.'

3. He gave us his Spirit,
   and now we can see.
   And he said: 'I'll never leave you.
   Put your trust in me.'

   Unknown

182

1. How lovely on the mountains
   are the feet of him
   who brings good news, good news,
   announcing peace,
   proclaiming news of happiness:
   our God reigns, our God reigns.

   Our God reigns, our God reigns,
   our God reigns, our God reigns.

2. You watchmen, lift your voices
   joyfully as one,
   shout for your king, your King!
   See eye to eye,
   the Lord restoring Sion:
   our God reigns, our God reigns.

3. Wasteplaces of Jerusalem,
   break forth with joy!
   We are redeemed, redeemed.
   The Lord has saved
   and comforted his people:
   our God reigns, our God reigns.

4. Ends of the earth, see the salvation
   of our God!
   Jesus is Lord, is Lord!
   Before the nations,
   he has bared his holy arm:
   our God reigns, our God reigns.

Based on Isaiah 52, 53.
Vs 1, Leonard E. Smith Jnr (b.1942)
Vv 2-4 Unknown
© 1974 Kingsway's Thankyou Music

183

1. I am the bread of life.
   He who comes to me shall not hunger.
   He who believes in me shall not thirst.
   No-one can come to me
   unless the Father draw him.

   And I will raise him up,
   and I will raise him up,
   and I will raise him up on the last day.

2. The bread that I will give
   is my flesh for the life of the world,
   and if you eat of this bread,
   you shall live for ever,
   you shall live for ever.

3. Unless you eat
   of the flesh of the Son of Man,
   and drink of his blood,
   and drink of his blood,
   you shall not have life within you.

4. I am the resurrection,
   I am the life.
   If you believe in me,
   even if you die,
   you shall live for ever.

5. Yes, Lord, I believe
   that you are the Christ,
   the Son of God,
   who has come
   into the world.

Suzanne Toolan (b. 1927), alt.

184

1. I give my hands to do your work
   and, Jesus, Lord, I give them willingly.
   I give my feet to go your way
   and ev'ry step I shall take cheerfully.

   O, the joy of the Lord
   is my strength, my strength!
   O, the joy of the Lord
   is my help, my help!
   For the pow'r of his Spirit
   is in my soul
   and the joy of the Lord
   is my strength.

2. I give my eyes to see the world
   and ev'ryone, in just the way you do.
   I give my tongue to speak your words,
   to spread your name and
      freedom-giving truth.

3. I give my mind in every way
   so that each thought I have will come
      from you.
   I give my spirit to you, Lord,
   and every day my prayer will
      spring anew.

4. I give my heart that you may love
   in me your Father and the
      human race.
   I give myself that you may grow
   in me and make my life a song
      of praise.

Estelle White (b. 1925)

185

1. **I** have made a **covenant**
   with my **cho**sen,
   given my **ser**vant my **word**.
   I have made your **name** to **last** for**ever**,
   built to out**last** all **time**.

   I will celebrate your love for ever,
   Yahweh.
   Age on age my words proclaim
   your love.
   For I claim that love is built to
   last forever,
   founded firm your faithfulness.

2. **Yah**weh, the assembly of **those**
   who **love** you
   ap**plaud** your **marvellous word**.
   Who in the **skies** can com**pare**
      with **Yah**weh?
   Which can **rival him**?

3. **Happy** the **people** who **learn**
   to ac**claim** you.
   They re**joice** in your **light**.
   You are our **glory and** our **cour**age.
   Our **hope** be**longs** to **you**.

4. **I** have re**vealed** my **cho**sen **servant**
   and **he** can re**ly** on **me**;
   given him my **love** to **last** for**ever**.
   He shall rise **in** my **name**.

5. **He** will call to **me**,
   'My **Father**! My **God**!'
   For **I make** him my **first** born **son**.
   I cannot take **back** my **given** promise.
   I've **called** him to **shine** like the **sun**.

Karen Barrie (b. 1948),
based on Psalm 89

186

1. I, the Lord of sea and sky,
   I have heard my people cry.
   All who dwell in dark and sin
   my hand will save.
   I who made the stars of night,
   I will make their darkness bright.
   Who will bear my light to them?
   Whom shall I send?

   Here I am, Lord. Is it I, Lord?
   I have heard you calling in the night.
   I will go, Lord, if you lead me.
   I will hold your people in my heart.

2. I, the Lord of snow and rain,
   I have borne my people's pain.
   I have wept for love of them.
   They turn away.
   I will break their hearts of stone,
   give them hearts for love alone.
   I will speak my word to them.
   Whom shall I send?

3. I, the Lord of wind and flame,
   I will tend the poor and lame.
   I will set a feast for them.
   My hand will save.
   Finest bread I will provide
   till their hearts be satisfied.
   I will give my life to them.
   Whom shall I send?

   Dan Schutte, based on Isaiah 6
   © 1981 New Dawn Music

187

1. I watch the sunrise lighting the sky,
   casting its shadows near.
   And on this morning, bright though
     it be,
   I feel those shadows near me.

But you are always close to me,
following all my ways.
May I be always close to you,
following all your ways, Lord.

2. I watch the sunlight shine through
     the clouds,
   warming the earth below.
   And at the mid-day, life seems to say:
   'I feel your brightness near me.'

   For you are always . . .

3. I watch the sunset fading away,
   lighting the clouds with sleep.
   And as the evening closes its eyes,
   I feel your presence near me.

   For you are always . . .

4. I watch the moonlight guarding
     the night,
   waiting till morning comes.
   The air is silent, earth is at rest
   – only your peace is near me.

   Yes, you are always . . .
   John Glynn (b. 1948)

188

I will be with you wherever you go.
Go now throughout the world!
I will be with you in all that you say.
Go now and spread my word!

1. Come, walk with me on stormy waters.
   Why fear? Reach out, and I'll be there.

2. And you, my friend, will you now
     leave me,
   or do you know me as your Lord?

3. Your life will be transformed
   with power
   by living truly in my name.

4. And if you say: 'Yes, Lord, I love you,'
   then feed my lambs and feed
   my sheep.

   Gerard Markland

189

1. I will never forget you, my people;
   I have carved you
   on the palm of my hand.
   I will never forget you;
   I will not leave you orphaned.
   I will never forget my own.

2. Does a mother forget her baby?
   Or a woman
   the child within her womb?
   Yet even if these forget,
   yes, even if these forget,
   I will never forget my own.

3. I will never forget you, my people;
   I have carved you
   on the palm of my hand.
   I will never forget you;
   I will not leave you orphaned.
   I will never forget my own.

   Carey Landry, based on Isaiah 49:15
   © 1975 North American Liturgy Resources

190

1. I will sing, I will sing
   a song unto the Lord.
   I will sing, I will sing
   a song unto the Lord.
   I will sing, I will sing
   a song unto the Lord.
   Alleluia, glory to the Lord.

Allelu, alleluia, glory to the Lord.
Allelu, alleluia, glory to the Lord.
Allelu, alleluia, glory to the Lord.
Alleluia, glory to the Lord.

2. We will come, we will come
   as one before the Lord.
   We will come, we will come
   as one before the Lord.
   We will come, we will come
   as one before the Lord.
   Alleluia, glory to the Lord.

3. If the Son, if the Son,
   if the Son shall make you free,
   if the Son, if the Son,
   if the Son shall make you free,
   if the Son, if the Son,
   if the Son shall make you free,
   you shall be free indeed.

4. They that sow, they that sow
   in tears shall reap in joy.
   They that sow, they that sow
   in tears shall reap in joy.
   They that sow, they that sow
   in tears shall reap in joy.
   Alleluia, glory to the Lord.

5. Ev'ry knee shall bow
   and ev'ry tongue confess,
   ev'ry knee shall bow
   and ev'ry tongue confess,
   ev'ry knee shall bow
   and ev'ry tongue confess
   that Jesus Christ is Lord.

6. In his name, in his name
   we have the victory.
   In his name, in his name
   we have the victory.
   In his name, in his name
   we have the victory.
   Alleluia, glory to the Lord.

   Max Dyer (b. 1951)
   © 1974 Celebration/Kingsway's Thankyou Music

191

1. I wonder as I wander
   out under the sky,
   how Jesus the Saviour
   did come for to die
   for poor ord'n'ry people
   like you and like I.
   I wonder as I wander
   out under the sky.

2. When Mary birthed Jesus,
   'twas in a cow's stall
   with wise men and farmers
   and shepherds and all.
   But high from God's heaven
   a star's light did fall,
   and the promise of ages
   it did then recall.

3. If Jesus had wanted
   for any wee thing,
   a star in the sky,
   or a bird on the wing,
   or all of God's angels
   in heav'n for to sing,
   he surely could have it,
   'cause he was the King.

Traditional North American

192

If God is for us, who can be against,
if the Spirit of God has set us free?
If God is for us, who can be against,
if the Spirit of God has set us free?

1. I know that nothing in this world
   can ever take us from his love.

2. Nothing can take us from his love,
   poured out on Jesus, the Lord.

3. And nothing present or to come
   can ever take us from his love.

4. I know that neither death nor life
   can ever take us from his love.

John Foley, based on Romans 8:31-39
© 1975 New Dawn Music

193

1. If I were a butterfly
   I'd thank you, Lord,
   for giving me wings,
   and if I were a robin in a tree
   I'd thank you, Lord, that I could sing,
   and if I were a fish in the sea
   I'd wiggle my tail
   and I'd giggle with glee,
   but I just thank you, Father,
   for making me me.

   For you gave me a heart
   and you gave me a smile,
   you gave me Jesus
   and you made me your child,
   and I just thank you, Father,
   for making me me.

2. If I were an elephant
   I'd thank you, Lord,
   by raising my trunk,
   and if I were a kangaroo
   you know I'd hop right up to you,
   and if I were an octopus
   I'd thank you, Lord,
   for my fine looks,
   but I just thank you, Father,
   for making me me.

3. If I were a wiggly worm
   I'd thank you, Lord,
   that I could squirm,
   and if I were a billy goat
   I'd thank you, Lord, for my
       strong throat,
   and if I were a fuzzy wuzzy bear
   I'd thank you, Lord,
   for my fuzzy wuzzy hair,
   but I just thank you, Father,
   for making me me.

Brian Howard
© 1974 Celebration/Kingsway's Thankyou Music

194

1. I'll sing a hymn to Mary,
   the mother of my God,
   the virgin of all virgins,
   of David's royal blood.
   O teach me, holy Mary,
   a loving song to frame,
   when wicked men blaspheme thee,
   to love and bless thy name.

2. O noble Tower of David,
   of gold and ivory,
   the Ark of God's own promise,
   the gate of heav'n to me,
   to live and not to love thee,
   would fill my soul with shame;
   when wicked men blaspheme thee,
   I'll love and bless thy name.

3. The saints are high in glory,
   with golden crowns so bright;
   but brighter far is Mary,
   upon her throne of light.
   O that which God did give thee,
   let mortal ne'er disclaim;
   when wicked men blaspheme thee,
   I'll love and bless thy name.

4. But in the crown of Mary,
   there lies a wondrous gem,
   as queen of all the angels,
   which Mary shares with them:
   no sin hath e'er defiled thee,
   so doth our faith proclaim;
   when wicked men blaspheme thee,
   I'll love and bless thy name.

John Wyse (1825-1898)

195

1. Immaculate Mary!
   Our hearts are on fire,
   that title so wondrous
   fills all our desire.

   Ave, ave, ave Maria!
   Ave, ave, ave Maria!

2. We pray for God's glory,
   may his kingdom come!
   We pray for his vicar,
   our father, and Rome.

3. We pray for our mother
   the church upon earth,
   and bless, sweetest lady,
   the land of our birth.

4. For poor, sick, afflicted
   thy mercy we crave;
   and comfort the dying,
   thou light of the grave.

5. In grief and temptation,
   in joy or in pain,
   we'll ask thee, our mother,
   nor seek thee in vain.

6. In death's solemn moment,
   our mother, be nigh;
   as children of Mary,
   O teach us to die.

Continued overleaf

7. And crown thy sweet mercy
   with this special grace,
   and worship in heaven
   God's ravishing face.

   Ave, ave, ave Maria!
   Ave, ave, ave Maria!

8. To God be all glory
   and worship for aye;
   to God's virgin mother
   an endless Ave.

   Unknown

196

1. Immortal, invisible,
   God only wise,
   in light inaccessible
   hid from our eyes,
   most blessèd, most gracious,
   the Ancient of Days,
   almighty, victorious,
   thy great name we praise.

2. Unresting, unhasting,
   and silent as light;
   not wanting, nor wasting,
   thou rulest in might;
   thy justice like mountains
   high soaring above
   thy clouds which are fountains
   of goodness and love.

3. To all life thou givest,
   to both great and small;
   in all life thou livest,
   the true life of all;
   we blossom and flourish
   as leaves on the tree,
   and wither and perish
   but naught changeth thee.

4. Great Father of glory,
   pure Father of light,
   thine angels adore thee,
   all veiling their sight;
   all laud we would render,
   O help us to see
   'tis only the splendour
   of light hideth thee.

   Walter Chalmers Smith (1824-1908), based on 1 Tim. 1:17

197

1. In bread we bring you, Lord,
   our bodies' labour.
   In wine we offer you
   our spirits' grief.
   We do not ask you, Lord,
   who is my neighbour,
   but stand united now,
   one in belief.
   O we have gladly heard
   your Word, your holy Word,
   and now in answer, Lord,
   our gifts we bring.
   Our selfish hearts make true,
   our failing faith renew,
   our lives belong to you,
   our Lord and King.

2. The bread we offer you
   is blessed and broken,
   and it becomes for us
   our spirits' food.
   Over the cup we bring
   your Word is spoken;
   make it your gift to us,
   your healing blood.
   Take all that daily toil
   plants in our hearts' poor soil,
   take all we start and spoil,
   each hopeful dream,
   the chances we have missed,
   the graces we resist,
   Lord, in thy Eucharist,
   take and redeem.

   Kevin Nichols (b. 1929)

198

1. In the bleak midwinter
   frosty wind made moan,
   earth stood hard as iron,
   water like a stone;
   snow had fallen, snow on snow,
   snow on snow,
   in the bleak midwinter long ago.

2. Our God, heav'n cannot hold him
   nor earth sustain;
   heav'n and earth shall flee away
   when he comes to reign.
   In the bleak midwinter
   a stable-place sufficed
   the Lord God almighty, Jesus Christ.

3. Enough for him, whom cherubim
   worship night and day,
   a breastful of milk,
   and a mangerful of hay:
   enough for him, whom angels
   fall down before,
   the ox and ass and camel which adore.

4. Angels and archangels
   may have gathered there,
   cherubim and seraphim
   thronged the air;
   but only his mother
   in her maiden bliss
   worshipped the belovèd with a kiss.

5. What can I give him,
   poor as I am?
   If I were a shepherd
   I would bring a lamb;
   if I were a wise man
   I would do my part,
   yet what I can I give him:
   give my heart.

   Christina Rossetti (1830-1894)

199

In the Lord I'll ever be thankful,
in the Lord I will rejoice!
Look to him, do not be afraid;
in him rejoicing: the Lord is near,
in him rejoicing: the Lord is near.

Taizé Community

200

1. In the love of God and neighbour
   we are gathered at his table:
   gifts of bread and wine
   will become a sign
   of the love our Father gave us,
   through the Son who came to save us,
   by the Spirit blest.

2. So we offer our tomorrows,
   all our present joys and sorrows,
   ev'ry heart and will,
   talent, gift and skill.
   For the riches we've been given
   to the Trinity of heaven
   we give thanks and praise.

   Estelle White (b. 1925)

201

1. Infant holy, infant lowly,
   for his bed a cattle stall;
   oxen lowing, little knowing
   Christ the babe is Lord of all.
   Swift are winging angels singing,
   nowells ringing, tidings bringing,
   Christ the babe is Lord of all,
   Christ the babe is Lord of all.

Continued overleaf

2. Flocks were sleeping, shepherds keeping
   vigil till the morning new;
   saw the glory, heard the story,
   tidings of a gospel true.
   Thus rejoicing, free from sorrow,
   praises voicing, greet the morrow,
   Christ the babe was born for you,
   Christ the babe was born for you.

   Tr. from the Polish
   by Edith M. G. Reed (1885-1933)

202

1. Into one we all are gathered
   through the love of Christ.
   Let us then rejoice with gladness.
   In him we find love.
   Let us fear and love the living God,
   and love and cherish all mankind.

   Where charity and love are,
   there is God.

2. Therefore, when we are together
   in the love of Christ,
   let our minds know no division,
   strife or bitterness;
   may the Christ our God be in our midst.
   Through Christ our Lord all love
      is found.

3. May we see your face in glory,
   Christ our loving God.
   With the blessèd saints of heaven
   give us lasting joy.
   We will then possess true happiness,
   and love for all eternity.

   Michael Cockett (b. 1938),
   adapted from 'Ubi Caritas et Amor'

203

1. It came upon the midnight clear,
   that glorious song of old,
   from angels bending near the earth
   to touch their harps of gold:
   'Peace on the earth, goodwill to all,
   from heav'n's all-gracious King!'
   The world in solemn stillness lay
   to hear the angels sing.

2. Yet with the woes of sin and strife
   the world has suffered long;
   beneath the angel-strain have rolled
   two thousand years of wrong;
   and warring humankind hears not
   the love-song which they bring:
   O hush the noise, and cease your strife,
   and hear the angels sing!

3. For lo, the days are hastening on,
   by prophets seen of old,
   when with the ever-circling years
   shall come the time foretold,
   when the new heav'n and earth
      shall own
   the Prince of Peace their King,
   and all the world send back the song
   which now the angels sing.

   Edmund Hamilton Sears (1810-1876) alt.

204

It's me, it's me, it's me, O Lord,
standing in the need of prayer.
It's me, it's me, it's me, O Lord,
standing in the need of prayer.

1. Not my brother or my sister,
   but it's me, O Lord,
   standing in the need of prayer.
   Not my brother or my sister,
   but it's me, O Lord,
   standing in the need of prayer.

2. Not my mother or my father,
   but it's me, O Lord,
   standing in the need of prayer.
   Not my mother or my father,
   but it's me, O Lord,
   standing in the need of prayer.

3. Not the stranger or my neighbour,
   but it's me, O Lord,
   standing in the need of prayer.
   Not the stranger or my neighbour,
   but it's me, O Lord,
   standing in the need of prayer.

Spiritual

205

1. Jerusalem the golden,
   with milk and honey blest,
   beneath thy contemplation
   sink heart and voice oppressed.
   I know not, ah, I know not
   what joys await us there,
   what radiancy of glory,
   what bliss beyond compare.

2. They stand, those halls of Sion,
   all jubilant with song,
   and bright with many an angel,
   and all the martyr throng;
   the prince is ever in them,
   the daylight is serene;
   the pastures of the blessèd
   are decked in glorious sheen.

3. There is the throne of David;
   and there, from care released,
   the shout of them that triumph,
   the song of them that feast;
   and they, who with their leader
   have conquered in the fight,
   for ever and for ever
   are clad in robes of white.

4. O sweet and blessèd country,
   the home of God's elect!
   O sweet and blessèd country
   that eager hearts expect!
   Jesus, in mercy, brings us
   to that dear land of rest;
   who art, with God the Father
   and Spirit, ever blest.

From 'De Contemptu Mundi'
by St Bernard of Cluny (12th cent)

206

1. Jesu, lover of my soul,
   let me to thy bosom fly,
   while the nearer waters roll,
   while the tempest still is high:
   hide me, O my Saviour, hide
   till the storm of life is past;
   safe into the haven guide,
   O receive my soul at last.

2. Other refuge have I none,
   hangs my helpless soul on thee;
   leave, ah, leave me not alone,
   still support and comfort me.
   All my trust on thee is stayed,
   all my help from thee I bring;
   cover my defenceless head
   with the shadow of thy wing.

3. Plenteous grace with thee is found,
   grace to cover all my sin;
   let the healing streams abound,
   make and keep me pure within.
   Thou of life the fountain art,
   freely let me take of thee,
   spring thou up within my heart,
   rise to all eternity.

Charles Wesley (1707-1788)

207

1. Jesu, the very thought of thee
   with sweetness fills my breast;
   but sweeter far thy face to see,
   and in thy presence rest.

2. No voice can sing, no heart can frame,
   nor can the memory find,
   a sweeter sound than thy blest name,
   O Saviour of mankind.

3. O hope of ev'ry contrite heart,
   O joy of all the meek,
   to those who fall, how kind thou art,
   how good to those who seek!

4. But what to those who find? Ah, this
   no tongue nor pen can show;
   the love of Jesus, what it is
   none but his lovers know.

5. Jesu, our only joy be thou,
   as thou our prize wilt be,
   Jesu, be thou our glory now,
   and through eternity.

   11th century, tr. Edward Caswall (1814-1878)

208

1. Jesus Christ is ris'n today, *alleluia!*
   our triumphant holy day, *alleluia!*
   who did once, upon the cross, *alleluia!*
   suffer to redeem our loss, *alleluia!*

2. Hymns of praise then let us sing
   unto Christ, our heavenly King,
   who endured the cross and grave,
   sinners to redeem and save.

3. But the pains that he endured
   our salvation have procured;
   now above the sky he's King
   where the angels ever sing.

   From 'Lyra Davidica', 1708

209

1. Jesus Christ is waiting,
   waiting in the streets:
   no-one is his neighbour,
   all alone he eats.
   Listen, Lord Jesus,
   I am lonely too;
   make me, friend or stranger,
   fit to wait on you.

2. Jesus Christ is raging,
   raging in the streets
   where injustice spirals
   and all hope retreats.
   Listen, Lord Jesus,
   I am angry too;
   in the kingdom's causes
   let me rage with you.

3. Jesus Christ is healing,
   healing in the streets;
   curing those who suffer,
   touching those he greets.
   Listen, Lord Jesus,
   I have pity too;
   let my care be active,
   healing just like you.

4. Jesus Christ is dancing,
   dancing in the streets,
   where each sign of hatred
   his strong love defeats.
   Listen, Lord Jesus,
   I feel triumph too;
   on suspicion's graveyard,
   let me dance with you.

5. Jesus Christ is calling,
   calling in the streets,
   'Come and walk faith's tightrope,
   I will guide your feet.'
   Listen, Lord Jesus,
   let my fears be few;
   walk one step before me,
   I will follow you.

John Bell (b. 1949)
and Graham Maule (b. 1958)

211

Jesus, Jesus,
can I tell you what I know?
You have given me your Spirit.
I love you so.

Unknown

210

1. Jesus, gentlest Saviour,
   God of might and power,
   thou thyself art dwelling
   in us at this hour.
   Nature cannot hold thee,
   heav'n is all too strait
   for thine endless glory,
   and thy royal state.

2. Yet the hearts of children,
   hold what worlds cannot,
   and the God of wonders
   loves the lowly spot.
   Jesus, gentlest Saviour,
   thou art in us now,
   fill us full of goodness,
   till our hearts o'erflow.

3. Pray the prayer within us
   that to heaven shall rise;
   sing the song that angels
   sing above the skies;
   multiply our graces,
   chiefly love and fear;
   and, dear Lord, the chiefest,
   grace to persevere.

Frederick William Faber (1814-1863)

212

1. Jesus, my Lord, my God, my all,
   how can I love thee as I ought?
   And how revere this wondrous gift
   so far surpassing hope or thought?

   Sweet Sacrament, we thee adore;
   O make us love thee more and more.

2. Had I but Mary's sinless heart
   to love thee with, my dearest King,
   O, with what bursts of fervent praise
   thy goodness, Jesus, would I sing!

3. Ah, see, within a creature's hand
   the vast Creator deigns to be,
   reposing, infant-like, as though
   on Joseph's arm, or Mary's knee.

4. Thy body, soul and Godhead, all;
   O mystery of love divine!
   I cannot compass all I have,
   for all thou hast and art are mine.

5. Sound, sound, his praises higher still,
   and come, ye angels, to our aid;
   'tis God, 'tis God, the very God
   whose pow'r both us and angels made.

Frederick William Faber (1814-1863)

213

Jesus, name above all names,
beautiful Saviour, glorious Lord,
Emmanuel, God is with us,
blessèd Redeemer, living Word.

Naida Hearn (b. 1944)
© 1974 Scripture in Song/CopyCare Ltd

214

Jesus, remember me
when you come into your kingdom.
Jesus, remember me
when you come into your kingdom.

Taizé Community, based on Scripture

215

1. Jesus, thou art coming,
   holy as thou art,
   thou, the God who made me,
   to my sinful heart.
   Jesus, I believe it,
   on thy only word;
   kneeling, I adore thee,
   as my King and Lord.

2. Put thy kind arms round me,
   feeble as I am;
   thou art my good shepherd:
   I, thy little lamb;
   since thou comest, Jesus,
   now to be my guest,
   I can trust thee always, Lord,
   for all the rest.

3. Dearest Lord, I love thee,
   with my whole heart,
   not for what thou givest,
   but for what thou art.
   Come, O come, sweet Saviour!
   Come to me, and stay,
   for I want thee, Jesus,
   more than I can say.

4. Ah, what gift or present,
   Jesus, can I bring?
   I have nothing worthy
   of my God and King;
   but thou art my shepherd:
   I, thy little lamb,
   take myself, dear Jesus,
   all I have and am.

5. Take my body, Jesus,
   eyes and ears and tongue;
   never let them, Jesus,
   help to do thee wrong.
   Take my heart and fill it
   full of love for thee;
   all I have I give thee,
   give thyself to me.

A Sister of Notre Dame

216

Jesus, you are Lord.
You are risen from the dead
and you are Lord.
Ev'ry knee shall bow,
and ev'ry tongue confess
that Jesus, you are Lord.
You are the Way.

1. I am the Way.
   No-one knows the Father
   but it be through me.
   I am in my Father, and my Father is
     in me,
   and we come in love
   to live within your heart.

2. I am the Truth,
   and I set my spirit
   deep within your hearts,
   and you will know me, and love me,
   and the truth I give to you
   will set you free.

3. I am the Life.
   The living waters
   I pour out for you.
   Anyone who drinks of the waters
      that I give
   will have eternal life.

4. I am the Word,
   the true light that shines
   brightly in the dark,
   a light that darkness
   could not overpow'r,
   the Word made Flesh,
   risen among you.

   Mary Barrett (born 1942), based on St John

3. He rules the world with truth
      and grace,
   and makes the nations prove
   the glories of his righteousness,
   and wonders of his love,
   and wonders of his love,
   and wonders, and wonders of
      his love.

   Isaac Watts (1674-1748), alt.

218

Jubilate, ev'rybody,
serve the Lord in all your ways and
come before his presence singing;
enter now his courts with praise.
For the Lord our God is gracious,
and his mercy everlasting.
Jubilate, jubilate, jubilate Deo!

Fred Dunn (1907-1979)
© 1977 Kingsway's Thankyou Music

217

1. Joy to the world! The Lord is come;
   let earth receive her King;
   let ev'ry heart prepare him room,
   and heav'n and nature sing,
   and heav'n and nature sing,
   and heaven, and heaven and nature sing.

2. Joy to the earth! The Saviour reigns;
   let us our songs employ;
   while fields and floods, rocks,
      hills and plains
   repeat the sounding joy,
   repeat the sounding joy,
   repeat, repeat the sounding joy.

219

1. Just as I am, without one plea
   but that thy blood was shed for me,
   and that thou bidst me come to thee,
   O Lamb of God, I come.

2. Just as I am, though tossed about
   with many a conflict, many a doubt,
   fightings and fears within, without,
   O Lamb of God, I come.

3. Just as I am, poor, wretched, blind;
   sight, riches, healing of the mind,
   yea, all I need, in thee to find,
   O Lamb of God, I come.

Continued overleaf

4. Just as I am, thou wilt receive,
   wilt welcome, pardon, cleanse, relieve:
   because thy promise I believe,
   O Lamb of God, I come.

5. Just as I am, thy love unknown
   has broken ev'ry barrier down,
   now to be thine, yea, thine alone,
   O Lamb of God, I come.

6. Just as I am, of that free love
   the breadth, length, depth and height
      to prove,
   here for a season, then above,
   O Lamb of God, I come.

   Charlotte Elliott (1789-1871)

220

*Keep in mind that Jesus Christ
has died for us
and is risen from the dead.
He is our saving Lord,
he is joy for all ages.*

1. If we die with the Lord,
   we shall live with the Lord.

2. If we endure with the Lord,
   we shall reign with the Lord.

3. In him hope of glory,
   in him all our love.

4. In him our redemption,
   in him all our grace.

5. In him our salvation,
   in him all our peace.

   Lucien Deiss (b. 1921), based on 2 Tim 2:8-11

221

1. King of glory, King of peace,
   I will love thee;
   and, that love may never cease,
   I will move thee.
   Thou hast granted my request,
   thou hast heard me;
   thou didst note my working breast,
   thou hast spared me.

2. Wherefore with my utmost art,
   I will sing thee,
   and the cream of all my heart
   I will bring thee.
   Though my sins against me cried,
   thou didst clear me,
   and alone, when they replied,
   thou didst hear me.

3. Seven whole days, not one in seven,
   I will praise thee;
   in my heart, though not in heaven,
   I can raise thee.
   Small it is, in this poor sort
   to enrol thee:
   e'en eternity's too short
   to extol thee.

   George Herbert (1593-1633)

222

1. Kum ba yah, my Lord, kum ba yah,
   kum ba yah, my Lord, kum ba yah,
   kum ba yah, my Lord, kum ba yah,
   O Lord, kum ba yah.

2. Someone's crying, Lord, kum ba yah,
   someone's crying, Lord, kum ba yah,
   someone's crying, Lord, kum ba yah,
   O Lord, kum ba yah.

3. Someone's singing, Lord, kum ba yah,
   someone's singing, Lord, kum ba yah,
   someone's singing, Lord, kum ba yah,
   O Lord, kum ba yah.

4. Someone's praying, Lord, kum ba yah,
   someone's praying, Lord, kum ba yah,
   someone's praying, Lord, kum ba yah,
   O Lord, kum ba yah.

Spiritual

223

Laudate Dominum,
laudate Dominum,
omnes gentes,
alleluia.

Taizé Community (Psalm 117)
The Latin 'Laudate Dominum omnes gentes'
translates as 'Praise the Lord, all peoples'.

224

Laudato sii, O mi Signore.
Laudato sii, O mi Signore.
Laudato sii, O mi Signore.
Laudato sii, O mi Signore.

1. Yes, be praised in all your creatures,
   brother sun and sister moon;
   in the stars and in the wind,
   air and fire and flowing water.

2. For our sister, mother earth,
   she who feeds us and sustains us;
   for her fruits, her grass, her flowers,
   for the mountains and the oceans.

3. Praise for those who spread forgiveness,
   those who share your peace with others,
   bearing trials and sickness bravely!
   Even sister death won't harm them.

4. For our life is but a song,
   and the reason for our singing
   is to praise you for the music;
   join the dance of your creation.

5. Praise to you, Father most holy,
   praise and thanks to you, Lord Jesus,
   praise to you, most Holy Spirit,
   life and joy of all creation!

Damian Lundy (b. 1944)
from St Francis of Assisi (1182-1226)
The Italian 'Laudato sii, O mi Signore'
translates as 'Praise be to you, O my Lord'.

225

Lay your hands gently upon us,
let their touch render your peace,
let them bring your forgiveness
and healing,
lay your hands, gently lay your hands.

1. You were sent to free the
   broken-hearted.
   You were sent to give sight to
   the blind.
   You desire to heal all our illness.
   Lay your hands,
   gently lay your hands.

2. Lord, we come to you through
   one another,
   Lord, we come to you in all our need.
   Lord, we come to you
   seeking wholeness.
   Lay your hands,
   gently lay your hands.

Carey Landry
© 1977 North American Liturgy Resources

226

1. Lead, kindly light,
   amid th'encircling gloom,
   lead thou me on;
   the night is dark,
   and I am far from home,
   lead thou me on.
   Keep thou my feet;
   I do not ask to see
   the distant scene;
   one step enough for me.

2. I was not ever thus,
   nor prayed that thou
   shouldst lead me on;
   I loved to choose
   and see my path; but now
   lead thou me on.
   I loved the garish day
   and, spite of fears,
   pride ruled my will;
   remember not past years.

3. So long thy power
   hath blest me, sure it still
   will lead me on
   o'er moor and fen,
   o'er crag and torrent, till
   the night is gone,
   and with the morn
   those angel faces smile
   which I have loved long since,
   and lost awhile.

   John Henry Newman (1801-1890)

227

1. Lead us, heav'nly Father, lead us
   o'er the world's tempestuous sea;
   guard us, guide us, keep us, feed us,
   for we have no help but thee;
   yet possessing ev'ry blessing
   if our God our Father be.

2. Saviour, breathe forgiveness o'er us,
   all our weakness thou dost know,
   thou didst tread this earth before us,
   thou didst feel its keenest woe;
   lone and dreary, faint and weary,
   through the desert thou didst go.

3. Spirit of our God, descending,
   fill our hearts with heav'nly joy,
   love with ev'ry passion blending,
   pleasure that can never cloy;
   thus provided, pardoned, guided,
   nothing can our peace destroy.

   James Edmeston (1791-1867)

228

1. Leader, now on earth no longer,
   soldier of th'eternal King,
   victor in the fight for heaven,
   we thy loving praises sing.

   Great Saint George, our patron, help us,
   in the conflict be thou nigh;
   help us in that daily battle,
   where each one must win or die.

2. Praise him who in deadly battle
   never shrank from foeman's sword,
   proof against all earthly weapon,
   gave his life for Christ the Lord.

3. Who, when earthly war was over,
   fought, but not for earth's renown;
   fought, and won a nobler glory,
   won the martyr's purple crown.

4. Help us when temptation presses,
   we have still our crown to win;
   help us when our soul is weary
   fighting with the pow'rs of sin.

5. Clothe us in thy shining armour,
   place thy good sword in our hand;
   teach us how to wield it, fighting
   onward t'wards the heav'nly land.

6. Onward till, our striving over,
   on life's battlefield we fall,
   resting then, but ever ready,
   waiting for the angel's call.

   Joseph W. Reeks (1849-1900)

229

1. Let all mortal flesh keep silence
   and with fear and trembling stand;
   ponder nothing earthly-minded,
   for with blessing in his hand
   Christ our God on earth descendeth,
   our full homage to demand.

2. King of kings, yet born of Mary,
   as of old on earth he stood,
   Lord of lords, in human vesture,
   in the body and the blood.
   He will give to all the faithful
   his own self for heav'nly food.

3. Rank on rank the host of heaven
   spreads its vanguard on the way,
   as the Light of light descendeth
   from the realms of endless day,
   that the pow'rs of hell may vanish
   as the darkness clears away.

4. At his feet the six-winged seraph;
   cherubim, with sleepless eye,
   veil their faces to the Presence,
   as with ceaseless voice they cry,
   alleluia, alleluia,
   alleluia, Lord most high.

   Liturgy of St James, tr. G. Moultrie (1829-1885)

230

1. Let all that is within me cry: holy.
   Let all that is within me cry: holy.
   Holy, holy, holy is the Lamb
   that was slain.

2. Let all that is within me cry: mighty.
   Let all that is within me cry: mighty.
   Mighty, mighty, mighty is the Lamb
   that was slain.

3. Let all that is within me cry: worthy.
   Let all that is within me cry: worthy.
   Worthy, worthy, worthy is the Lamb
   that was slain.

4. Let all that is within me cry: blessèd.
   Let all that is within me cry: blessèd.
   Blessèd, blessèd, blessèd is the Lamb
   that was slain.

5. Let all that is within me cry: Jesus.
   Let all that is within me cry: Jesus.
   Jesus, Jesus, Jesus is the Lamb
   that was slain.

   Unknown

231

1. Let all the world in ev'ry corner sing,
   my God and King!
   The heav'ns are not too high,
   his praise may thither fly;
   the earth is not too low,
   his praises there may grow.
   Let all the world in ev'ry corner sing,
   my God and King!

Continued overleaf

2. Let all the world in ev'ry corner sing,
   my God and King!
   The church with psalms must shout,
   no door can keep them out;
   but, above all, the heart must bear
   the longest part.
   Let all the world in ev'ry corner sing,
   my God and King!

   George Herbert (1593-1633)

232

1. Let there be love shared among us,
   let there be love in our eyes.
   May now your love sweep this nation;
   cause us, O Lord, to arise.
   Give us a fresh understanding,
   brotherly love that is real.
   Let there be love shared among us,
   let there be love.

2. Let there be peace shared among us,
   let there be peace in our eyes.
   May now your peace sweep this nation;
   cause us, O Lord, to arise.
   Give us a fresh understanding,
   sisterly love that is real.
   Let there be peace shared among us,
   let there be peace.

3. Let there be hope shared among us,
   let there be hope in our eyes.
   May now your hope sweep this nation;
   cause us, O Lord, to arise.
   Give us a fresh understanding,
   brotherly love that is real.
   Let there be hope shared among us,
   let there be hope.

4. Let there be joy shared among us,
   let there be joy in our eyes.
   May now your joy sweep this nation;
   cause us, O Lord, to arise.
   Give us a fresh understanding,
   sisterly love that is real.
   Let there be joy shared among us,
   let there be joy.

5. Let there be love shared among us,
   let there be love in our eyes.
   May now your love sweep this nation;
   cause us, O Lord, to arise.
   Give us a fresh understanding,
   brotherly love that is real.
   Let there be love shared among us,
   let there be love.

   Dave Bilbrough
   © 1979 Kingsway's Thankyou Music

233

1. Let us, with a gladsome mind,
   praise the Lord, for he is kind;

   for his mercies aye endure,
   ever faithful, ever sure.

2. Let us blaze his name abroad,
   for of gods he is the God;

3. He, with all-commanding might,
   filled the new-made world with light;

4. He the golden-tressèd sun
   caused all day his course to run;

5. And the moon to shine at night,
   'mid her starry sisters bright;

6. All things living he doth feed,
   his full hand supplies their need;

7. Let us, with a gladsome mind,
   praise the Lord, for he is kind;

John Milton (1608-1674)
based on Psalm 136

234

1. Let's all join together in
   communion sweet,
   walk, walk in the light,
   and love one another till our
   Saviour we meet,
   walk, walk in the light.

Walk in the light,
walk in the light,
walk in the light,
walk in the light of the Lord.

2. The Spirit lives to set us free,
   walk, walk in the light.
   He binds us all in unity,
   walk, walk in the light.

3. When Jesus died on Calvary,
   walk, walk in the light,
   he saved the lost like you and me,
   walk, walk in the light.

4. And Jesus did just what he said,
   walk, walk in the light,
   he healed the sick and he raised
   the dead,
   walk, walk in the light.

5. He left his Spirit our friend to be,
   walk, walk in the light;
   he prays in you and he prays in me,
   walk, walk in the light.

Unknown

235

1. Like a sea without a shore
   love divine is boundless.
   Time is now and ever more,
   and his love surrounds us.

Maranatha! Maranatha!
Maranatha! Come, Lord Jesus, come!

2. So that mankind could be free
   he appeared among us.
   Blest are those who have not seen,
   yet believe his promise.

3. All our visions, all our dreams,
   are but ghostly shadows
   of the radiant clarity
   waiting at life's close.

4. Death where is your victory?
   Death where is your sting?
   Closer than the air we breathe
   is our risen King.

Estelle White (b. 1925)
'Maranatha' is an Aramaic word meaning 'Lord,
come!' See 1 Corinthians 16: 22.

236

Like a shepherd he feeds his flock
and gathers the lambs in his arms,
holding them carefully,
close to his heart,
leading them home.

1. Say to the cities of Judah:
   'Prepare the way of the Lord.'
   Go to the mountain top,
   lift your voice;
   Jerusalem, here is your God.

Continued overleaf

2. I myself will shepherd them,
   for others have led them astray.
   The lost I will rescue
   and heal their wounds and pasture them,
   giving them rest.

   Like a shepherd he feeds his flock
   and gathers the lambs in his arms,
   holding them carefully,
   close to his heart,
   leading them home.

3. Come unto me if you are
   heavily burdened,
   and take my yoke upon your shoulders.
   I will give you rest.

   Bob Dufford, based on Scripture
   © 1976 New Dawn Music

237

1. Like the deer that yearns for water,
   O God, I long for you.
   Weeping I have heard them taunt me:
   'What help is in your God?'

2. Gladly I would lead your people,
   rejoicing to your house.
   Trust in God, my soul, and praise him,
   and he will dry your tears.

3. Grief and pain, like roaring torrents,
   had swept my soul away.
   But his mercy is my rescue,
   I will praise him all my days.

4. Weeping, I have heard them taunt me:
   'What help is in your God?'
   Rock of strength, do not forget me,
   in you alone I trust.

5. To the Father praise and honour,
   all glory to the Son,
   honour to the Holy Spirit:
   let God be glorified.

   Luke Connaughton (1917-1979)
   and Kevin Mayhew (b. 1942) based on Psalm 41

238

Listen, let your heart keep seeking;
listen to his constant speaking;
listen to the Spirit calling you.
Listen to his inspiration;
listen to his invitation;
listen to the Spirit calling you.

1. He's in the sound of the thunder,
   in the whisper of the breeze.
   He's in the might of the whirlwind,
   in the roaring of the seas.

2. He's in the laughter of the children,
   in the patter of the rain.
   Hear him in cries of the suff'ring,
   in their moaning and their pain.

3. He's in the noise of the city,
   in the singing of the birds.
   And in the night-time the stillness
   helps you listen to his word.

   Aniceto Nazareth

239

1. Little Jesus, sweetly sleep, do not stir;
   we will lend a coat of fur;
   we will rock you, rock you, rock you,
   we will rock you, rock you, rock you;
   see the fur to keep you warm,
   snugly round your tiny form.

2. Mary's little baby sleep, sweetly sleep,
   sleep in comfort, slumber deep;
   we will rock you, rock you, rock you,
   we will rock you, rock you, rock you;
   we will serve you all we can,
   darling, darling little man.

Traditional Czech Carol,
tr. Percy Dearmer (1867-1936)

240

1. Lo, he comes with clouds descending,
   once for favoured sinners slain;
   thousand thousand saints attending
   swell the triumph of his train.
   Alleluia! Alleluia!
   Alleluia!
   Christ appears on earth to reign.

2. Ev'ry eye shall now behold him
   robed in dreadful majesty;
   those who set at naught and sold him,
   pierced and nailed him to the tree,
   deeply wailing, deeply wailing,
   deeply wailing,
   shall the true Messiah see.

3. Those dear tokens of his passion
   still his dazzling body bears,
   cause of endless exultation
   to his ransomed worshippers:
   with what rapture, with what rapture,
   with what rapture
   gaze we on those glorious scars!

4. Yea, amen, let all adore thee,
   high on thine eternal throne;
   Saviour, take the pow'r and glory,
   claim the kingdom for thine own.
   Alleluia! Alleluia!
   Alleluia!
   Thou shalt reign, and thou alone.

Charles Wesley (1707-1788), John Cenrick
(1718-1755) and Martin Madan (1726-1790)

241

1. Look around you, can you see?
   Times are troubled, people grieve.
   See the violence, feel the hardness;
   all my people, weep with me.

   Kyrie eleison. Christe eleison.
   Kyrie eleison.

2. Walk among them, I'll go with you.
   Reach out to them with my hands.
   Suffer with me, and together
   we will serve them, help them stand.

3. Forgive us, Father; hear our prayer.
   We'll walk with you anywhere,
   through your suff'ring,
     with forgiveness,
   take your life into the world.

Jodi Page Clark (b. 1941)
© 1976 Celebration/Kingsway's Thankyou Music

242

1. Look down, O mother Mary,
   from thy bright throne above;
   cast down upon thy children
   one only glance of love;
   and if a heart so tender
   with pity flows not o'er,
   then turn away, O mother,
   and look on us no more.

   Look down, O mother Mary,
   from thy bright throne above,
   cast down upon thy children
   one only glance of love.

Continued overleaf

2. See how, ungrateful sinners,
   we stand before thy Son;
   his loving heart upbraids us
   the evil we have done,
   but if thou wilt appease him,
   speak for us but one word;
   for thus thou canst obtain us,
   the pardon of our Lord.

   Look down, O mother Mary,
   from thy bright throne above,
   cast down upon thy children
   one only glance of love.

3. O Mary, dearest mother,
   if thou wouldst have us live,
   say that we are thy children,
   and Jesus will forgive.
   Our sins make us unworthy
   that title still to bear,
   but thou art still our mother;
   then show a mother's care.

4. Unfold to us thy mantle,
   there stay we without fear;
   what evil can befall us
   if, mother, thou art near?
   O kindest, dearest mother,
   thy sinful children save;
   look down on us with pity,
   who thy protection crave.

   St Alphonsus (1696-1787),
   tr Edmund Vaughan (1827-1908)

243

1. Lord, accept the gifts we offer
   at this Eucharistic feast,
   bread and wine to be transformed now
   through the action of thy priest.
   Take us too, Lord, and transform us,
   be thy grace in us increased.

2. May our souls be pure and spotless
   as the host of wheat so fine;
   may all stain of sin be crushed out,
   like the grape that forms the wine,
   as we, too, become partakers,
   in the sacrifice divine.

3. Take our gifts, almighty Father,
   living God, eternal, true,
   which we give through Christ
      our Saviour,
   pleading here for us anew.
   Grant salvation to all present,
   and our faith and love renew.

   Sister M. Teresine

244

1. Lord, enthroned in heav'nly splendour,
   first begotten from the dead,
   thou alone, our strong defender,
   liftest up thy people's head;
   alleluia, alleluia,
   Jesus, true and living bread!

2. Prince of life, for us thou livest,
   by thy body souls are healed;
   Prince of peace, thy peace thou givest,
   by thy blood is pardon sealed;
   alleluia, alleluia,
   Word of God, in flesh revealed.

3. Paschal Lamb! Thine off'ring finished,
   once for all, when thou wast slain,
   in its fullness undiminished
   shall for ever more remain,
   alleluia, alleluia,
   cleansing souls from ev'ry stain.

4. Great high priest of our profession,
   through the veil thou enteredst in;
   by thy mighty intercession
   grace and mercy thou canst win:
   alleluia, alleluia,
   only sacrifice for sin.

5. Life-imparting heav'nly manna,
   stricken rock, with streaming side,
   heav'n and earth, with loud hosanna,
   worship thee, the Lamb who died;
   alleluia, alleluia,
   ris'n, ascended, glorified!

   George Hugh Bourne (1840-1925)

245

1. Lord, for tomorrow and its needs
   I do not pray;
   keep me, my God, from stain of sin,
   just for today.

2. Let me both diligently work
   and duly pray;
   let me be kind in word and deed,
   just for today.

3. Let me no wrong or idle word
   unthinking say;
   set thou a seal upon my lips,
   just for today.

4. And if today my tide of life
   should ebb away,
   give me thy sacraments divine,
   sweet Lord, today.

5. So, for tomorrow and its needs
   I do not pray;
   but keep me, guide me,
      love me, Lord,
   just for today.

   Sister M. Xavier

246

Lord, have mercy. Lord, have mercy.
Lord, have mercy on your people.
Lord, have mercy. Lord, have mercy.
Lord, have mercy on your people.

1. Give me the heart of stone within you,
   and I'll give you a heart of flesh.
   Clean water I will use to cleanse all
      your wounds.
   My Spirit I give to you.

2. You'll find me near the
      broken-hearted:
   those crushed in spirit I will save.
   So turn to me, for my pardon is great;
   my word will heal all your wounds.

   Gerard Markland, based on Ezekiel

247

1. Lord Jesus Christ,
   you have come to us,
   you are one with us,
   Mary's Son.
   Cleansing our souls from all their sin,
   pouring your love and goodness in,
   Jesus, our love for you we sing,
   living Lord.

2. Lord Jesus Christ,
   now and ev'ry day
   teach us how to pray,
   Son of God.
   You have commanded us to do
   this in remembrance, Lord, of you.
   Into our lives your pow'r
      breaks through,
   living Lord.

Continued overleaf

3. Lord Jesus Christ,
   you have come to us,
   born as one of us,
   Mary's Son.
   Led out to die on Calvary,
   risen from death to set us free,
   living Lord Jesus, help us see
   you are Lord.

4. Lord Jesus Christ,
   I would come to you,
   live my life for you,
   Son of God.
   All your commands I know are true,
   your many gifts will make me new,
   into my life your pow'r breaks through,
   living Lord.

Patrick Appleford (b. 1925)

248

1. Lord Jesus, think on me,
   and purge away my sin;
   from earth-born passions set me free,
   and make me pure within.

2. Lord Jesus, think on me,
   with care and woe oppressed;
   let me thy loving servant be
   and taste thy promised rest.

3. Lord Jesus, think on me
   amid the battle's strife;
   in all my pain and misery
   be thou my health and life.

4. Lord Jesus, think on me,
   nor let me go astray;
   through darkness and perplexity
   point thou the heav'nly way.

5. Lord Jesus, think on me,
   when flows the tempest high:
   when on doth rush the enemy,
   O Saviour, be thou nigh.

6. Lord Jesus, think on me,
   that, when the flood is past,
   I may th'eternal brightness see,
   and share thy joy at last.

Bishop Synesius (375-430),
tr. A. W. Chatfield (1808-1896)

249

1. Lord, make me a means of your peace.
   Where there's hatred grown,
     let me sow your love.
   Where there's inj'ry, Lord,
     let forgiveness be my sword.
   Lord, make me a means of your peace.

2. Lord, make me a means of your peace.
   Where there's doubt and fear,
     let me sow your faith.
   In this world's despair,
     give me hope in you to share.
   Lord, make me a means of your peace.

3. Lord, make me a means of your peace.
   When there's sadness here,
     let me sow your joy.
   When the darkness nears,
     may your light dispel our fears.
   Lord, make me a means of your peace.

4. Lord, grant me to seek and to share:
   less to be consoled
     than to help console,
   less be understood
     than to understand your good.
   Lord, make me a means of your peace.

5. Lord, grant me to seek and to share:
   to receive love less
      than to give love free,
   just to give in thee,
      just receiving from your tree.
   Lord, make me a means of your peace.

6. Lord, grant me to seek and to share:
   to forgive in thee, you've forgiven me;
   for to die in thee is eternal life to me.
   Lord, make me a means of your peace.

John Foley based on the 'Prayer of St Francis'
© 1985 New Dawn Music

250

1. Lord of all hopefulness,
   Lord of all joy,
   whose trust, ever child-like,
   no cares could destroy,
   be there at our waking,
   and give us, we pray,
   your bliss in our hearts, Lord,
   at the break of the day.

2. Lord of all eagerness,
   Lord of all faith,
   whose strong hands were skilled
   at the plane and the lathe,
   be there at our labours,
   and give us, we pray,
   your strength in our hearts, Lord,
   at the noon of the day.

3. Lord of all kindliness,
   Lord of all grace,
   your hands swift to welcome,
   your arms to embrace,
   be there at our homing,
   and give us, we pray,
   your love in our hearts, Lord,
   at the eve of the day.

4. Lord of all gentleness,
   Lord of all calm,
   whose voice is contentment,
   whose presence is balm,
   be there at our sleeping,
   and give us, we pray,
   your peace in our hearts, Lord,
   at the end of the day.

Jan Struther (1901-1953)

251

Lord of creation,
may your will be done.
Lord of creation,
may your will be done.

Colin Mawby (b. 1936)

252

1. Lord our God, O Lord our Father,
   Lord of love and Lord of fear,
   now we gather round your altar
   and we know your Word is near.

2. All our lives lie open to you,
   Lord of age and Lord of youth,
   as we bring our sins and falsehoods
   to the judgement of your truth.

3. Lord of times and Lord of seasons,
   Lord of calmness, Lord of stress,
   heart that sees our secret terrors,
   Lord of strength and gentleness.

4. Lord of storms and Lord of sunsets,
   Lord of darkness, Lord of light,
   cast the shadow of your blessing
   on us gathered in your sight.

Continued overleaf

5. Lord of foes and Lord of friendships,
   Lord of laughter, Lord of tears,
   Lord of toil and Lord of Sabbath,
   Master of the hurrying years.

6. Lord of hope and Lord of hunger,
   Lord of atoms, Lord of space,
   take this world we bring before you
   to the haven of your grace.

   Kevin Nichols (b. 1929)

253

1. Lord, the light of your love is shining,
   in the midst of the darkness, shining;
   Jesus, Light of the World, shine upon us,
   set us free by the truth
   you now bring us,
   shine on me, shine on me.

   Shine, Jesus, shine,
   fill this land with the Father's glory;
   blaze, Spirit, blaze,
   set our hearts on fire.
   Flow, river, flow,
   flood the nations with grace and mercy;
   send forth your Word, Lord,
   and let there be light.

2. Lord, I come to your
      awesome presence,
   from the shadows into your radiance;
   by the blood I may enter
      your brightness,
   search me, try me, consume
   all my darkness.
   Shine on me, shine on me.

3. As we gaze on your kingly brightness
   so our faces display your likeness,
   ever changing from glory to glory,
   mirrored here may our lives
   tell your story.
   Shine on me, shine on me.

   Graham Kendrick (b. 1950)
   © 1987 Make Way Music

254

1. Lord, thy word abideth,
   and our footsteps guideth;
   who its truth believeth,
   light and joy receiveth.

2. When our foes are near us,
   then thy word doth cheer us,
   word of consolation,
   message of salvation.

3. When the storms are o'er us,
   and dark clouds before us,
   then its light directeth
   and our way protecteth.

4. Who can tell the pleasure,
   who recount the treasure,
   by thy word imparted
   to the simple-hearted?

5. Word of mercy, giving
   succour to the living;
   word of life, supplying
   comfort to the dying.

6. O that we, discerning
   its most holy learning,
   Lord, may love and fear thee,
   evermore be near thee.

   Henry Williams Baker (1821-1877)

255

1. Lord, when I wake I turn to you,
   yourself my day's first thought
      and prayer,
   your strength to help, your peace
      to bless,
   your will to guide me ev'rywhere!

2. I live with many in our world
   – their worldly eyes too blind to see –
   who never think what is your will,
   or why you brought our world to be!

3. Your thought for me, your loving care,
   those favours I could never earn,
   call for my thanks in praise and prayer,
   call me to love you in return!

4. There is no blessing, Lord, from you
   for those who make their will
      their way,
   no praise for those who do not praise,
   no peace for those who do not pray!

5. Make then my life a life of love,
   keep me from sin in all I do,
   your way to be my only way,
   your will my will for love of you!

   Brian Foley (b. 1919) based on Psalm 5

256

1. Lord, who throughout these forty days
   for us didst fast and pray,
   teach us with thee to mourn our sins,
   and at thy side to stay.

2. As thou with Satan didst contend
   and didst the vict'ry win,
   O give us strength in thee to fight,
   in thee to conquer sin.

3. As thirst and hunger thou didst bear,
   so teach us, gracious Lord,
   to die to self, and daily live
   by thy most holy word.

4. And through these days of penitence,
   and through thy Passiontide,
   yea, ever more, in life and death,
   Lord Christ, with us abide.

   Claudia Frances Hernaman (1838-1898)

257

1. Love divine, all loves excelling,
   joy of heav'n, to earth come down,
   fix in us thy humble dwelling,
   all thy faithful mercies crown.

2. Jesus, thou art all compassion,
   pure unbounded love thou art;
   visit us with thy salvation,
   enter ev'ry trembling heart.

3. Come, almighty to deliver,
   let us all thy life receive;
   suddenly return, and never,
   never more thy temples leave.

4. Thee we would be always blessing,
   serve thee as thy hosts above;
   pray, and praise thee without ceasing,
   glory in thy perfect love.

5. Finish then thy new creation,
   pure and sinless let us be;
   let us see thy great salvation
   perfectly restored in thee.

6. Changed from glory into glory,
   till in heav'n we take our place,
   till we cast our crowns before thee,
   lost in wonder, love and praise.

   Charles Wesley (1707-1788)

258

1. Love is his word, love is his way,
   feasting with all, fasting alone,
   living and dying, rising again,
   love, only love, is his way.

   *Richer than gold is the love of my Lord:
   better than splendour and wealth.*

Continued overleaf

2. Love is his way, love is his mark,
   sharing his last Passover feast,
   Christ at the table, host to the twelve,
   love, only love, is his mark.

   Richer than gold is the love of my Lord:
   better than splendour and wealth.

3. Love is his mark, love is his sign,
   bread for our strength, wine for our joy,
   'This is my body, this is my blood.'
   Love, only love, is his sign.

4. Love is his sign, love is his news,
   'Do this,' he said, 'lest you forget
   all my deep sorrow, all my dear blood.'
   Love, only love, is his news.

5. Love is his news, love is his name,
   we are his own, chosen and called,
   family, brethren, cousins and kin.
   Love, only love, is his name.

6. Love is his name, love is his law,
   hear his command, all who are his,
   'Love one another, I have loved you.'
   Love, only love, is his law.

7. Love is his law, love is his word:
   love of the Lord, Father and Word,
   love of the Spirit, God ever one,
   love, only love, is his word.

   Luke Connaughton (1917-1979), alt.

259

1. Loving shepherd of thy sheep,
   keep me, Lord, in safety keep;
   nothing can thy pow'r withstand,
   none can pluck me from thy hand.

2. Loving shepherd, thou didst give
   thine own life that I might live;
   may I love thee day by day,
   gladly thy sweet will obey.

3. Loving shepherd, ever near,
   teach me still thy voice to hear;
   suffer not my steps to stray
   from the straight and narrow way.

4. Where thou leadest may I go,
   walking in thy steps below;
   then, before thy Father's throne,
   Jesu, claim me for thine own.

   Jane Elizabeth Leeson (1809-1881)

260

Lumen Christi, alleluia! Amen!

1. I am the light of the world:
   everyone who follows me will have
      the light of life.

2. You are the light of the world:
   your light must shine in the light of men.

3. You will shine in the world like
      bright stars
   because you are offering it the word
      of life.

4. The sheep that belong to me listen to
      my voice:
   I know them and they follow me.

5. I call you friends because I have made
      known to you
   everything I have learnt from my Father.

6. I am the resurrection and the life;
   whoever lives and believes in me
      will never die.

7. You believe, Thomas, because you can
   see me.
   Happy are those who have not seen
   and yet believe.

8. Go, make disciples of all the nations:
   I am with you always; yes, to the end
   of time.

From Scripture

261

Majesty, worship his majesty;
unto Jesus be glory,
honour and praise.
Majesty, kingdom, authority
flow from his throne unto his own:
his anthem raise.
So exalt, lift up on high
the name of Jesus;
magnify, come glorify
Christ Jesus the King.
Majesty, worship his majesty,
Jesus who died, now glorified,
King of all kings.

Jack W. Hayford (b. 1934)

262

1. Make me a channel of your peace.
   Where there is hatred,
      let me bring your love.
   Where there is injury,
      your pardon, Lord;
   and where there's doubt,
      true faith in you.

2. Make me a channel of your peace.
   Where there's despair in life,
      let me bring hope.
   Where there is darkness, only light,
   and where there's sadness, ever joy.

3. O, Master, grant that I may never seek
   so much to be consoled as to console,
   to be understood as to understand,
   to be loved as to love with all my soul.

4. Make me a channel of your peace.
   It is in pardoning
      that we are pardoned,
   in giving to all men that we receive,
   and in dying that we're born to
      eternal life.

Sebastian Temple (b. 1928),
based on the Prayer of St Francis

263

1. Many times I have turned
   from the way of the Lord,
   many times I have
   chosen the darkness.
   In the light of the day,
   when the shadows are gone,
   all I see is my sin in its starkness.

   Jesus came to bring us mercy.
   Jesus came to bring us life again.
   He loves us, he loves us, he loves us!

2. I confess I have sinned
   in the sight of the Lord,
   through my pride,
   through my malice and weakness.
   I've rejected the promise
   that comes from the cross
   where the Lord hung above us
   in meekness.

3. With a word, with a deed,
   with a failure to act,
   with a thought that was evil
   and hateful,
   I confess to you,
   brothers and sisters of mine,
   I have sinned and been
   proven ungrateful.

Continued overleaf

4. Through my fault, through my fault,
   through my serious fault,
   I confess to you, Lord, all my sinning.
   But look down on me, Lord,
   grant your pardon and peace;
   with your help,
   I've a new life beginning.

   Jesus came to bring us mercy.
   Jesus came to bring us life again.
   He loves us, he loves us, he loves us!
   Willard F. Jabusch (b. 1930)

264

1. Mary had a baby, yes, Lord,
   Mary had a baby, yes, my Lord,
   Mary had a baby, yes, Lord!
   The people keep a-coming,
   but the train has gone!

2. What did she name him, yes, Lord,
   what did she name him, yes, my Lord,
   what did she name him, yes, Lord?
   The people keep a-coming,
   but the train has gone!

3. Mary named him Jesus, yes, Lord,
   Mary named him Jesus, yes, my Lord,
   Mary named him Jesus, yes, Lord!
   The people keep a-coming,
   but the train has gone!

4. Where was he born, yes, Lord,
   where was he born, yes, my Lord,
   where was he born, yes, Lord?
   The people keep a-coming
   but the train has gone!

5. Born in a stable, yes, Lord,
   born in a stable, yes, my Lord,
   born in a stable, yes, Lord!
   The people keep a-coming,
   but the train has gone!

6. Where did she lay him, yes, Lord,
   where did she lay him, yes, my Lord,
   where did she lay him, yes, Lord?
   The people keep a-coming,
   but the train has gone!

7. Laid him in a manger, yes, Lord,
   laid him in a manger, yes, my Lord,
   laid him in a manger, yes, Lord!
   The people keep a-coming,
   but the train has gone!
   West Indian Spiritual

265

1. Mary immaculate,
   star of the morning,
   chosen before
   the creation began,
   chosen to bring,
   for thy bridal adorning,
   woe to the serpent
   and rescue to man.

2. Here, in an orbit
   of shadow and sadness
   veiling thy splendour,
   thy course thou hast run;
   now thou art throned
   in all glory and gladness,
   crowned by the hand of
   thy Saviour and Son.

3. Sinners, we worship
   thy sinless perfection,
   fallen and weak,
   for thy pity we plead;
   grant us the shield
   of thy sovereign protection,
   measure thine aid
   by the depth of our need.

4. Frail is our nature
and strict our probation,
watchful the foe
that would lure us to wrong,
succour our souls
in the hour of temptation,
Mary immaculate,
tender and strong.

5. See how the wiles
of the serpent assail us,
see how we waver
and flinch in the fight;
let thine immaculate
merit avail us,
make of our weakness
a proof of thy might.

6. Bend from thy throne
at the voice of our crying;
bend to this earth
which thy footsteps have trod;
stretch out thine arms
to us living and dying,
Mary immaculate,
mother of God.

F. W. Weatherell

266

May the peace of Christ
be with you today,
may the peace of Christ
be with you today,
may the love of Christ,
the joy of Christ,
may the peace of Christ be yours.

Kevin Mayhew (b. 1942)

267

1. Meekness and majesty,
manhood and deity,
in perfect harmony,
the man who is God.
Lord of eternity
dwells in humanity,
kneels in humility
and washes our feet.

*O, what a mystery,
meekness and majesty,
bow down and worship,
for this is your God.
This is your God.*

2. Father's pure radiance,
perfect in innocence,
yet learns obedience
to death on a cross.
Suff'ring to give us life,
conqu'ring through sacrifice;
and as they crucify
prays: 'Father forgive'.

3. Wisdom unsearchable,
God the invisible;
love indestructible
in frailty appears.
Lord of infinity,
stooping so tenderly,
lifts our humanity
to the heights of his throne.

Graham Kendrick (b. 1950)

268

1. Mine eyes have seen the glory
   of the coming of the Lord.
   He is tramping out the vintage
   where the grapes of wrath are stored.
   He has loosed the fateful lightning
   of his terrible swift sword.
   His truth is marching on.

   Glory, glory hallelujah!
   Glory, glory hallelujah!
   Glory, glory hallelujah!
   His truth is marching on.

2. I have seen him in the watchfires
   of a hundred circling camps.
   They have gilded him an altar
   in the evening dews and damps.
   I can read his righteous sentence
   by the dim and flaring lamps.
   His day is marching on.

3. He has sounded forth the trumpet
   that shall never sound retreat.
   He is sifting out all human hearts
   before his judgement seat.
   O, be swift my soul to answer him,
   be jubilant my feet!
   Our God is marching on.

4. In the beauty of the lilies
   Christ was born across the sea,
   with a glory in his bosom
   that transfigures you and me.
   As he died to make us holy,
   let us live that all be free,
   whilst God is marching on.

   Julia Ward Howe (1819-1910), alt.

269

1. Morning has broken
   like the first morning,
   blackbird has spoken
   like the first bird.
   Praise for the singing!
   Praise for the morning!
   Praise for them, springing
   fresh from the Word!

2. Sweet the rain's new fall,
   sunlit from heaven,
   like the first dew-fall
   on the first grass.
   Praise for the sweetness
   of the wet garden,
   sprung in completeness
   where his feet pass.

3. Mine is the sunlight!
   Mine is the morning
   born of the one light
   Eden saw play!
   Praise with elation
   praise ev'ry morning,
   God's re-creation
   of the new day!

   Eleanor Farjeon (1881-1965)

270

1. 'Moses, I know you're the man,'
   the Lord said.
   'You're going to work out my plan,'
   the Lord said.
   'Lead all the Israelites
   out of slavery,
   and I shall make them a
   wandering race
   called the people of God.'

So ev'ry day we're on our way,
for we're a travelling,
wandering race
called the people of God.

2. 'Don't get too set in your ways,'
the Lord said.
'Each step is only a phase,'
the Lord said.
'I'll go before you and
I shall be a sign
to guide my travelling,
wandering race.
You're the people of God.'

3. 'No matter what you may do,'
the Lord said,
'I shall be faithful and true,'
the Lord said.
'My love will strengthen you
as you go along,
for you're my travelling,
wandering race.
You're the people of God.'

4. 'Look at the birds in the air,'
the Lord said.
'They fly unhampered by care,'
the Lord said.
'You will move easier
if you're travelling light,
for you're a wandering,
vagabond race.
You're the people of God.'

5. 'Foxes have places to go,'
the Lord said,
'but I've no home here below,'
the Lord said.
'So if you want to be with me
all your days,
keep up the moving and
travelling on.
You're the people of God.'

Estelle White (b. 1925)

271

1. Most ancient of all mysteries,
before thy throne we lie;
have mercy now, most merciful,
most Holy Trinity.

2. When heav'n and earth were
     yet unmade,
when time was yet unknown,
thou, in thy bliss and majesty,
didst love and love alone.

3. Thou wert not born; there was
     no fount,
from which thy being flowed;
there is no end which thou canst reach:
but thou art simply God.

4. How wonderful creation is,
the work that thou didst bless;
and O, what then must thou be like,
Eternal Loveliness!

5. Most ancient of all mysteries,
still at thy throne we lie;
have mercy now, most merciful,
most Holy Trinity.

Frederick William Faber (1814-1863)

272

1. Mother of God's living Word,
glorifying Christ your Lord;
full of joy, God's people sing,
grateful for your mothering.

2. Virgin soil, untouched by sin,
for God's seed to flourish in;
watered by the Spirit's dew,
in your womb the Saviour grew.

Continued overleaf

3. Sharing his humility,
   Bethlehem and Calvary,
   with him in his bitter pain,
   now as queen with him you reign.

4. We are God's new chosen race,
   new-born children of his grace,
   citizens of heaven who
   imitate and honour you.

5. We, God's people on our way,
   travelling by night and day,
   moving to our promised land,
   walk beside you hand in hand.

6. Christ, your Son, is always near,
   so we journey without fear,
   singing as we walk along:
   Christ our joy, and Christ our song!

7. Sing aloud to Christ with joy,
   who was once a little boy.
   Sing aloud to Mary, sing,
   grateful for her mothering.

   Damian Lundy (b. 1944)

273

1. My God, accept my heart this day,
   and make it wholly thine,
   that I from thee no more may stray,
   no more from thee decline.

2. Before the cross of him who died,
   behold, I prostrate fall;
   let ev'ry sin be crucified,
   and Christ be all in all.

3. Anoint me with thy heav'nly grace,
   and seal me for thine own,
   that I may see thy glorious face,
   and worship at thy throne.

4. Let ev'ry thought and work and word
   to thee be ever given,
   then life shall be thy service, Lord,
   and death the gate of heaven.

5. All glory to the Father be,
   all glory to the Son,
   all glory, Holy Ghost, to thee,
   while endless ages run.

   Matthew Bridges (1800-1894)

274

1. My God, and is thy table spread
   and does thy cup with love o'erflow?
   Thither be all thy children led,
   and let them all thy sweetness know.

2. Hail, sacred feast, which Jesus makes!
   Rich banquet of his flesh and blood!
   Thrice happy he, who here partakes
   that sacred stream, that heav'nly food.

3. O let thy table honoured be,
   and furnished well with joyful guests:
   and may each soul salvation see,
   that here its sacred pledges tastes.

   Philip Doddridge (1702-1751)

275

1. My God loves me,
   his love will never end.
   He rests within my heart,
   for my God loves me.

2. His gentle hand
   he stretches over me.
   Though storm-clouds threaten the day,
   he will set me free.

3. He comes to me
   in sharing bread and wine.
   He brings me life that will reach
   past the end of time.

4. My God loves me,
   his faithful love endures,
   and I will live like a child
   held in love secure.

5. The joys of love
   as off'rings now we bring.
   The pains of love will be lost
   in the praise we sing.

   Vs 1 Unknown,
   vv 2-5 Sandra Joan Billington (b. 1946)

276

My shepherd is the Lord,
nothing indeed shall I want.

or

His goodness shall follow me always,
to the end of my days.

1. The **Lord** is my **shep**herd;
   there is **no**thing I shall **want**.
   Fresh and **green** are the **pas**tures
   where he **gives** me re**pose**.
   Near **rest**ful **wat**ers he **leads** me,
   to re**vive** my drooping **spirit**.

2. He **guides** me a**long** the right **path**;
   he is **true** to his **name**.
   If I should **walk** in the **vall**ey
     of **dark**ness
   no **evil** would I **fear**.
   You are **there** with your **crook** and
     your **staff**;
   with **these** you give me **comfort**.

3. You have pre**pared** a **ban**quet for **me**
   in the **sight** of my **foes**.
   My **head** you have a**noin**ted with **oil**;
   my **cup** is over**flowing**.

4. Surely **good**ness and **kind**ness
     shall **fol**low me
   all the **days** of my **life**.
   In the **Lord's** own **house** shall I **dwell**
   for **ev**er and **ever**.

5. To the **Father** and **Son** give **glor**y,
   give **glor**y to the **Spir**it.
   To God who **is**, who **was**,
     and who **will** be
   for **ev**er and **ever**.

   Psalm 22 (23), Grail translation

277

1. My song is love unknown,
   my Saviour's love to me,
   love to the loveless shown,
   that they might lovely be.
   O who am I, that for my sake,
   my Lord should take frail flesh
     and die?

2. He came from his blest throne,
   salvation to bestow;
   but men made strange, and none
   the longed-for Christ would know,
   but O, my friend, my friend indeed,
   who at my need his life did spend!

3. Sometimes they strew his way,
   and his sweet praises sing;
   resounding all the day
   hosannas to their King;
   then 'Crucify!' is all their breath,
   and for his death they thirst and cry.

   Continued overleaf

4. Why, what hath my Lord done?
   What makes this rage and spite?
   He made the lame to run,
   he gave the blind their sight.
   Sweet injuries! Yet they at these
   themselves displease, and 'gainst
     him rise.

5. They rise, and needs will have
   my dear Lord made away;
   a murderer they save,
   the Prince of Life they slay.
   Yet cheerful he to suff'ring goes,
   that he his foes from thence
     might free.

6. Here might I stay and sing,
   no story so divine;
   never was love, dear King,
   never was grief like thine.
   This is my friend in whose sweet praise
   I all my days could gladly spend.

   Samuel Crossman (c. 1624-1684)

278

1. My soul doth magnify the Lord,
   and my spirit hath rejoiced
   in God my Saviour,
   for he that is mighty hath done
     great things,
   and holy is his name.

   My soul doth magnify the Lord,
   my soul doth magnify the Lord,
   and my spirit hath rejoiced
   in God my Saviour,
   for he that is mighty
   hath done great things,
   and holy is his name.

2. From age to age he shows his love,
   and his mercy is for ever
   to his servants,
   for he stretches out his arm,
     casts down the mighty,
   and raises up the meek.

3. He fills the hungry with good food.
   When the rich demand their share,
   their hands are empty.
   He has kept all his promises to Israel:
   his mercy is made known.

4. To God the Father we sing praise,
   and to Jesus, whom he sent
   to be our Saviour!
   To the Spirit of God be all glory,
   for holy is his name!

   Based on Luke 1:46-55, vs 1 Unknown,
   vv 2-4 Damian Lundy (b. 1944)

279

1. My soul is filled with joy
   as I sing to God my Saviour:
   he has looked upon his servant,
   he has visited his people.

   And holy is his name
   through all generations!
   Everlasting is his mercy
   to the people he has chosen,
   and holy is his name!

2. I am lowly as a child,
   but I know from this day forward
   that my name will be remembered
   and the world will call me blessèd.

3. I proclaim the pow'r of God!
   He does marvels for his servants;
   though he scatters the proud-hearted
   and destroys the might of princes.

4. To the hungry he gives food,
sends the rich away empty.
In his mercy he is mindful
of the people he has chosen.

5. In his love he now fulfills
what he promised to our fathers.
I will praise the Lord, my Saviour.
Everlasting is his mercy.

Unknown, based on Luke 1:46-55

280

*My soul is longing for your peace,
near to you, my God.*

1. Lord, you know that my
heart is not proud
and my eyes are not
lifted from the earth.

2. Lofty thoughts have
never filled my mind,
far beyond my sight
all ambitious deeds.

3. In your peace I have
maintained my soul,
I have kept my heart
in your quiet peace.

4. As a child rests on
his mother's knee,
so I place my soul
in your loving care.

5. Israel, put all your
hope in God,
place your trust in him,
now and evermore.

Lucien Deiss (b. 1921) based on Psalm 131

281

1. My soul proclaims you, mighty God.
My spirit sings your praise.
You look on me, you lift me up,
and gladness fills my days.

2. All nations now will share my joy;
your gifts you have outpoured.
Your little one you have made great;
I magnify my God.

3. For those who love your holy name,
your mercy will not die.
Your strong right arm puts down
   the proud
and lifts the lowly high.

4. You fill the hungry with good things,
the rich you send away.
The promise made to Abraham
is filled to endless day.

5. Magnificat, magnificat,
magnificat, praise God!
Praise God, praise God, praise God,
   praise God,
magnificat, praise God!

*Anne Carter (1944-1993)
based on Luke 1:46-55*

282

1. New daytime dawning,
breaking like the spring.
New voices singing,
and new songs to sing!
Christ has come back, alleluia!
He is risen, like the spring-time!
Say, what does he bring?

Continued overleaf

2. Death in the tree tops!
   Jesus cried with pain,
   hanging in the branches.
   Now he lives again!
   For the tree of death has flowered,
   life has filled the furthest branches!
   Sunlight follows rain.

3. The man of sorrows,
   sleeping in his tomb,
   the man of sorrows,
   he is coming home.
   He is coming like the springtime.
   Suddenly you'll hear him talking,
   you will see him come.

4. Say are you hungry?
   Come and eat today!
   Come to the table,
   nothing to pay!
   Take your place, the meal is waiting.
   Come and share the birthday party,
   and the holiday.

5. Look where the garden
   door is open wide!
   Come to the garden,
   there's no need to hide.
   God has broken down the fences
   and he stands with arms wide open.
   Come along inside!

   Damian Lundy (b. 1944) based on a French poem

283

1. New praises be given
   to Christ newly crowned,
   who back to his heaven
   a new way hath found;
   God's blessedness sharing
   before us he goes,
   what mansions preparing,
   what endless repose!

2. His glory still praising
   on thrice holy ground,
   th' apostles stood gazing,
   his mother around;
   with hearts that beat faster,
   with eyes full of love,
   they watched while their master
   ascended above.

3. 'No star can disclose him,'
   the bright angels said;
   'eternity knows him,
   your conquering head;
   those high habitations,
   he leaves not again,
   till, judging all nations,
   on earth he shall reign.'

4. Thus spoke they and straightway,
   where legions defend
   heav'n's glittering gateway,
   their Lord they attend,
   and cry, looking thither,
   'Your portals let down
   for him who rides hither
   in peace and renown.'

5. They asked, who keep sentry
   in that blessèd town,
   'Who thus claimeth entry,
   a king of renown?'
   'The Lord of all valiance,'
   that herald replied,
   'who Satan's battalions
   laid low in their pride.'

6. Grant, Lord, that our longing
   may follow thee there,
   on earth who are thronging
   thy temples with prayer;
   and unto thee gather,
   Redeemer, thine own,
   where thou with thy Father
   dost sit on the throne.

   The Venerable Bede (673-735)
   tr. Ronald Arbuthnott Knox (1888-1957)

284

1. Now thank we all our God,
with heart and hands and voices,
who wondrous things hath done,
in whom this world rejoices;
who from our mother's arms
hath blessed us on our way
with countless gifts of love,
and still is ours today.

2. O may this bounteous God
through all our life be near us,
with ever joyful hearts
and blessèd peace to cheer us;
and keep us in his grace,
and guide us when perplexed,
and free us from all ills
in this world and the next.

3. All praise and thanks to God
the Father now be given,
the Son and him who reigns
with them in highest heaven,
the one eternal God,
whom earth and heav'n adore;
for thus it was, is now,
and shall be evermore.

Martin Rinkart (1586-1649)
tr. Catherine Winkworth (1827-1878)

285

1. Now the green blade riseth
from the buried grain,
wheat that in the dark earth
many days has lain;
love lives again,
that with the dead has been:
love is come again
like wheat that springeth green.

2. In the grave they laid him,
love by hatred slain,
thinking that never
he would wake again,
laid in the earth
like grain that sleeps unseen:
love is come again
like wheat that springeth green.

3. Forth he came at Easter,
like the risen grain,
he that for three days
in the grave had lain;
quick from the dead
my risen Lord is seen:
love is come again
like wheat that springeth green.

4. When our hearts are wintry,
grieving or in pain,
thy touch can call us
back to life again;
fields of our hearts
that dead and bare have been:
love is come again
like wheat that springeth green.

John M. C. Crum (1872-1958), alt.

286

1. Now with the fast-departing light,
maker of all, we ask of thee,
of thy great mercy, through the night
our guardian and defence to be.

2. Far off let idle visions fly,
no phantom of the night molest;
curb thou our raging enemy,
that we in chaste repose may rest.

Continued overleaf

3. Father of mercies, hear our cry,
   hear us, O sole-begotten Son
   who, with the Holy Ghost most high,
   reignest while endless ages run.

   7th century, tr. Edward Caswall (1814-1878)

287

1. O bread of heav'n, beneath this veil
   thou dost my very God conceal;
   my Jesus, dearest treasure, hail;
   I love thee and adoring kneel;
   each loving soul by thee is fed
   with thine own self in form of bread.

2. O food of life, thou who dost give
   the pledge of immortality;
   I live; no, 'tis not I that live;
   God gives me life, God lives in me:
   he feeds my soul, he guides my ways,
   and ev'ry grief with joy repays.

3. O bond of love, that dost unite
   the servant to his living Lord;
   could I dare live, and not requite
   such love – then death were
      meet reward:
   I cannot live unless to prove
   some love for such unmeasured love.

4. Belovèd Lord in heav'n above,
   there, Jesus, thou awaitest me;
   to gaze on thee with changeless love,
   yes, thus I hope, thus shall it be:
   for how can he deny me heaven
   who here on earth himself hath given?

   St Alphonsus (1696-1787)
   tr. Edmund Vaughan (1827-1908)

288

1. O come, all ye faithful,
   joyful and triumphant,
   O come ye, O come ye to Bethlehem;
   come and behold him,
   born the king of angels:

   O come, let us adore him,
   O come, let us adore him,
   O come, let us adore him,
   Christ the Lord.

2. God of God,
   Light of Light,
   lo, he abhors not the virgin's womb;
   Very God,
   begotten not created:

3. Sing, choirs of angels,
   sing in exultation,
   sing all ye citizens of heav'n above:
   glory to God
   in the highest:

4. Yea, Lord, we greet thee,
   born this happy morning,
   Jesu, to thee be glory given;
   Word of the Father,
   now in flesh appearing:

   John F. Wade (1711-1786),
   tr. Frederick Oakeley (1802-1880)

289

1. O come and mourn with me awhile;
   see, Mary calls us to her side;
   O come and let us mourn with her;

   Jesus our love, Jesus our love,
   is crucified.

2. Have we no tears to shed for him
   while soldiers scoff and men deride?
   Ah, look how patiently he hangs!

3. How fast his feet and hands are nailed,
   his blessèd tongue with thirst is tied;
   his failing eyes are blind with blood;

4. Sev'n times he spoke, sev'n words
     of love,
   and all three hours his silence cried
   for mercy on the souls of men;

5. O break, O break, hard heart of mine:
   thy weak self-love and guilty pride
   his Pilate and his Judas were;

6. A broken heart, a fount of tears,
   ask, and they will not be denied;
   a broken heart, love's cradle is;

7. O love of God! O sin of man!
   In this dread act your strength is tried;
   and victory remains with love;

Frederick William Faber (1814-1863)

290

1. O come, O come, Emmanuel,
   and ransom captive Israel,
   that mourns in lonely exile here
   until the Son of God appear.

   *Rejoice, rejoice! Emmanuel
   shall come to thee, O Israel.*

2. O come, thou Rod of Jesse, free
   thine own from Satan's tyranny;
   from depths of hell thy people save,
   and give them vict'ry o'er the grave.

3. O come, thou dayspring, come
     and cheer
   our spirits by thine advent here;
   disperse the gloomy clouds of night,
   and death's dark shadows put
     to flight.

4. O come, thou key of David, come
   and open wide our heav'nly home;
   make safe the way that leads on high,
   and close the path to misery.

5. O come, O come, thou Lord of might,
   who to thy tribes on Sinai's height
   in ancient times didst give the Law,
   in cloud and majesty and awe.

*From the Great O Antiphons,
(12th-13th century),
tr. John Mason Neale (1818-1866)*

291

*O, come to the water,
all you who are thirsty,
and drink, drink deeply.
Though you don't have a penny
and your clothes are in rags,
you'll be welcome to drink all you can.*

1. Come, take your choice of wine
     and milk:
   ev'rything here is free!
   Why spend your money on
     worthless food:
   ev'rything here is free!

2. Now, listen well and you will find
   food that will feed your soul.
   Just come to me to receive your share,
   food that will feed your soul.

Continued overleaf

3. I promise you good things to come;
   you are my chosen ones.
   I name you witnesses to my world;
   you are my chosen ones.

   O, come to the water,
   all you who are thirsty,
   and drink, drink deeply.
   Though you don't have a penny
   and your clothes are in rags,
   you'll be welcome to drink all you can.

   Kevin Mayhew (b. 1942) based on Isaiah 55:1-4

292

1. O comfort my people
   and calm all their fear,
   and tell them the time
   of salvation draws near.
   O tell them I come
   to remove all their shame.
   Then they will for ever
   give praise to my name.

2. Proclaim to the cities
   of Judah my word:
   that gentle yet strong
   is the hand of the Lord.
   I rescue the captives,
   my people defend,
   and bring them to justice
   and joy without end.

3. All mountains and hills
   shall become as a plain,
   for vanished are mourning
   and hunger and pain.
   And never again shall
   these war against you.
   Behold I come quickly
   to make all things new.

   Chrysogonous Waddell, based on Isaiah 40

293

1. O food of trav'llers, angels' bread,
   manna wherewith the blest are fed,
   come nigh, and with thy sweetness fill
   the hungry hearts that seek thee still.

2. O fount of love, O well unpriced,
   outpouring from the heart of Christ,
   give us to drink of very thee,
   and all we pray shall answered be.

3. O Jesus Christ, we pray to thee
   that this thy presence which we see,
   though now in form of bread concealed,
   to us may be in heav'n revealed.

   From Maintzisch Gesangbuch (1661)
   tr. Walter H. Shewring and others

294

1. O for a closer walk with God,
   a calm and heav'nly frame;
   a light to shine upon the road
   that leads me to the Lamb.

2. What peaceful hours I once enjoyed,
   how sweet their memory still!
   But they have left an aching void
   the world can never fill.

3. Return, O holy Dove, return,
   sweet messenger of rest:
   I hate the sins that made thee mourn,
   and drove thee from my breast.

4. The dearest idol I have known,
   whate'er that idol be,
   help me to tear it from thy throne,
   and worship only thee.

5. So shall my walk be close with God,
   calm and serene my frame;
   so purer light shall mark the road
   that leads me to the Lamb.
   William Cowper (1731-1800)

295

1. O for a thousand tongues to sing
   my dear Redeemer's praise,
   the glories of my God and King,
   the triumphs of his grace!

2. Jesus, the name that charms our fears,
   that bids our sorrows cease;
   'tis music in the sinner's ears,
   'tis life and health and peace.

3. He speaks; and, listening to his voice,
   new life the dead receive,
   the mournful broken hearts rejoice,
   the humble poor believe.

4. Hear him, ye deaf; his praise, ye dumb,
   your loosened tongue employ;
   ye blind, behold your Saviour come;
   and leap, ye lame, for joy!

5. My gracious Master and my God,
   assist me to proclaim
   and spread through all the earth abroad
   the honours of thy name.
   Charles Wesley (1707-1788)

296

1. O God of earth and altar,
   bow down and hear our cry,
   our earthly rulers falter,
   our people drift and die;
   the walls of gold entomb us,
   the swords of scorn divide,
   take not thy thunder from us,
   but take away our pride.

2. From all that terror teaches,
   from lies of tongue and pen,
   from all the easy speeches
   that comfort cruel men,
   from sale and profanation
   of honour and the sword,
   from sleep and from damnation,
   deliver us, good Lord!

3. Tie in a living tether
   the prince and priest and thrall,
   bind all our lives together,
   smite us and save us all;
   in ire and exultation
   aflame with faith and free,
   lift up a living nation,
   a single sword to thee.
   Gilbert Keith Chesterton (1874-1936)

297

1. O God, our help in ages past,
   our hope for years to come,
   our shelter from the stormy blast,
   and our eternal home.

2. Beneath the shadow of thy throne,
   thy saints have dwelt secure;
   sufficient is thine arm alone,
   and our defence is sure.

3. Before the hills in order stood,
   or earth received her frame,
   from everlasting thou art God,
   to endless years the same.

4. A thousand ages in thy sight
   are like an evening gone;
   short as the watch that ends the night
   before the rising sun.

Continued overleaf

5. Time, like an ever-rolling stream,
   bears all its sons away;
   they fly forgotten, as a dream
   dies at the opening day.

6. O God, our help in ages past,
   our hope for years to come,
   be thou our guard while troubles last,
   and our eternal home.

Isaac Watts (1674-1748)

298

1. O God, we give ourselves today
   with this pure host to thee,
   the selfsame gift which thy dear Son
   gave once on Calvary.

2. Entire and whole, our life and love
   with heart and soul and mind,
   for all our sins and faults and needs,
   thy Church and all mankind.

3. With humble and with contrite heart
   this bread and wine we give
   because thy Son once gave himself
   and died that we might live.

4. Though lowly now, soon by thy word
   these offered gifts will be
   the very body of our Lord,
   his soul and deity.

5. His very body, offered up,
   a gift beyond all price,
   he gives to us, that we may give,
   in loving sacrifice.

6. O Lord, who took our human life,
   as water mixed with wine,
   grant through this sacrifice that we
   may share thy life divine.

Anthony Nye (b. 1932)

299

1. O Godhead hid,
   devoutly I adore thee,
   who truly art within
   the forms before me;
   to thee my heart
   I bow with bended knee,
   as failing quite
   in contemplating thee.

2. Sight, touch and taste
   in thee are each deceived,
   the ear alone most
   safely is believed:
   I believe all
   the Son of God has spoken;
   than truth's own word
   there is no truer token.

3. God only on the cross
   lay hid from view;
   but here lies hid
   at once the manhood too:
   and I, in both
   professing my belief,
   make the same pray'r
   as the repentant thief.

4. Thy wounds, as Thomas saw,
   I do not see;
   yet thee confess
   my Lord and God to be;
   make me believe thee
   ever more and more,
   in thee my hope,
   in thee my love to store.

5. O thou memorial
   of our Lord's own dying!
   O bread that living art
   and vivifying!
   Make ever thou my soul
   on thee to live;
   ever a taste
   of heav'nly sweetness give.

6. O loving Pelican!
   O Jesus, Lord!
   Unclean I am,
   but cleanse me in thy blood,
   of which a single drop,
   for sinners spilt,
   is ransom for
   a world's entire guilt.

7. Jesus, whom for the present
   veiled I see,
   what I so thirst for,
    O, vouchsafe to me:
   that I may see thy
   countenance unfolding,
   and may be blest
   thy glory in beholding.

St Thomas Aquinas (1227-1274)
tr. Edward Caswall (1814-1878)

300

1. O holy Lord, by all adored,
   our trespasses confessing,
   to thee this day thy children pray,
   our holy faith professing!
   Accept, O King, the gifts we bring,
   our songs of praise, the prayers
     we raise,
   and grant us, Lord, thy blessing.

2. To God on high be thanks
     and praise,
   who deigns our bond to sever;
   his care shall guide us all our days,
   and harm shall reach us never;
   on him we rest with faith assured
   of all that live he is the Lord,
   for ever and for ever.

Maurice F. Bell (1862-1947)

301

O, how good is the Lord!
O, how good is the Lord!
O, how good is the Lord!
I never will forget
what he has done for me.

1. He gives us salvation,
   how good is the Lord.
   He gives us salvation,
   how good is the Lord.
   He gives us salvation,
   how good is the Lord.
   I never will forget
   what he has done for me.

2. He gives us his Spirit,
   how good is the Lord.
   He gives us his Spirit,
   how good is the Lord.
   He gives us his Spirit,
   how good is the Lord.
   I never will forget
   what he has done for me.

3. He gives us his healing,
   how good is the Lord.
   He gives us his healing,
   how good is the Lord.
   He gives us his healing,
   how good is the Lord.
   I never will forget
   what he has done for me.

4. He gives us his body,
   how good is the Lord.
   He gives us his body,
   how good is the Lord.
   He gives us his body,
   how good is the Lord.
   I never will forget
   what he has done for me.

Continued overleaf

5. He gives us his freedom,
   how good is the Lord.
   He gives us his freedom,
   how good is the Lord.
   He gives us his freedom,
   how good is the Lord.
   I never will forget
   what he has done for me.

   O, how good is the Lord!
   O, how good is the Lord!
   O, how good is the Lord!
   I never will forget
   what he has done for me.

6. He gives us each other,
   how good is the Lord.
   He gives us each other,
   how good is the Lord.
   He gives us each other,
   how good is the Lord.
   I never will forget
   what he has done for me.

7. He gives us his glory,
   how good is the Lord.
   He gives us his glory,
   how good is the Lord.
   He gives us his glory,
   how good is the Lord.
   I never will forget
   what he has done for me.
   Traditional

302

1. O Jesus Christ, remember,
   when thou shalt come again
   upon the clouds of heaven,
   with all thy shining train;
   when ev'ry eye shall see thee
   in deity revealed,
   who now upon this altar
   in silence art concealed.

2. Remember then, O Saviour,
   I supplicate of thee,
   that here I bowed before thee
   upon my bended knee;
   that here I owned thy presence,
   and did not thee deny,
   and glorified thy greatness
   though hid from human eye.

3. Accept, divine Redeemer,
   the homage of my praise;
   be thou the light and honour
   and glory of my days.
   Be thou my consolation
   when death is drawing nigh;
   be thou my only treasure
   through all eternity.
   Edward Caswall (1814-1878)

303

1. O Jesus, I have promised
   to serve thee to the end;
   be thou for ever near me,
   my Master and my friend:
   I shall not fear the battle
   if thou art by my side,
   nor wander from the pathway
   if thou wilt be my guide.

2. O let me feel thee near me:
   the world is ever near;
   I see the sights that dazzle,
   the tempting sounds I hear;
   my foes are ever near me,
   around me and within;
   but, Jesus, draw thou nearer,
   and shield my soul from sin.

3. O let me hear thee speaking
in accents clear and still,
above the storms of passion,
the murmurs of self-will;
O speak to reassure me,
to hasten or control;
O speak and make me listen,
thou guardian of my soul.

4. O Jesus, thou hast promised,
to all who follow thee,
that where thou art in glory
there shall thy servant be;
and, Jesus, I have promised
to serve thee to the end:
O give me grace to follow,
my Master and my friend.

5. O let me see thy foot-marks,
and in them plant mine own;
my hope to follow duly
is in thy strength alone:
O guide me, call me, draw me,
uphold me to the end;
and then in heav'n receive me,
my Saviour and my friend.

John E. Bode (1816-1874)

304

1. O King of might and splendour,
creator most adored,
this sacrifice we render
to thee as sov'reign Lord.
May these our gifts be pleasing
unto thy majesty,
mankind from sin releasing
who have offended thee.

2. Thy body thou hast given,
thy blood thou hast outpoured,
that sin might be forgiven,
O Jesus, loving Lord.
As now with love most tender,
thy death we celebrate,
our lives in self-surrender
to thee we consecrate.

Dom Gregory Murray (1905-1992)

305

1. O lady, full of God's own grace,
whose caring hands the child embraced,
who listened to the Spirit's word,
believed and trusted in the Lord.

*O virgin fair, star of the sea,
my dearest mother, pray for me.
O virgin fair, star of the sea,
my dearest mother, pray for me.*

2. O lady, who felt daily joy
in caring for the holy boy,
whose home was plain and shorn
of wealth,
yet was enriched by God's own breath.

3. O lady, who bore living's pain
but still believed that love would reign,
who on a hill watched Jesus die,
as on the cross they raised him high.

4. O lady, who, on Easter day,
had all your sorrow wiped away
as God the Father's will was done
when from death's hold he freed
your Son.

Estelle White (b. 1925)

306

1. O let the Son of God enfold you
   with his Spirit and his love,
   let him fill your heart
   and satisfy your soul.
   O let him have the things that
      hold you,
   and his Spirit, like a dove,
   will descend upon your life and make
      you whole.

   Jesus, O Jesus,
   come and fill your lambs.
   Jesus, O Jesus,
   come and fill your lambs.

2. O come and sing this song with gladness
   as your hearts are filled with joy;
   lift your hands in sweet
   surrender to his name.
   O give him all your tears and sadness,
   give him all your years of pain,
   and you'll enter into life in Jesus' name.

   John Wimber (b. 1933)
   © 1979 Mercy Publishing/Kingsway's Thankyou Music

2. O morning stars, together
   proclaim the holy birth,
   and praises sing to God the King,
   and peace to all on earth;
   for Christ is born of Mary;
   and, gathered all above,
   while mortals sleep, the angels keep
   their watch of wond'ring love.

3. How silently, how silently,
   the wondrous gift is given!
   So God imparts to human hearts
   the blessings of his heaven.
   No ear may hear his coming;
   but in this world of sin,
   where meek souls will receive him, still
   the dear Christ enters in.

4. O holy child of Bethlehem,
   descend to us, we pray;
   cast out our sin, and enter in,
   be born in us today.
   We hear the Christmas angels
   the great glad tidings tell:
   O come to us, abide with us,
   our Lord Emmanuel.

   Phillips Brooks (1835-1893), alt.

307

1. O little town of Bethlehem,
   how still we see thee lie!
   Above thy deep and dreamless sleep
   the silent stars go by.
   Yet, in thy dark streets shineth
   the everlasting light;
   the hopes and fears of all the years
   are met in thee tonight.

308

O living water, refresh my soul.
O living water, refresh my soul.
Spirit of joy, Lord of creation.
Spirit of hope, Spirit of peace.

1. Spirit of God. Spirit of God.

2. O set us free. O set us free.

3. Come, pray in us. Come, pray in us.

   Sister Virginia Vissing

309

1. O Lord, all the world
   belongs to you,
   and you are always
   making all things new.
   What is wrong you forgive,
   and the new life you give
   is what's turning
   the world upside down.

2. The world's only
   loving to its friends,
   but you have brought us
   love that never ends;
   loving enemies too,
   and this loving with you
   is what's turning
   the world upside down.

3. This world lives divided
   and apart.
   You draw us all together
   and we start
   in your body to see
   that in fellowship we
   can be turning
   the world upside down.

4. The world wants the wealth
   to live in state,
   but you show us a new way
   to be great:
   like a servant you came,
   and if we do the same,
   we'll be turning
   the world upside down.

5. O Lord, all the world
   belongs to you,
   and you are always
   making all things new.
   Send your Spirit on all
   in your Church whom you call
   to be turning
   the world upside down.

Patrick Appleford (b. 1925), alt.

310

O Lord, hear my prayer,
O Lord, hear my prayer:
when I call answer me.
O Lord, hear my prayer,
O Lord, hear my prayer.
Come and listen to me.

Taizé Community, based on Psalm 55:1,2

311

1. O Lord, my God,
   when I in awesome wonder
   consider all the worlds
   thy hand has made,
   I see the stars,
   I hear the rolling thunder,
   thy pow'r throughout
   the universe displayed.

   Then sings my soul,
   my Saviour God, to thee:
   how great thou art,
   how great thou art.
   Then sings my soul,
   my Saviour God, to thee:
   how great thou art,
   how great thou art.

3. When through the woods
   and forest glades I wander
   and hear the birds sing sweetly
   in the trees;
   when I look down
   from lofty mountain grandeur,
   and hear the brook,
   and feel the gentle breeze.

Continued overleaf

3. And when I think that God,
   his Son not sparing,
   sent him to die,
   I scarce can take it in
   that on the cross,
   my burden gladly bearing,
   he bled and died
   to take away my sin.

   Then sings my soul,
   my Saviour God, to thee:
   how great thou art,
   how great thou art.
   Then sings my soul,
   my Saviour God, to thee:
   how great thou art,
   how great thou art.

4. When Christ shall come
   with shout of acclamation
   and take me home,
   what joy shall fill my heart;
   when I shall bow
   in humble adoration,
   and there proclaim:
   my God, how great thou art.

   Karl Boberg (1859-1940),
   tr. Stuart K. Hine (1899-1989)
   © 1953 Stuart K. Hine/Kingsway's Thankyou Music

312

O Lord, your tenderness,
melting all my bitterness,
O Lord, I receive your love.
O Lord, your loveliness,
changing all my ugliness,
O Lord, I receive your love.
O Lord, I receive your love.
O Lord, I receive your love.

Graham Kendrick (b. 1950)
© 1986 Kingsway's Thankyou Music

313

1. O Mary, when our God chose you
   to bring his dear Son to birth,
   a new creation made in you
   gave joy to all the earth.

   Alleluia, alleluia, alleluia, alleluia.
   A new creation made in you
   gave joy to all the earth.

2. When he was born on Christmas night
   and music made the rafters ring,
   the stars were dancing with delight;
   now all God's children sing.

3. One winter's night, a heap of straw
   becomes a place where ages meet,
   when kings come knocking at the door
   and kneeling at your feet.

4. In you, our God confounds the strong
   and makes the crippled dance with joy;
   and to our barren world belong
   his mother and her boy.

5. In empty streets and broken hearts
   you call to mind what he has done;
   where all his loving kindness starts
   in sending you a Son.

6. And, Mary, while we stand with you,
   may once again his Spirit come,
   and all his brethren follow you
   to reach our Father's home.

Damian Lundy (b. 1944)

314

1. O Mother blest, whom God bestows
on sinners and on just,
what joy, what hope thou givest those
who in thy mercy trust.

Thou art clement, thou art chaste,
Mary, thou art fair;
of all mothers sweetest, best,
none with thee compare.

2. O heav'nly mother, mistress sweet!
It never yet was told
that suppliant sinner left thy feet
unpitied, unconsoled.

3. O mother pitiful and mild,
cease not to pray for me;
for I do love thee as a child
and sigh for love of thee.

4. O mother blest, for me obtain,
ungrateful though I be,
to love that God who first
     could deign
to show such love for me.

St Alphonsus (1696-1787),
tr. Edmund Vaughan (1827-1908)

315

O my people, what have I done to you?
How have I hurt you? Answer me.

1. I led you out of Egypt;
from slavery I set you free.
I brought you into a land of promise;
you have prepared a cross for me.

2. I led you as a shepherd,
I brought you safely through the sea,
fed you with manna in the desert;
you have prepared a cross for me.

3. I fought for you in battles,
I won you strength and victory,
gave you a royal crown and sceptre:
you have prepared a cross for me.

4. I planted you, my vineyard,
and cared for you most tenderly,
looked for abundant fruit,
     and found none
– only the cross you made for me.

5. Then listen to my pleading,
and do not turn away from me.
You are my people: will you reject me?
For you I suffer bitterly.

Damian Lundy (b. 1944),
based on the Good Friday 'Reproaches'

316

1. O perfect love,
all human thought transcending,
lowly we kneel
in prayer before thy throne,
that theirs may be
the love which knows no ending,
whom thou for ever more
dost join in one.

2. O perfect life,
be thou their full assurance
of tender charity
and steadfast faith,
of patient hope
and quiet, brave endurance,
with childlike trust that fears
not pain nor death.

Continued overleaf

3. Grant them the joy
   which brightens earthly sorrow,
   grant them the peace
   which calms all earthly strife;
   and to life's day
   the glorious unknown morrow
   that dawns upon
   eternal love and life.

   Dorothy F. Gurney (1858-1932)

4. O praise ye the Lord,
   thanksgiving and song
   to him be outpoured
   all ages along;
   for love in creation,
   for heavens restored,
   for grace of salvation,
   O praise ye the Lord!

   Henry Williams Baker (1821-1877),
   based on Psalms 148 and 150

317

1. O praise ye the Lord,
   praise him in the height;
   rejoice in his word,
   ye angels of light;
   ye heavens, adore him,
   by whom ye were made,
   and worship before him,
   in brightness arrayed.

2. O praise ye the Lord,
   praise him upon earth,
   in tuneful accord,
   ye saints of new birth.
   Praise him who hath brought you
   his grace from above,
   praise him who hath taught you
   to sing of his love.

3. O praise ye the Lord,
   all things that give sound;
   each jubilant chord
   re-echo around;
   loud organs his glory
   forth tell in deep tone,
   and, sweet harp, the story
   of what he hath done.

318

1. O purest of creatures!
   Sweet mother, sweet maid;
   the one spotless womb
   wherein Jesus was laid.
   Dark night hath come down
   on us, mother, and we
   look out for thy shining,
   sweet star of the sea.

2. Earth gave him one lodging;
   'twas deep in thy breast,
   and God found a home where
   the sinner finds rest;
   his home and his hiding-place,
   both were in thee;
   he was won by thy shining,
   sweet star of the sea.

3. O, blissful and calm
   was the wonderful rest
   that thou gavest thy God
   in thy virginal breast;
   for the heaven he left
   he found heaven in thee,
   and he shone in thy shining,
   sweet star of the sea.

   Frederick William Faber (1814-1863)

319

O Sacrament most holy,
O Sacrament divine,
all praise and all thanksgiving
be ev'ry moment thine.

Traditional

320

1. O sacred head ill-usèd,
   by reed and bramble scarred,
   that idle blows have bruisèd,
   and mocking lips have marred,
   how dimmed that eye so tender,
   how wan those cheeks appear,
   how overcast the splendour
   that angel hosts revere!

2. What marvel if thou languish,
   vigour and virtue fled,
   wasted and spent with anguish,
   and pale as are the dead?
   O by thy foes' derision,
   that death endured for me,
   grant that thy open vision
   a sinner's eyes may see.

3. Good Shepherd, spent with loving,
   look on me, who have strayed,
   oft by those lips unmoving
   with milk and honey stayed;
   spurn not a sinner's crying
   nor from thy love outcast,
   but rest thy head in dying
   on these frail arms at last.

4. In this thy sacred passion
   O, that some share had I!
   O, may thy Cross's fashion
   o'erlook me when I die!
   For these dear pains that rack thee
   a sinner's thanks receive;
   O, lest in death I lack thee,
   a sinner's care relieve.

5. Since death must be my ending,
   in that dread hour of need,
   my friendless cause befriending,
   Lord, to my rescue speed;
   thyself, dear Jesus, trace me
   that passage to the grave,
   and from thy cross embrace me
   with arms outstretched to save.

13th century,
tr. Ronald Arbuthnott Knox (1888-1957)

321

1. O sacred head sore wounded,
   defiled and put to scorn;
   O kingly head surrounded
   with mocking crown of thorn:
   what sorrow mars thy grandeur?
   Can death thy bloom deflower?
   O countenance whose splendour
   the hosts of heav'n adore.

2. Thy beauty, long-desirèd,
   hath vanished from our sight;
   thy pow'r is all expirèd,
   and quenched the light of light.
   Ah me, for whom thou diest,
   hide not so far thy grace:
   show me, O love most highest,
   the brightness of thy face.

3. I pray thee, Jesus, own me,
   me, shepherd good, for thine;
   who to thy fold hast won me,
   and fed with truth divine.
   Me guilty, me refuse not,
   incline thy face to me,
   this comfort that I lose not,
   on earth to comfort thee.

Continued overleaf

4. In thy most bitter passion
   my heart to share doth cry,
   with thee for my salvation
   upon the cross to die.
   Ah, keep my heart thus movèd
   to stand thy cross beneath,
   to mourn thee, well-belovèd,
   yet thank thee for thy death.

5. My days are few, O fail not,
   with thine immortal power,
   to hold me that I quail not
   in death's most fearful hour:
   that I may fight befriended,
   and see in my last strife
   to me thine arms extended
   upon the cross of life.

   Paul Gerhardt (1607-1676)
   tr. Robert Bridges (1844-1930)

322

1. O Sacred Heart,
   our home lies deep in thee;
   on earth thou art an exile's rest,
   in heav'n the glory of the blest,
   O Sacred Heart.

2. O Sacred Heart,
   thou fount of contrite tears;
   where'er those living waters flow,
   new life to sinners they bestow,
   O Sacred Heart.

3. O Sacred Heart,
   our trust is all in thee,
   for though earth's night be dark
      and drear,
   thou breathest rest where thou
      art near,
   O Sacred Heart.

4. O Sacred Heart,
   lead exiled children home,
   where we may ever rest near thee,
   in peace and joy eternally,
   O Sacred Heart.

   Francis Stanfield (1835-1914)

323

1. O, the love of my Lord is the essence
   of all that I love here on earth.
   All the beauty I see he has given to me,
   and his giving is gentle as silence.

2. Ev'ry day, ev'ry hour, ev'ry moment
   have been blessed by the strength of
      his love.
   At the turn of each tide he is there at
      my side,
   and his touch is as gentle as silence.

3. There've been times when I've turned
      from his presence
   and I've walked other paths, other ways;
   but I've called on his name in the dark
      of my shame,
   and his mercy was gentle as silence.

   Estelle White (b. 1925)

324

O the word of my Lord,
deep within my being,
O the word of my Lord,
you have filled my mind.

1. Before I formed you in the womb
   I knew you through and through,
   I chose you to be mine.
   Before you left your mother's side
   I called to you, my child,
   to be my sign.

2. I know that you are very young,
   but I will make you strong,
   I'll fill you with my word;
   and you will travel through the land,
   fulfilling my command
   which you have heard.

3. And ev'rywhere you are to go
   my hand will follow you;
   you will not be alone.
   In all the danger that you fear
   you'll find me very near,
   your words my own.

4. With all my strength you will be filled:
   you will destroy and build,
   for that is my design.
   You will create and overthrow,
   reap harvests I will sow,
   your word is mine.

Damian Lundy (b. 1944),
based on Jeremiah 1

325

1. O worship the King,
   all glorious above;
   O gratefully sing
   his pow'r and his love:
   our shield and defender,
   the ancient of days,
   pavilioned in splendour,
   and girded with praise.

2. O tell of his might,
   O sing of his grace,
   whose robe is the light,
   whose canopy space.
   His chariots of wrath
   the deep thunder-clouds form,
   and dark is his path
   on the wings of the storm.

3. This earth, with its store
   of wonders untold,
   almighty, thy pow'r
   hath founded of old;
   hath 'stablished it fast
   by a changeless decree,
   and round it hath cast,
   like a mantle, the sea.

4. Thy bountiful care
   what tongue can recite?
   It breathes in the air,
   it shines in the light;
   it streams from the hills,
   it descends to the plain,
   and sweetly distils
   in the dew and the rain.

5. O measureless might,
   ineffable love,
   while angels delight
   to hymn thee above,
   thy humbler creation,
   though feeble their lays,
   with true adoration
   shall sing to thy praise.

Robert Grant (1799-1838) based on Psalm 104

326

1. O worship the Lord
   in the beauty of holiness;
   bow down before him,
   his glory proclaim;
   with gold of obedience
   and incense of lowliness,
   kneel and adore him:
   the Lord is his name.

Continued overleaf

2. Low at his feet lay
   thy burden of carefulness:
   high on his heart
   he will bear it for thee,
   comfort thy sorrows,
   and answer thy prayerfulness,
   guiding thy steps
   as may best for thee be.

3. Fear not to enter
   his courts in the slenderness
   of the poor wealth
   thou wouldst reckon as thine:
   truth in its beauty,
   and love in its tenderness,
   these are the off'rings
   to lay on his shrine.

4. These, though we bring them
   in trembling and fearfulness,
   he will accept
   for the name that is dear;
   mornings of joy give
   for evenings of tearfulness,
   trust for our trembling
   and hope for our fear.

   John Samuel Bewley Monsell (1811-1875)

327

1. Of the Father's love begotten,
   ere the worlds began to be,
   he is Alpha and Omega,
   he the source, the ending he,
   of all things that are and have been
   and that future years shall see:
   evermore and evermore.

2. By his word was all created;
   he commanded, it was done:
   heav'n and earth and depth of ocean,
   universe of three in one,
   all that grows beneath the shining
   of the light of moon and sun:
   evermore and evermore.

3. Blessèd was that day for ever
   when the virgin, full of grace,
   by the Spirit's pow'r conceiving,
   bore the Saviour of our race,
   and the child, the world's Redeemer,
   first revealed his sacred face:
   evermore and evermore.

4. O, ye heights of heav'n, adore him,
   angels and archangels sing!
   Ev'ry creature bow before him
   singing praise to God our King;
   let no earthly tongue be silent,
   all the world with homage ring:
   evermore and evermore.

5. He, by prophets sung, is here now,
   promised since the world began,
   now on earth in flesh descended
   to atone for sins of man.
   All creation praise its Master,
   see fulfilment of his plan:
   evermore and evermore.

6. Glory be to God the Father,
   glory be to God the Son,
   glory to thee Holy Spirit,
   persons three, yet Godhead one.
   Glory be from all creation
   while eternal ages run:
   evermore and evermore.

   Aurelius Clemens Prudentius (348-413),
   tr. John Mason Neale (1818-1866)

328

1. Of the glorious body telling,
   O my tongue, its myst'ries sing,
   and the blood, all price excelling,
   which the world's eternal King,
   in a noble womb once dwelling,
   shed for this world's ransoming.

2. Giv'n for us, for us descending,
   of a virgin to proceed,
   he with us in converse blending,
   scattered he the gospel seed,
   till his sojourn drew to ending,
   which he closed in wondrous deed.

3. At the last great supper lying,
   circled by his brethren's band,
   meekly with the law complying,
   first he finished its command.
   Then, immortal food supplying,
   gave himself with his own hand.

4. Word made flesh, by word he maketh
   very bread his flesh to be;
   we, in wine, Christ's blood partaketh,
   and if senses fail to see,
   faith alone the true heart waketh,
   to behold the mystery.

5. Therefore, we before him bending,
   this great sacrament revere;
   types and shadows have their ending,
   for the newer rite is here;
   faith, our outward sense befriending,
   makes the inward vision clear.

6. Glory let us give, and blessing,
   to the Father and the Son,
   honour, might and praise addressing,
   while eternal ages run;
   ever too his love confessing,
   who from both, with both is one.

   St Thomas Aquinas (1227-1274),
   tr. John Mason Neale (1818-1866), alt.

329

1. On a hill far away
   stood an old rugged cross,
   the emblem of suff'ring and shame;
   and I loved that old cross
   where the dearest and best
   for a world of lost sinners was slain.

   So I'll cherish the old rugged cross,
   till my trophies at last I lay down;
   I will cling to the old rugged cross
   and exchange it some day for a crown.

2. O that old rugged cross,
   so despised by the world,
   has a wondrous attraction for me:
   for the dear Lamb of God
   left his glory above
   to bear it to dark Calvary.

3. In the old rugged cross,
   stained with blood so divine,
   a wondrous beauty I see.
   For 'twas on that old cross
   Jesus suffered and died
   to pardon and sanctify me.

4. To the old rugged cross
   I will ever be true,
   its shame and reproach gladly bear.
   Then he'll call me some day
   to my home far away;
   there his glory for ever I'll share.

   George Bennard (1873-1958)
   © 1913 Rodeheaver Co/Word Music Inc./Word Music (UK)

330

1. On Christmas night all Christians sing,
   to hear the news the angels bring,
   on Christmas night all Christians sing,
   to hear the news the angels bring,
   news of great joy, news of great mirth,
   news of our merciful King's birth.

Continued overleaf

2. Then why should we on earth be so sad,
   since our Redeemer made us glad,
   then why should we on earth be so sad,
   since our Redeemer made us glad,
   when from our sin he set us free,
   all for to gain our liberty?

3. When sin departs before his grace,
   then life and health come in its place,
   when sin departs before his grace,
   then life and health come in its place,
   angels and earth with joy may sing,
   all for to see the new-born King.

4. All out of darkness we have light,
   which made the angels sing this night:
   all out of darkness we have light,
   which made the angels sing this night:
   'Glory to God and peace to men,
   now and for evermore. Amen.'

   Traditional English Carol, alt.

331

1. On Jordan's bank the Baptist's cry
   announces that the Lord is nigh,
   come then and hearken, for he brings
   glad tidings from the King of kings.

2. Then cleansed be ev'ry Christian breast,
   and furnished for so great a guest!
   Yea, let us each our hearts prepare
   for Christ to come and enter there.

3. For thou art our salvation, Lord,
   our refuge and our great reward;
   without thy grace our souls must fade
   and wither like a flower decayed.

4. Stretch forth thy hand, to heal our sore,
   and make us rise, to fall no more;
   once more upon thy people shine,
   and fill the world with love divine.

5. All praise, eternal Son, to thee
   whose advent sets thy people free,
   whom, with the Father, we adore,
   and Holy Ghost, for evermore.

   Charles Coffin (1676-1749),
   tr. John Chandler (1806-1876)

332

1. On this house your blessing, Lord,
   on this house your grace bestow.
   On this house your blessing, Lord,
   may it come and never go.
   Bringing peace and joy and happiness,
   bringing love that knows no end.
   On this house your blessing, Lord,
   on this house your blessing send.

2. On this house your loving, Lord,
   may it overflow each day.
   On this house your loving, Lord,
   may it come and with us stay.
   Drawing us in love and unity
   by the love received from you.
   On this house your loving, Lord,
   may it come each day anew.

3. On this house your giving, Lord,
   may it turn and ever flow.
   On this house your giving, Lord,
   on this house your wealth bestow.
   Filling all our hopes and wishes, Lord,
   in the way you know is best.
   On this house your giving, Lord,
   may it come and with us rest.

4. On this house your calling, Lord,
   may it come to us each day.
   On this house your calling, Lord,
   may it come to lead the way.
   Filling us with nobler yearnings, Lord,
   calling us to live in you.
   On this house your calling, Lord,
   may it come each day anew.

*The word 'house' may be replaced
throughout by 'school', 'church', etc.*

Marie Lydia Pereira (b. 1920)

333

1. Once in royal David's city
   stood a lowly cattle shed,
   where a mother laid her baby
   in a manger for his bed:
   Mary was that mother mild,
   Jesus Christ her little child.

2. He came down to earth from heaven,
   who is God and Lord of all,
   and his shelter was a stable
   and his cradle was a stall;
   with the poor, and mean, and lowly,
   lived on earth our Saviour holy.

3. And through all his wondrous childhood
   he would honour and obey,
   love and watch the lowly maiden
   in whose gentle arms he lay;
   Christian children all must be
   mild, obedient, good as he.

4. For he is our childhood's pattern,
   day by day like us he grew;
   he was little, weak and helpless,
   tears and smiles like us he knew;
   and he feeleth for our sadness,
   and he shareth in our gladness.

5. And our eyes at last shall see him
   through his own redeeming love,
   for that child so dear and gentle
   is our Lord in heaven above;
   and he leads his children on
   to the place where he is gone.

6. Not in that poor lowly stable,
   with the oxen standing by,
   we shall see him; but in heaven,
   set at God's right hand on high;
   when like stars his children crowned
   all in white shall wait around.

Cecil Frances Alexander (1818-1895)

334

*One bread, one body, one Lord of all,
one cup of blessing which we bless;
and we, though many,
throughout the earth,
we are one body in this one Lord.*

1. Gentile or Jew,
   servant or free,
   woman or man, no more.

2. Many the gifts,
   many the works,
   one in the Lord of all.

3. Grain for the fields,
   scattered and grown,
   gathered to one, for all.

*John Foley, based on 1 Cor. 10:16,
17; 12:4; Gal 3:28; The Didache 9*
© 1978 New Dawn Music

335

1. One cold night in spring the wind
   blew strong;
   then the darkness had its hour.
   A man was eating with his friends,
   for he knew his death was near.

Continued overleaf

2. And he broke a wheaten loaf to share,
   for his friends a last goodbye.
   'My body is the bread I break.
   O, my heart will break and die.'

3. Then he poured good wine into a cup,
   blessed it gently, passed it round.
   'This cup is brimming with my blood.
   Soon the drops will stain the ground.'

4. See a dying man with arms outstretched
   at the setting of the sun.
   He stretches healing hands to you.
   Will you take them for your own?

5. Soon a man will come with
       arms outstretched
   at the rising of the sun.
   His wounded hands will set you free
   if you take them for your own.

   Damian Lundy (b. 1944)

336

Open our eyes, Lord,
we want to see Jesus,
to reach out and touch him
and say that we love him;
open our ears, Lord,
and help us to listen;
O open our eyes, Lord,
we want to see Jesus!

Robert Cull (b. 1949)
© 1976 Maranatha! Music/CopyCare Ltd

337

1. Open your ears, O Christian people,
   open your ears and hear Good News!
   Open your hearts, O royal priesthood,
   God has come to you!

*God has spoken to his people, alleluia,
and his words are words of wisdom,
alleluia.*

2. Israel comes to greet the Saviour,
   Judah is glad to see his day.
   From east and west the peoples travel,
   he will show the way.

3. He who has ears to hear his message;
   he who has ears, then let him hear.
   He who would learn the way of wisdom,
   let him hear God's words.

   Willard F. Jabusch (b. 1930)

338

*Our hearts were made for you, Lord,
our hearts were made for you;
they'll never find, never find,
never find rest
until they find their rest in you.*

1. When you call me I will answer,
   when you seek me you will find.
   I will lead you back from exile
   and reveal to you my mind.

2. I will take you from the nations,
   and will bring you to your land.
   From your idols I will cleanse you
   and you'll cherish my command.

3. I will put my law within you,
   I will write it on your heart;
   I will be your God and Saviour,
   you, my people set apart.

   Aniceto Nazareth, based on Scripture

339

1. Pange lingua gloriosi,
   Corporis Mysterium,
   Sanguinisque pretiosi
   quem in mundi pretium,
   fructus ventris generosi
   Rex effudit gentium.

2. Nobis datus, nobis natus
   ex intacta Virgine;
   et in mundo conversatus,
   sparso verbi semine,
   sui moras incolatus
   miro clausit ordine.

3. In supremæ nocte coenæ
   recumbens cum fratribus,
   observata lege plene
   cibis in legalibus:
   cibum turbæ duodenæ
   se dat suis manibus.

4. Verbum caro, panem verum,
   Verbo carnem efficit:
   fitque sanguis Christi merum;
   et si sensus deficit,
   ad firmandum cor sincerum
   sola fides sufficit.

5. Tantum ergo Sacramentum
   veneremur cernui:
   et antiquum documentum
   novo cedat ritui;
   præstet fides supplementum
   sensuum defectui.

6. Genitori, genitoque
   laus, et jubilatio,
   salus, honor, virtus quoque
   sit et benedictio;
   procedenti ab utroque
   compar sit laudatio. Amen.
   St Thomas Aquinas (1227-1274)

340

Peace I leave with you,
peace I give to you;
not as the world gives peace,
do I give.
Take and pass it on,
on to ev'ryone;
thus the world will know,
you are my friends.
Peter Madden

341

1. Peace is flowing like a river,
   flowing out through you and me,
   spreading out into the desert,
   setting all the captives free.

2. Love is flowing like a river,
   flowing out through you and me,
   spreading out into the desert,
   setting all the captives free.

3. Joy is flowing like a river,
   flowing out through you and me,
   spreading out into the desert,
   setting all the captives free.

4. Hope is flowing like a river,
   flowing out through you and me,
   spreading out into the desert,
   setting all the captives free.
   Unknown

342

1. Peace is the gift of heaven to earth,
   softly enfolding our fears.
   Peace is the gift of Christ to the world,
   given for us:
   he is the Lamb who bore
   the pain of peace.

Continued overleaf

2. Peace is the gift of Christ to his Church,
   wound of the lance of his love.
   Love is the pain he suffered for all,
   offered to us:
   O, to accept the wound
   that brings us peace!

3. Joy is the gift the Spirit imparts,
   born of the heavens and earth.
   We are his children, children of joy,
   people of God:
   he is our Lord, our peace,
   our love, our joy!

   John Glynn (b. 1948)

343

1. Peace, perfect peace,
   is the gift of Christ our Lord.
   Peace, perfect peace,
   is the gift of Christ our Lord.
   Thus, says the Lord,
   will the world know my friends.
   Peace, perfect peace,
   is the gift of Christ our Lord.

2. Love, perfect love,
   is the gift of Christ our Lord.
   Love, perfect love,
   is the gift of Christ our Lord.
   Thus, says the Lord,
   will the world know my friends.
   Love, perfect love,
   is the gift of Christ our Lord.

3. Faith, perfect faith,
   is the gift of Christ our Lord.
   Faith, perfect faith,
   is the gift of Christ our Lord.
   Thus, says the Lord,
   will the world know my friends.
   Faith, perfect faith,
   is the gift of Christ our Lord.

4. Hope, perfect hope,
   is the gift of Christ our Lord.
   Hope, perfect hope,
   is the gift of Christ our Lord.
   Thus, says the Lord,
   will the world know my friends.
   Hope, perfect hope,
   is the gift of Christ our Lord.

5. Joy, perfect joy,
   is the gift of Christ our Lord.
   Joy, perfect joy,
   is the gift of Christ our Lord.
   Thus, says the Lord,
   will the world know my friends.
   Joy, perfect joy,
   is the gift of Christ our Lord.

   Kevin Mayhew (b. 1942)

344

1. Praise him, praise him,
   praise him in the morning,
   praise him in the noontime.
   Praise him, praise him,
   praise him when the sun goes down.

2. Love him, love him,
   love him in the morning,
   love him in the noontime.
   Love him, love him,
   love him when the sun goes down.

3. Trust him, trust him,
   trust him in the morning,
   trust him in the noontime.
   Trust him, trust him,
   trust him when the sun goes down.

4. Serve him, serve him,
   serve him in the morning,
   serve him in the noontime.
   Serve him, serve him,
   serve him when the sun goes down.

5. Jesus, Jesus,
   Jesus in the morning,
   Jesus in the noontime.
   Jesus, Jesus,
   Jesus when the sun goes down.

Unknown

345

1. Praise, my soul, the King of heaven!
   To his feet thy tribute bring.
   Ransomed, healed, restored, forgiven,
   who like me his praise should sing?
   Praise him! Praise him!
   Praise him! Praise him!
   Praise the everlasting King!

2. Praise him for his grace and favour
   to our fathers in distress;
   praise him still the same for ever,
   slow to chide and swift to bless.
   Praise him! Praise him!
   Praise him! Praise him!
   Glorious in his faithfulness!

3. Father-like he tends and spares us;
   well our feeble frame he knows;
   in his hands he gently bears us,
   rescues us from all our foes.
   Praise him! Praise him!
   Praise him! Praise him!
   Widely as his mercy flows!

4. Angels, help us to adore him;
   ye behold him face to face;
   sun and moon bow down before him,
   dwellers all in time and space.
   Praise him! Praise him!
   Praise him! Praise him!
   Praise with us the God of grace!

Henry Francis Lyte (1793-1847)

346

1. Praise the Lord, ye heav'ns adore him!
   Praise him, angels in the height;
   sun and moon, rejoice before him,
   praise him, all ye stars and light.
   Praise the Lord, for he hath spoken;
   worlds his mighty voice obeyed:
   laws, which never shall be broken,
   for their guidance he hath made.

2. Praise the Lord, for he is glorious!
   Never shall his promise fail.
   God hath made his saints victorious;
   sin and death shall not prevail.
   Praise the God of our salvation,
   hosts on high, his pow'r proclaim;
   heav'n and earth and all creation,
   laud and magnify his name!

3. Worship, honour, glory, blessing,
   Lord, we offer to thy name;
   young and old, thy praise expressing,
   join their Saviour to proclaim.
   As the saints in heav'n adore thee,
   we would bow before thy throne;
   as thine angels serve before thee,
   so on earth thy will be done.

Vv 1 and 2 from 'Foundling Hospital Collection'
(1796), vs 3 Edward Osler (1798-1863)

347

1. Praise to the Holiest in the height,
   and in the depth be praise,
   in all his words most wonderful,
   most sure in all his ways.

2. O loving wisdom of our God!
   When all was sin and shame,
   a second Adam to the fight,
   and to the rescue came.

Continued overleaf

3. O wisest love, that flesh and blood
which did in Adam fail,
should strive afresh against the foe,
should strive and should prevail.

4. And that a higher gift than grace
should flesh and blood refine,
God's presence and his very self,
and Essence all divine.

5. O generous love, that he who smote
in man for man the foe,
the double agony in man
for man should undergo.

6. And in the garden secretly
and on the cross on high,
should teach his brethren, and inspire
to suffer and to die.

7. Praise to the Holiest in the height,
and in the depth be praise,
in all his words most wonderful,
most sure in all his ways.

John Henry Newman (1801-1890)

348

1. Praise to the Lord,
the Almighty, the King of creation!
O my soul, praise him,
for he is your health and salvation.
All you who hear,
now to his altar draw near;
join in profound adoration.

2. Praise to the Lord,
let us offer our gifts at his altar;
let not our sins and transgressions
now cause us to falter.
Christ, the High Priest,
bids us all join in his feast;
victims with him on the altar.

3. Praise to the Lord,
O let all that is in us adore him!
All that has life and breath,
come now in praises before him.
Let the Amen
sound from his people again,
now as we worship before him.

Joachim Neander (1650-1680)
tr. Catherine Winkworth (1827-1878), alt.

349

1. Praise to the Lord,
the Almighty, the King of creation!
O my soul, praise him,
for he is thy health and salvation.
All ye who hear,
now to his temple draw near,
joining in glad adoration.

2. Praise to the Lord,
who o'er all things so
wondrously reigneth,
shieldeth thee gently from harm,
or when fainting sustaineth:
hast thou not seen
how thy heart's wishes have been
granted in what he ordaineth?

3. Praise to the Lord,
who doth prosper thy work and
defend thee,
surely his goodness and mercy
shall daily attend thee:
ponder anew
what the Almighty can do,
if to the end he befriend thee.

4. Praise to the Lord,
O let all that is in us adore him!
All that hath life and breath,
come now in praises before him.
Let the Amen
sound from his people again,
gladly for ay we adore him.

Joachim Neander (1650-1680),
tr. Catherine Winkworth (1827-1878)

350

1. Praise we our God with joy
and gladness never-ending;
angels and saints with us
their grateful voices blending.
He is our Father dear,
o'er-filled with parent's love;
mercies unsought, unknown,
he showers from above.

2. He is our shepherd true;
with watchful care unsleeping,
on us, his erring sheep,
an eye of pity keeping;
he with a mighty arm
the bonds of sin doth break,
and to our burdened hearts
in words of peace doth speak.

3. Graces in copious stream
from that pure fount are welling,
where, in our heart of hearts,
our God hath set his dwelling.
His word our lantern is;
his peace our comfort still;
his sweetness all our rest;
our law, our life, his will.

Frederick Oakeley (1802-1880) and others

351

Regina cæli, lætare, alleluia,
quia quem meruisti portare, alleluia,
resurrexit sicut dixit, alleluia.
Ora pro nobis Deum, alleluia.

Unknown 12th century

352

Rejoice in the Lord always
and again I say rejoice.
Rejoice in the Lord always
and again I say rejoice.
Rejoice, rejoice
and again I say rejoice.
Rejoice, rejoice
and again I say rejoice.

Based on Phil. 4:4

353

Rejoice! Rejoice! Christ is in you,
the hope of glory in our hearts.
He lives! He lives! His breath is in you,
arise, a mighty army, we arise.

1. Now is the time for us
to march upon the land,
into our hands he will give
the ground we claim.
He rides in majesty
to lead us into victory,
the world shall see
that Christ is Lord!

2. God is at work in us
his purpose to perform,
building a kingdom of power
not of words,
where things impossible
by faith shall be made possible;
let's give the glory
to him now.

Continued overleaf

3. Though we are weak,
   his grace is ev'rything we need;
   we're made of clay
   but this treasure is within.
   He turns our weaknesses
   into his opportunities,
   so that the glory
   goes to him.

   Rejoice! Rejoice! Christ is in you,
   the hope of glory in our hearts.
   He lives! He lives! His breath is in you,
   arise, a mighty army, we arise.

   Graham Kendrick (b. 1950)
   based on the Letters of St Paul
   © 1983 Kingsway's Thankyou Music

354

1. Rejoice, the Lord is King!
   Your Lord and King adore;
   mortals, give thanks and sing,
   and triumph evermore.

   Lift up your heart, lift up your voice;
   rejoice, again I say, rejoice.

2. Jesus the Saviour reigns,
   the God of truth and love;
   when he had purged our stains,
   he took his seat above.

3. His kingdom cannot fail;
   he rules o'er earth and heaven;
   the keys of death and hell
   are to our Jesus given.

4. He sits at God's right hand
   till all his foes submit,
   and bow to his command,
   and fall beneath his feet.

   Charles Wesley (1707-1788)

355

1. Ride on, ride on in majesty!
   Hark, all the tribes hosanna cry;
   thy humble beast pursues his road
   with palms and scattered
       garments strowed.

2. Ride on, ride on in majesty!
   In lowly pomp ride on to die;
   O Christ, thy triumphs now begin
   o'er captive death and conquered sin.

3. Ride on, ride on in majesty!
   The wingèd squadrons of the sky
   look down with sad and wond'ring eyes
   to see th'approaching sacrifice.

4. Ride on, ride on in majesty!
   Thy last and fiercest strife is nigh;
   the Father, on his sapphire throne,
   expects his own anointed Son.

5. Ride on, ride on in majesty!
   In lowly pomp ride on to die;
   bow thy meek head to mortal pain,
   then take, O God, thy pow'r, and reign.

   H. H. Milman (1791-1868)

356

Ring out your joy, give glory to God.
Lift up your hearts and sing.
Let all creation tell of his name.
Praise him for evermore!

1. Blessèd are you, God of our fathers;
   glory and praise for evermore!
   Blest be your holy, glorious, great name;
   glory and praise for evermore!

2. Blest in the temple of your glory;
   glory and praise for evermore!
   Blessèd, enthroned over
      your kingdom;
   glory and praise for evermore!

3. Blest, you who know the deeps
      and highest;
   glory and praise for evermore!
   Blest in the firmament of heaven;
   glory and praise for evermore!

4. All things the Lord has made,
      now bless him;
   glory and praise for evermore!
   Angels and saints, now bless
      and praise him;
   glory and praise for evermore!

   Aniceto Nazareth, based on the Canticle of Daniel

357

Salve, Regina, mater misericordiæ;
vita, dulcedo, et spes nostra, salve.
Ad te clamamus, exules filii hevæ.
Ad te suspiramus, gementes et flentes
in hac lacrimarum valle.
Eia ergo, advocata nostra,
illos tuos misericordes oculos
ad nos converte.
Et Jesum, benedictum fructum
   ventris tui,
nobis post hoc exilium ostende.
O clemens, O pia, O dulcis
   Virgo Maria.

   Hermann the Lame (d. 1054)

358

1. See, amid the winter's snow,
   born for us on earth below,
   see, the tender Lamb appears,
   promised from eternal years.

Hail, thou ever-blessèd morn,
hail, redemption's happy dawn!
Sing through all Jerusalem,
Christ is born in Bethlehem.

2. Lo, within a manger lies
   he who built the starry skies;
   he who, throned in heights sublime,
   sits amid the cherubim.

3. Say, ye holy shepherds, say,
   what your joyful news today?
   Wherefore have ye left your sheep
   on the lonely mountain steep?

4. 'As we watched at dead of night,
   lo, we saw a wondrous light;
   angels, singing peace on earth,
   told us of the Saviour's birth.'

5. Sacred infant, all divine,
   what a tender love was thine,
   thus to come from highest bliss,
   down to such a world as this!

6. Virgin mother, Mary blest,
   by the joys that fill thy breast,
   pray for us, that we may prove
   worthy of the Saviour's love.

   Edward Caswall (1814-1878)

359

1. See, Christ was wounded for our sake,
   and bruised and beaten for our sin,
   so by his suff'rings we are healed,
   for God has laid our guilt on him.

2. Look on his face, come close to him
   – see, you will find no beauty there;
   despised, rejected, who can tell
   the grief and sorrow he must bear?

Continued overleaf

3. Like sheep that stray we leave
   God's path,
   to choose our own and not his will;
   like lamb to slaughter he has gone,
   obedient to his Father's will.

4. Cast out to die by those he loved,
   reviled by those he died to save,
   see how sin's pride has sought his death,
   see how sin's hate has made his grave.

5. For on his shoulders God has laid
   the weight of sin that we should bear;
   so by his passion we have peace,
   through his obedience and his prayer.

   Brian Foley (b. 1919)

360

1. See him lying on a bed of straw:
   a draughty stable with an open door;
   Mary cradling the babe she bore:
   the Prince of Glory is his name.

   O now carry me to Bethlehem
   to see the Lord appear to men,
   just as poor as was the stable then,
   the Prince of Glory when he came.

2. Star of silver, sweep across the skies,
   show where Jesus in the manger lies;
   shepherds swiftly from your stupor rise
   to see the Saviour of the world!

3. Angels, sing again the song you sang,
   bring God's glory to the heart of man;
   sing that Bethl'em's little baby can
   be salvation to the soul.

4. Mine are riches, from your poverty;
   from your innocence, eternity;
   mine, forgiveness by your death for me,
   child of sorrow for my joy.

   Michael Perry (b. 1942)

361

1. See us, Lord, about thine altar;
   though so many, we are one;
   many souls by love united
   in the heart of Christ thy Son.

2. Hear our prayers, O loving Father,
   hear in them thy Son, our Lord;
   hear him speak our love and worship,
   as we sing with one accord.

3. Once were seen the blood and water;
   now he seems but bread and wine;
   then in human form he suffered,
   now his form is but a sign.

4. Wheat and grape contain the meaning;
   food and drink he is to all;
   one in him, we kneel adoring,
   gathered by his loving call.

5. Hear us yet; so much is needful
   in our frail, disordered life;
   stay with us and tend our weakness
   till that day of no more strife.

6. Members of his mystic body,
   now we know our prayer is heard,
   heard by thee, because thy children
   have received th'eternal Word.

   John Greally

362

1. Seek ye first the kingdom of God,
   and his righteousness,
   and all these things shall be added
      unto you;
   allelu, alleluia.

   Alleluia, alleluia, alleluia,
   allelu, alleluia.

2. You shall not live by bread alone,
   but by every word
   that proceeds from the mouth of God;
   allelu, alleluia.

3. Ask and it shall be given unto you,
   seek and ye shall find;
   knock, and it shall be opened
      unto you;
   allelu, alleluia.

Vs 1 Karen Lafferty (b. 1948), vv 2 and 3 unknown,
based on Matt. 6:33; 7:7
© 1972 Maranatha! Music/CopyCare Ltd

363

Send forth your Spirit, O Lord,
that the face of the earth be renewed.

1. O my soul, arise and bless
      the Lord God.
   Say to him: 'My God, how great
      you are.
   You are clothed with majesty
      and splendour,
   and light is the garment you wear.'

2. 'You have built your palace on
      the waters.
   Like the winds, the angels do
      your word.
   You have set the earth on
      its foundations,
   so firm, to be shaken no more.'

3. 'All your creatures look to you
      for comfort;
   from your open hand they have
      their fill.
   You send forth your Spirit
      and revive them,
   the face of the earth you renew.'

4. While I live, I sing the Lord
      God's praises;
   I will thank the author of
      these marvels.
   Praise to God, the Father, Son
      and Spirit
   both now and for ever. Amen.

Aniceto Nazareth, based on Psalm 104

364

Shalom, my friend,
shalom, my friend, shalom, shalom.
The peace of Christ
I give you today, shalom, shalom.

Sandra Joan Billington (b. 1946)

365

1. Silent night, holy night.
   All is calm, all is bright,
   round yon virgin mother and child;
   holy infant, so tender and mild,
   sleep in heavenly peace,
   sleep in heavenly peace.

2. Silent night, holy night.
   Shepherds quake at the sight,
   glories stream from heaven afar,
   heav'nly hosts sing alleluia:
   Christ, the Saviour is born,
   Christ, the Saviour is born.

3. Silent night, holy night.
   Son of God, love's pure light,
   radiant beams from thy holy face,
   with the dawn of redeeming grace:
   Jesus, Lord, at thy birth,
   Jesus, Lord, at thy birth.

Joseph Mohr (1792-1848),
tr. John Freeman Young (1820-1885)

366

Sing a new song unto the Lord,
let your song be sung
from mountains high.
Sing a new song unto the Lord,
singing alleluia.

1. Yahweh's people dance for joy,
   O come before the Lord,
   and play for him on glad tambourines,
   and let your trumpet sound.

2. Rise, O children, from your sleep,
   your Saviour now has come,
   and he has turned your sorrow to joy,
   and filled your soul with song.

3. Glad my soul, for I have seen
   the glory of the Lord.
   The trumpet sounds, the dead shall
     be raised.
   I know my Saviour lives.

Dan Schutte, based on Psalm 98
© 1972, 1974 New Dawn Music

367

1. Sing alleluia.
   Sing alleluia.
   Sing alleluia.
   You are my Lord.

2. Father, I thank you.
   Father, I thank you.
   Father, I thank you.
   You are my Lord.

3. Jesus, I love you.
   Jesus, I love you.
   Jesus, I love you.
   You are my Lord.

4. Spirit, I need you.
   Spirit, I need you.
   Spirit, I need you.
   You are my Lord.

5. Sing alleluia.
   Sing alleluia.
   Sing alleluia.
   You are my Lord.

Unknown

368

1. Sing, my tongue, the glorious battle,
   sing the last, the dread affray;
   o'er the cross, the victor's trophy,
   sound the high triumphal lay;
   how, the pains of death enduring,
   earth's redeemer won the day.

2. Faithful cross, above all other,
   one and only noble tree!
   None in foliage, none in blossom,
   none in fruit thy peer may be;
   sweetest wood and sweetest iron,
   sweetest weight is hung on thee!

3. Bend, O lofty tree, thy branches,
   thy too rigid sinews bend;
   and awhile the stubborn hardness,
   which thy birth bestowed, suspend;
   and the limbs of heaven's high monarch
   gently on thine arms extend.

4. Thou alone wast counted worthy
   this world's ransom to sustain,
   that by thee a wrecked creation
   might its ark and haven gain,
   with the sacred blood anointed
   of the Lamb that hath been slain.

5. Praise and honour to the Father,
   praise and honour to the Son,
   praise and honour to the Spirit,
   ever three and ever one,
   one in might and one in glory,
   while eternal ages run.

   Venantius Fortunatus (530-609),
   tr. John Mason Neale (1818-1866)

369

1. Sing of Mary, pure and lowly,
   virgin mother undefiled.
   Sing of God's own Son most holy,
   who became her little child.
   Fairest child of fairest mother,
   God, the Lord, who came to earth,
   Word made flesh, our very brother,
   takes our nature by his birth.

2. Sing of Jesus, son of Mary,
   in the home at Nazareth.
   Toil and labour cannot weary
   love enduring unto death.
   Constant was the love he gave her,
   though he went forth from her side,
   forth to preach and heal and suffer,
   till on Calvary he died.

3. Glory be to God the Father,
   glory be to God the Son,
   glory be to God the Spirit,
   glory to the three in one.
   From the heart of blessèd Mary,
   from all saints the song ascends,
   and the Church the strain re-echoes
   unto earth's remotest ends.

   Anonymous (c. 1914)

370

1. Sing of the Lord's goodness,
   Father of all wisdom,
   come to him and bless his name.
   Mercy he has shown us,
   his love is for ever,
   faithful to the end of days.

   Come then, all you nations,
   sing of your Lord's goodness,
   melodies of praise and thanks to God.
   Ring out the Lord's glory,
   praise him with your music,
   worship him and bless his name.

2. Power he has wielded,
   honour is his garment,
   risen from the snares of death.
   His word he has spoken,
   one bread he has broken,
   new life he now gives to all.

3. Courage in our darkness,
   comfort in our sorrow,
   Spirit of our God most high;
   solace for the weary,
   pardon for the sinner,
   splendour of the living God.

4. Praise him with your singing,
   praise him with the trumpet,
   praise him with the lute and harp;
   praise him with the cymbals,
   praise him with your dancing,
   praise God till the end of days.

   Ernest Sands (b. 1949)
   © 1981 OCP Publications

371

1. Sing praises to the Lord, alleluia,
   sing praise to greet the Word, alleluia.
   The Word is a sign
   of God's wisdom and love,
   alleluia, alleluia.

2. God's truth can set us free, alleluia,
   Christ Jesus is the key, alleluia.
   Our ears hear the Word,
   but it lives in our hearts,
   alleluia, alleluia.

3. We listen to your voice, alleluia,
   we praise you and rejoice, alleluia.
   Your Spirit is with us,
   she breathes in your Word:
   alleluia, alleluia.

4. Sing praises to the Lord, alleluia,
   sing praise to greet the Word, alleluia.
   Creator and Son
   with the Spirit adored:
   alleluia, alleluia.

Christopher Walker (b. 1947)
© 1985 OCP Publications

372

1. Sing to God a song of glory,
   peace he brings to all on earth.
   Worship we the King of heaven;
   praise and bless his holy name.

   Glory, glory, sing his glory.
   Glory to our God on high.

2. Sing to Christ, the Father's loved one,
   Jesus, Lord and Lamb of God:
   hear our prayer, O Lord, have mercy,
   you who bear the sins of all.

3. Sing to Christ, the Lord and Saviour,
   seated there at God's right hand:
   hear our prayer, O Lord, have mercy,
   you alone the Holy One.

4. Glory sing to God the Father,
   glory to his only Son,
   glory to the Holy Spirit,
   glory to the three in one.

Francesca Leftley (b. 1955), based on the 'Gloria'

373

Sing to the mountains, sing to the sea,
raise your voices, lift your hearts.
This is the day the Lord has made,
let all the earth rejoice.

1. I will give thanks to you, my Lord,
   you have answered my plea;
   you have saved my soul from death,
   you are my strength and my song.

2. Holy, holy, holy Lord,
   heaven and earth are full of your glory.

3. This is the day that the Lord has made,
   let us be glad and rejoice.
   He has turned all death to life,
   sing of the glory of God.

Bob Dufford, based on Psalm 118
© 1975 New Dawn Music

374

1. Sleep, holy babe,
   upon thy mother's breast;
   great Lord of earth and sea and sky,
   how sweet it is to see thee lie
   in such a place of rest.

2. Sleep, holy babe,
   thine angels watch around,
   all bending low, with folded wings,
   before th'incarnate King of kings,
   in reverent awe profound.

3. Sleep, holy babe,
   while I with Mary gaze
   in joy upon that face awhile,
   upon the loving infant smile,
   which there divinely plays.

4. Sleep, holy babe,
   ah, take thy brief repose;
   too quickly will thy slumbers break,
   and thou to lengthened pains awake,
   that death alone shall close.

5. O lady blest,
   sweet virgin, hear my cry;
   forgive the wrong that I have done
   to thee, in causing thy dear Son
   upon the cross to die.

   Edward Caswall (1814-1878)

375

1. Songs of thankfulness and praise,
   Jesus, Lord to thee we raise,
   manifested by the star
   to the sages from afar;
   branch of royal David's stem,
   in thy birth at Bethlehem;
   anthems be to thee addressed;
   God in man made manifest.

2. Manifest at Jordan's stream,
   prophet, priest and King supreme,
   and at Cana wedding-guest,
   in thy Godhead manifest,
   manifest in pow'r divine,
   changing water into wine;
   anthems be to thee addressed;
   God in man made manifest.

3. Manifest in making whole,
   palsied limbs and fainting soul,
   manifest in valiant fight,
   quelling all the devil's might,
   manifest in gracious will,
   ever bringing good from ill;
   anthems be to thee addressed;
   God in man made manifest.

4. Sun and moon shall darkened be,
   stars shall fall, the heav'ns shall flee.
   Christ will then like lightning strike;
   all will see his glorious sign.
   All will see the judge appear;
   all will then the trumpet hear;
   thou by all wilt be confessed;
   God in man made manifest.

5. Grant us grace to see thee, Lord,
   mirrored in thy holy word;
   may we imitate thee now
   and be pure, as pure art thou;
   that we like to thee may be
   at thy great Epiphany,
   and may praise thee, ever blest,
   God in man made manifest.

   Christopher Wordsworth (1807-1885)

376

1. Soul of my Saviour,
   sanctify my breast;
   Body of Christ,
   be thou my saving guest;
   Blood of my Saviour,
   bathe me in thy tide,
   wash me with water
   flowing from thy side.

Continued overleaf

2. Strength and protection
   may thy passion be;
   O blessèd Jesus,
   hear and answer me;
   deep in thy wounds, Lord,
   hide and shelter me;
   so shall I never,
   never part from thee.

3. Guard and defend me
   from the foe malign;
   in death's dread moments
   make me only thine;
   call me, and bid me
   come to thee on high,
   when I may praise thee
   with thy saints for aye.

   Ascribed to John XXII (1249-1334),
   tr. Unknown

377

1. Spirit of the living God,
   fall afresh on me.
   Spirit of the living God,
   fall afresh on me.
   Melt me, mould me,
   fill me, use me.
   Spirit of the living God,
   fall afresh on me.

2. Spirit of the living God,
   fall afresh on us.
   Spirit of the living God,
   fall afresh on us.
   Melt us, mould us,
   fill us, use us.
   Spirit of the living God,
   fall afresh on us.

At Confirmation, or a Service for the sick:

3. Spirit of the living God,
   fall afresh on them.
   Spirit of the living God,
   fall afresh on them.
   Melt them, mould them,
   fill them, use them.
   Spirit of the living God,
   fall afresh on them.

   Daniel Iverson (1890-1972)

378

1. Spread, O spread, thou mighty word,
   spread the kingdom of the Lord,
   wheresoe'er his breath has given
   life to beings meant for heaven.

2. Tell them how the Father's will
   made the world, and keeps it still,
   how he sent his Son to save
   all who help and comfort crave.

3. Tell of our Redeemer's love,
   who for ever doth remove
   by his holy sacrifice
   all the guilt that on us lies.

4. Tell them of the Spirit given
   now to guide us up to heaven,
   strong and holy, just and true,
   working both to will and do.

5. Lord of harvest, let there be
   joy and strength to work for thee,
   till the nations, far and near,
   see thy light and learn thy fear.

   Jonathan Bahnmaier (1774-1841),
   tr. Catherine Winkworth (1827-1878)

379

Springs of water, bless the Lord!
Praise be God for evermore!

1. With this gift of water, Lord,
   you have given us a sign,
   our baptismal sacrament.

2. At the wat'ry dawn of all,
   order out of chaos came,
   when your Spirit hovered there.

3. With the waters of the flood
   you renewed baptismal sign.
   Sin gave way to spring of life.

4. Through the waters of the sea
   you led Israel, set her free,
   image of your baptised Church.

5. In the Jordan waters, John
   saw your Son baptised and sealed
   with your Spirit resting there.

6. Blood and water from his side,
   symbols of his life outpoured,
   as he hung upon the cross.

7. Then the risen Lord proclaimed:
   'Go and teach, baptising all.
   I will always be with you!'

Noel Donnelly (b. 1932), based on the 'Roman Missal'

380

1. Star of ocean, lead us;
   God for mother claims thee,
   ever virgin names thee;
   gate of heaven, speed us.

2. Ave to thee crying
   Gabriel went before us;
   peace do thou restore us,
   Eva's knot untying.

3. Loose the bonds that chain us,
   darkened eyes enlighten,
   clouded prospects brighten,
   heav'nly mercies gain us.

4. For thy sons thou carest;
   offer Christ our praying
   – still thy word obeying –
   whom on earth thou barest.

5. Purer, kinder maiden
   God did never fashion;
   pureness and compassion
   grant to hearts sin-laden.

6. From that sin release us,
   shield us, heav'nward faring;
   heav'n, that is but sharing
   in thy joy with Jesus.

7. Honour, praise and merit
   to our God address we;
   three in one confess we,
   Father, Son and Spirit.

Ave Maris Stella, 9th century,
tr. Ronald Arbuthnott Knox (1888-1957)

381

Stay with me,
remain here with me,
watch and pray,
watch and pray.

Taizé Community

382

Steal away, steal away,
steal away to Jesus.
Steal away, steal away home.
I ain't got long to stay here.

1. My Lord, he calls me,
   he calls me by the thunder.
   The trumpet sounds within my soul;
   I ain't got long to stay here.

2. Green trees are bending,
   the sinner stands a-trembling.
   The trumpet sounds within my soul;
   I ain't got long to stay here.

3. My Lord, he calls me,
   he calls me by the lightning.
   The trumpet sounds within my soul;
   I ain't got long to stay here.

Spiritual

383

1. Sweet heart of Jesus,
   fount of love and mercy,
   today we come,
   thy blessing to implore;
   O touch our hearts,
   so cold and so ungrateful,
   and make them, Lord,
   thine own for evermore.

   Sweet heart of Jesus,
   we implore,
   O make us love thee
   more and more.

2. Sweet heart of Jesus,
   make us know and love thee,
   unfold to us
   the treasures of thy grace;
   that so our hearts,
   from things of earth uplifted,
   may long alone
   to gaze upon thy face.

3. Sweet heart of Jesus,
   make us pure and gentle,
   and teach us how
   to do thy blessèd will;
   to follow close
   the print of thy dear footsteps,
   and when we fall
   – sweet heart, O love us still.

4. Sweet heart of Jesus,
   bless all hearts that love thee,
   and may thine own heart
   ever blessèd be;
   bless us, dear Lord,
   and bless the friends we cherish,
   and keep us true
   to Mary and to thee.

   Sister Marie Josephine

384

1. Sweet sacrament divine,
   hid in thy earthly home,
   lo, round thy lowly shrine,
   with suppliant hearts we come;
   Jesus, to thee our voice we raise,
   in songs of love and heartfelt praise,
   sweet sacrament divine,
   sweet sacrament divine.

2. Sweet sacrament of peace,
   dear home of ev'ry heart,
   where restless yearnings cease,
   and sorrows all depart,
   there in thine ear all trustfully
   we tell our tale of misery,
   sweet sacrament of peace,
   sweet sacrament of peace.

3. Sweet sacrament of rest,
   Ark from the ocean's roar,
   within thy shelter blest
   soon may we reach the shore;
   save us, for still the tempest raves;
   save, lest we sink beneath the waves,
   sweet sacrament of rest,
   sweet sacrament of rest.

4. Sweet sacrament divine,
   earth's light and jubilee,
   in thy far depths doth shine
   thy Godhead's majesty;
   sweet light, so shine on us, we pray,
   that earthly joys may fade away,
   sweet sacrament divine,
   sweet sacrament divine.

Francis Stanfield (1835-1914)

385

1. Sweet Saviour, bless us ere we go,
   thy word into our minds instil;
   and make our lukewarm hearts
      to glow
   with lowly love and fervent will.

*Through life's long day
and death's dark night,
O gentle Jesus, be our light.*

2. The day is done; its hours have run,
   and thou hast taken count of all
   the scanty triumphs grace has won,
   the broken vow, the frequent fall.

3. Grant us, dear Lord, from evil ways,
   true absolution and release;
   and bless us more than in past days
   with purity and inward peace.

4. Do more than pardon; give us joy,
   sweet fear and sober liberty,
   and loving hearts without alloy,
   that only long to be like thee.

5. Labour is sweet, for thou hast toiled,
   and care is light, for thou hast cared;
   let not our works with self be soiled,
   nor in unsimple ways ensnared.

6. For all we love – the poor, the sad,
   the sinful – unto thee we call;
   O let thy mercy make us glad,
   thou art our Jesus and our all.

Frederick William Faber (1814-1863)

386

1. Take my hands
   and make them as your own,
   and use them for your
   kingdom here on earth.
   Consecrate them to your care,
   anoint them for your service where
   you may need your
   gospel to be sown.

2. Take my hands,
   they speak now for my heart,
   and by their actions
   they will show their love.
   Guard them on their daily course,
   be their strength and guiding force
   to ever serve the
   Trinity above.

Continued overleaf

3. Take my hands,
   I give them to you, Lord.
   Prepare them for the
   service of your name.
   Open them to human need
   and by their love they'll sow your seed
   so all may know the love
   and hope you give.

Sebastian Temple (b. 1928)

387

Take our bread, we ask you,
take our hearts, we love you,
take our lives, O Father,
we are yours, we are yours.

1. Yours as we stand
   at the table you set,
   yours as we eat the bread
   our hearts can't forget.
   We are the signs
   of your life with us yet;
   we are yours, we are yours.

2. Your holy people stand
   washed in your blood,
   Spirit-filled, yet hungry,
   we await your food.
   Poor though we are,
   we have brought ourselves to you:
   we are yours, we are yours.

Joe Wise (b. 1939)

388

1. Tell out, my soul,
   the greatness of the Lord!
   Unnumbered blessings,
   give my spirit voice;
   tender to me
   the promise of his word;
   in God my Saviour
   shall my heart rejoice.

2. Tell out, my soul,
   the greatness of his name!
   Make known his might,
   the deeds his arm has done;
   his mercy sure,
   from age to age the same;
   his holy name the Lord,
   the mighty one.

3. Tell out, my soul,
   the greatness of his might!
   Pow'rs and dominions
   lay their glory by.
   Proud hearts and stubborn
   wills are put to flight,
   the hungry fed,
   the humble lifted high.

4. Tell out, my soul,
   the glories of his word!
   Firm is his promise,
   and his mercy sure.
   Tell out, my soul,
   the greatness of the Lord;
   to children's children
   and for evermore!

Timothy Dudley-Smith (b. 1926)
based on Luke 1:46-55

389

Thanks for the fellowship
found at this meal,
thanks for a day refreshed;
thanks to the Lord
for his presence we feel,
thanks for the food he blessed.
Joyfully sing praise to the Lord,
praise to the risen Son,
alleluia, ever adored,
pray that his will be done.

As he was known
in the breaking of bread,
now is he known again;
and by his hand
have the hungry been fed,
thanks be to Christ. Amen!

Jean Holloway (b. 1939)

390

1. The angel Gabriel from heaven came,
   his wings as drifted snow,
      his eyes as flame.
   'All hail,' said he, 'thou lowly
      maiden, Mary,
   most highly favoured lady.' Gloria!

2. 'For know, a blessèd Mother thou
      shalt be.
   All generations laud
      and honour thee.
   Thy Son shall be Emmanuel,
      by seers foretold,
   most highly favoured lady.' Gloria!

3. Then gentle Mary meekly bowed
      her head.
   'To me be, as it pleaseth God,'
      she said.
   'My soul shall laud and magnify his
      holy name!'
   Most highly favoured lady! Gloria!

4. Of her, Emmanuel, the Christ,
      was born
   in Bethlehem,
      all on a Christmas morn;
   and Christian folk throughout the
      world will ever say:
   'Most highly favoured lady!' Gloria!

Sabine Baring-Gould (1834-1924)

391

1. The Church's one foundation
   is Jesus Christ, her Lord;
   she is his new creation,
   by water and the word;
   from heav'n he came and sought her
   to be his holy bride,
   with his own blood he bought her,
   and for her life he died.

2. Elect from ev'ry nation,
   yet one o'er all the earth,
   her charter of salvation,
   one Lord, one faith, one birth;
   one holy name she blesses,
   partakes one holy food,
   and to one hope she presses,
   with ev'ry grace endued.

3. 'Mid toil, and tribulation,
   and tumult of her war,
   she waits the consummation
   of peace for evermore;
   till with the vision glorious
   her longing eyes are blest,
   and the great Church victorious
   shall be the Church at rest.

4. Yet she on earth hath union
   with God the Three in One,
   and mystic sweet communion
   with those whose rest is won:
   O happy ones and holy!
   Lord, give us grace that we
   like them, the meek and lowly,
   on high may dwell with thee.

Samuel J. Stone (1839-1900)

392

1. The coming of our God
   our thoughts must now employ;
   then let us meet him on the road
   with songs of holy joy.

2. The co-eternal Son,
   a maiden's offspring see;
   a servant's form Christ putteth on,
   to set his people free.

3. Daughter of Sion, rise
   to greet thine infant king,
   nor let thy stubborn heart despise
   the pardon he doth bring.

4. In glory from his throne
   again will Christ descend,
   and summon all that are his own
   to joys that never end.

5. Let deeds of darkness fly
   before th'approaching morn,
   for unto sin 'tis ours to die,
   and serve the virgin-born.

6. Our joyful praises sing
   to Christ, that set us free;
   like tribute to the Father bring
   and, Holy Ghost, to thee.

   Charles Coffin (1676-1749),
   tr. Robert Campbell (1814-1868)

393

1. The day of resurrection!
   Earth, tell it out abroad;
   the passover of gladness,
   the passover of God!
   From death to life eternal,
   from earth unto the sky,
   our Christ hath brought us over
   with hymns of victory.

2. Our hearts be pure from evil,
   that we may see aright
   the Lord in rays eternal
   of resurrection-light;
   and list'ning to his accents,
   may hear so calm and plain
   his own 'All hail' and, hearing,
   may raise the victor strain.

3. Now let the heav'ns be joyful,
   and earth her song begin,
   the round world keep high triumph,
   and all that is therein;
   let all things, seen and unseen,
   their notes of gladness blend,
   for Christ the Lord hath risen,
   our joy that hath no end.

   St John Damascene (c. 750),
   tr. John Mason Neale (1818-1866)

394

1. The day thou gavest, Lord, is ended:
   the darkness falls at thy behest;
   to thee our morning hymns ascended;
   thy praise shall sanctify our rest.

2. We thank thee that thy Church
      unsleeping,
   while earth rolls onward into light,
   through all the world her watch
      is keeping,
   and rests not now by day or night.

3. As o'er each continent and island
   the dawn leads on another day,
   the voice of prayer is never silent,
   nor dies the strain of praise away.

4. The sun that bids us rest is waking
   our brethren 'neath the western sky,
   and hour by hour fresh lips are making
   thy wondrous doings heard on high.

5. So be it, Lord; thy throne shall never,
   like earth's proud empire, pass away;
   thy kingdom stands, and grows
      for ever,
   till all thy creatures own thy sway.

   John Ellerton (1826-1893)

6. Then let us all with one accord
   sing praises to our heav'nly Lord,
   that hath made heav'n and earth
      of nought,
   and with his blood mankind
   hath bought.

   From William Sandys' 'Christmas Carols,
   Ancient and Modern' (1833)

395

1. The first Nowell the angel did say
   was to certain poor shepherds in
      fields as they lay:
   in fields where they lay keeping
      their sheep,
   on a cold winter's night that was
      so deep.

   Nowell, Nowell, Nowell, Nowell,
   born is the King of Israel!

2. They lookèd up and saw a star,
   shining in the east, beyond them far,
   and to the earth it gave great light,
   and so it continued both day
      and night.

3. And by the light of that same star,
   three wise men came from country far;
   to seek for a king was their intent,
   and to follow the star wherever it went.

4. This star drew nigh to the north-west,
   o'er Bethlehem it took its rest,
   and there it did both stop and stay
   right over the place where Jesus lay.

5. Then entered in those wise men three,
   full rev'rently upon their knee,
   and offered there in his presence,
   their gold and myrrh and frankincense.

396

1. The head that once was crowned
      with thorns
   is crowned with glory now:
   a royal diadem adorns
   the mighty victor's brow.

2. The highest place that heav'n affords
   is his, is his by right.
   The King of kings and Lord of lords,
   and heav'n's eternal light.

3. The joy of all who dwell above,
   the joy of all below,
   to whom he manifests his love,
   and grants his name to know.

4. To them the cross, with all its shame,
   with all its grace is given;
   their name an everlasting name,
   their joy the joy of heaven.

5. They suffer with their Lord below,
   they reign with him above,
   their profit and their joy to know
   the myst'ry of his love.

6. The cross he bore is life and health,
   though shame and death to him;
   his people's hope, his people's wealth,
   their everlasting theme.

   Thomas Kelly (1769-1855)

397

1. The holly and the ivy,
   when they are both full grown,
   of all the trees that are in the wood
   the holly bears the crown.

   The rising of the sun
   and the running of the deer,
   the playing of the merry organ,
   sweet singing in the choir.

2. The holly bears a blossom,
   white as the lily flower,
   and Mary bore sweet Jesus Christ
   to be our sweet Saviour.

3. The holly bears a berry,
   as red as any blood,
   and Mary bore sweet Jesus Christ
   to do poor sinners good.

4. The holly bears a prickle,
   as sharp as any thorn,
   and Mary bore sweet Jesus Christ
   on Christmas day in the morn.

5. The holly bears a bark,
   as bitter as any gall,
   and Mary bore sweet Jesus Christ
   for to redeem us all.

6. The holly and the ivy,
   when they are both full grown,
   of all the trees that are in the wood
   the holly bears the crown.

   Traditional

398

1. The King is among us,
   his Spirit is here,
   let's draw near and worship,
   let songs fill the air.

2. He looks down upon us,
   delight in his face,
   enjoying his children's love,
   enthralled by our praise.

3. For each child is special,
   accepted and loved,
   a love gift from Jesus
   to his Father above.

4. And now he is giving
   his gifts to us all,
   for no one is worthless
   and each one is called.

5. The Spirit's anointing
   on all flesh comes down,
   and we shall be channels
   for worlds like his own.

6. We come now believing
   your promise of power,
   for we are your people
   and this is your hour.

7. The King is among us,
   his Spirit is here,
   let's draw near and worship,
   let songs fill the air.

Graham Kendrick (b. 1950)
© 1981 Kingsway's Thankyou Music

399

The King of glory comes,
the nation rejoices,
open the gates before him,
lift up your voices.

1. Who is the King of glory,
   how shall we call him?
   He is Emmanuel,
   the promised of ages.

2. In all of Galilee,
   in city and village,
   he goes among his people,
   curing their illness.

3. Sing then of David's Son,
   our Saviour and brother;
   in all of Galilee
   was never another.

4. He gave his life for us,
   the pledge of salvation.
   He took upon himself
   the sins of the nation.

5. He conquered sin and death;
   he truly has risen;
   and he will share with us
   his heavenly vision.

   William F. Jabusch (b. 1930)

400

1. The King of love my shepherd is,
   whose goodness faileth never;
   I nothing lack if I am his
   and he is mine for ever.

2. Where streams of living waters flow
   my ransomed soul he leadeth,
   and where the verdant pastures grow
   with food celestial feedeth.

3. Perverse and foolish oft I strayed,
   but yet in love he sought me,
   and on his shoulder gently laid,
   and home, rejoicing, brought me.

4. In death's dark vale I fear no ill
   with thee, dear Lord, beside me;
   thy rod and staff my comfort still,
   thy cross before to guide me.

5. Thou spread'st a table in my sight,
   thy unction grace bestoweth:
   and O what transport of delight
   from thy pure chalice floweth!

6. And so through all the length of days
   thy goodness faileth never;
   good Shepherd, may I sing thy praise
   within thy house for ever.

   Henry Williams Baker (1821-1877)

401

*The light of Christ
has come into the world.
The light of Christ
has come into the world.*

1. We must all be born again
   to see the kingdom of God.
   The water and the Spirit bring
   new life in God's love.

2. God gave up his only Son
   out of love for the world,
   so that all who believe in him
   will live for ever.

3. The light of God has come to us
   so that we might have salvation;
   from the darkness of our sins we walk
   into glory with Christ Jesus.

   Donald Fishel (b. 1950)

402

*The Lord hears the cry of the poor.
Blessèd be the Lord.*

1. I will bless the Lord at all times,
   his praise ever in my mouth.
   Let my soul glory in the Lord,
   for he hears the cry of the poor.

Continued overleaf

2. Let the lowly hear and be glad:
   the Lord listens to their pleas;
   and to hearts broken he is near,
   for he hears the cry of the poor.

   The Lord hears the cry of the poor.
   Blessèd be the Lord.

3. Ev'ry spirit crushed he will save;
   will be ransom for their lives;
   will be safe shelter for their fears,
   for he hears the cry of the poor.

4. We proclaim the greatness of God,
   his praise ever in our mouth;
   ev'ry face brightened in his light,
   for he hears the cry of the poor.

   John Foley, based on Psalm 33
   © 1978 New Dawn Music

403

1. The Lord is alive! Alleluia!
   He dwells in our midst! Alleluia!
   Give praise to his name
   throughout all the world!
   Alleluia! Alleluia!

2. He brings us great joy! Alleluia!
   He fills us with hope! Alleluia!
   He comes as our food,
   he gives us our life!
   Alleluia! Alleluia!

3. So let us rejoice! Alleluia!
   Give praise to the Lord! Alleluia!
   He showed us his love,
   by him we are saved!
   Alleluia! Alleluia!

4. The Lord is alive! Alleluia!
   So let us proclaim, alleluia,
   the Good News of Christ
   throughout all the world!
   Alleluia! Alleluia!

5. Christ Jesus has died! Alleluia!
   Christ Jesus is ris'n! Alleluia!
   Christ Jesus will come
   again as the Lord!
   Alleluia! Alleluia!

6. Sing praises to God, alleluia,
   who reigns without end! Alleluia!
   The Father, the Son,
   and Spirit – all One!
   Alleluia! Alleluia!

   Jean-Paul Lécot (b. 1947), tr. W. R. Lawrence (b. 1925)

404

1. The Lord is present in his sanctuary,
   let us praise the Lord.
   The Lord is present
   in his people gathered here,
   let us praise the Lord.
   Praise him, praise him,
   let us praise the Lord.
   Praise him, praise him,
   let us praise Jesus!

2. The Lord is present in his sanctuary,
   let us sing to the Lord.
   The Lord is present
   in his people gathered here,
   let us sing to the Lord.
   Sing to him, sing to him,
   let us sing to the Lord.
   Sing to him, sing to him,
   let us sing to Jesus!

3. The Lord is present in his sanctuary,
   let us love the Lord.
   The Lord is present
   in his people gathered here,
   let us love the Lord.
   Love him, love him,
   let us love the Lord.
   Love him, love him,
   let us love the Lord.

   Gail Cole
   © 1975 Church of the Messiah

405

1. The Lord's my shepherd, I'll not want.
   He makes me down to lie
   in pastures green. He leadeth me
   the quiet waters by.

2. My soul he doth restore again,
   and me to walk doth make
   within the paths of righteousness,
   e'en for his own name's sake.

3. Yea, though I walk in death's dark vale,
   yet will I fear none ill.
   For thou art with me, and thy rod
   and staff me comfort still.

4. My table thou hast furnishèd
   in presence of my foes,
   my head thou dost with oil anoint,
   and my cup overflows.

5. Goodness and mercy all my life
   shall surely follow me.
   And in God's house for evermore
   my dwelling-place shall be.

   Psalm 22 (23), from The Scottish Psalter (1650)

406

1. The Lord's my shepherd, I'll not want.
   He makes me down to lie
   in pastures green. He leadeth me
   the quiet waters by.
   In pastures green, he leadeth me
   the quiet waters by.

2. My soul he doth restore again,
   and me to walk doth make
   within the paths of righteousness,
   e'en for his own name's sake.
   Within the paths of righteousness,
   e'en for his own name's sake.

3. Yea, though I walk in death's dark vale,
   yet will I fear none ill.
   For thou art with me, and thy rod
   and staff me comfort still.
   For thou art with me, and thy rod
   and staff me comfort still.

4. My table thou hast furnishèd
   in presence of my foes,
   my head thou dost with oil anoint,
   and my cup overflows.
   My head thou dost with oil anoint,
   and my cup overflows.

5. Goodness and mercy all my life
   shall surely follow me.
   And in God's house for evermore
   my dwelling-place shall be.
   And in God's house for evermore
   my dwelling-place shall be.

   Psalm 22 (23), from The Scottish Psalter (1650)

407

1. The love I have for you, my Lord,
   is only a shadow of your love for me;
   only a shadow of your love for me;
   your deep abiding love.

2. My own belief in you, my Lord,
   is only a shadow of your faith in me;
   only a shadow of your faith in me;
   your deep and lasting faith.

3. My life is in your hands;
   my life is in your hands.
   My love for you will grow, my God.
   Your light in me will shine.

4. The dream I have today, my Lord,
   is only a shadow of your dreams
      for me;
   only a shadow of all that will be;
   if I but follow you.

Continued overleaf

5. The joy I feel today, my Lord,
   is only a shadow of your joys for me;
   only a shadow of your joys for me;
   when we meet face to face.

6. My life is in your hands;
   my life is in your hands.
   My love for you will grow, my God.
   Your light in me will shine.

   Carey Landry
   © 1971 North American Liturgy Resources

408

1. The race that long in darkness pined
   has seen a glorious light:
   the people dwell in day, who dwelt
   in death's surrounding night.

2. To hail thy rise, thou better sun,
   the gath'ring nations come,
   joyous as when the reapers bear
   the harvest treasures home.

3. To us a child of hope is born,
   to us a Son is given;
   him shall the tribes of earth obey,
   him all the hosts of heaven.

4. His name shall be the Prince of Peace
   for evermore adored,
   the Wonderful, the Counsellor,
   the great and mighty Lord.

5. His pow'r increasing still shall spread,
   his reign no end shall know;
   justice shall guard his throne above,
   and peace abound below.

   John Morrison (1750-1798), based on Isaiah 9:2-7

409

1. The royal banners forward go,
   the cross shines forth in mystic glow,
   where he in flesh, our flesh who made,
   our sentence bore, our ransom paid.

2. There whilst he hung, his sacred side
   by soldier's spear was opened wide,
   to cleanse us in the precious flood
   of water mingled with his blood.

3. Fulfilled is now what David told
   in true prophetic song of old,
   how God the heathen's king should be;
   for God is reigning from the tree.

4. O tree of glory, tree most fair,
   ordained those holy limbs to bear,
   how bright in purple robe it stood,
   the purple of a Saviour's blood!

5. Upon its arms, like balance true,
   he weighed the price for sinners due,
   the price which none but he could pay:
   and spoiled the spoiler of his prey.

6. To thee, eternal Three in One,
   let homage meet by all be done,
   as by the cross thou dost restore,
   so rule and guide us evermore.

   Venantius Fortunatus (530-609),
   tr. John Mason Neale (1818-1866) and others

410

1. The Spirit lives to set us free,
   walk, walk in the light.
   He binds us all in unity,
   walk, walk in the light.

   Walk in the light,
   walk in the light,
   walk in the light,
   walk in the light of the Lord.

2. Jesus promised life to all,
   walk, walk in the light.
   The dead were wakened by his call,
   walk, walk in the light.

3. He died in pain on Calvary,
   walk, walk in the light,
   to save the lost like you and me,
   walk, walk in the light.

4. We know his death was not the end,
   walk, walk in the light.
   He gave his Spirit to be our friend,
   walk, walk in the light.

5. By Jesus' love our wounds are healed,
   walk, walk in the light.
   The Father's kindness is revealed,
   walk, walk in the light.

6. The Spirit lives in you and me,
   walk, walk in the light.
   His light will shine for all to see,
   walk, walk in the light.

Damian Lundy (b. 1944)

411

1. The Virgin Mary had a baby boy,
   the Virgin Mary had a baby boy,
   the Virgin Mary had a baby boy,
   and they said that his name was Jesus.

   He came from the glory,
   he came from the glorious kingdom.
   He came from the glory,
   he came from the glorious kingdom.
   O yes, believer.
   O yes, believer.
   He came from the glory,
   he came from the glorious kingdom.

2. The angels sang when the baby
      was born,
   the angels sang when the baby
      was born,
   the angels sang when the baby
      was born,
   and proclaimed him the
      Saviour Jesus.

3. The wise men saw where the baby
      was born,
   the wise men saw where the baby
      was born,
   the wise men saw where the baby
      was born,
   and they saw that his name was Jesus.

Traditional West Indian

412

1. There is a green hill far away,
   without a city wall,
   where the dear Lord was crucified
   who died to save us all.

2. We may not know, we cannot tell
   what pains he had to bear,
   but we believe it was for us
   he hung and suffered there.

3. He died that we might be forgiven,
   he died to make us good;
   that we might go at last to heaven,
   saved by his precious blood.

4. There was no other good enough
   to pay the price of sin;
   he only could unlock the gate
   of heav'n, and let us in.

5. O, dearly, dearly has he loved,
   and we must love him too,
   and trust in his redeeming blood,
   and try his works to do.

Cecil Frances Alexander (1818-1895)

413

1. There is a Redeemer,
   Jesus, God's own Son,
   precious Lamb of God,
   Messiah, Holy One.

   Thank you, O my Father,
   for giving us your Son,
   and leaving your Spirit till
   the work on earth is done.

2. Jesus, my Redeemer,
   name above all names,
   precious Lamb of God,
   Messiah, O for sinners slain.

3. When I stand in glory
   I will see his face,
   and there I'll serve my King for ever,
   in that holy place.

   Melody Green, based on Scripture

414

1. There is a world
   where people come and go
   about their ways,
   and never care to know
   that ev'ry step they take
   is placed on roads
   made out of those who had to carry
   loads too hard to bear.

   'That world's not ours,'
   that's what we always say.
   'We'll build a new one,
   but some other day.'
   When will we wake
   from comfort and from ease,
   and strive together to create
   a world of love and peace?

2. There is a world
   where people walk alone
   and have around them
   those with hearts of stone
   who would not spare
   one second of their day,
   or spend their breath, in order
   just to say: 'Your pain is mine'.

3. There is a world
   where people cannot meet
   with one another,
   where the tramp of feet
   brings men of ice,
   men who would force apart
   friends of all races having but one
   heart, a heart of love.

   Estelle White (b. 1925)

415

1. Thine be the glory,
   risen, conqu'ring Son,
   endless is the vict'ry
   thou o'er death hast won;
   angels in bright raiment
   rolled the stone away,
   kept the folded grave-clothes
   where thy body lay.

   Thine be the glory,
   risen, conqu'ring Son,
   endless is the vict'ry
   thou o'er death hast won.

2. Lo! Jesus meets us,
   risen from the tomb;
   lovingly he greets us,
   scatters fear and gloom.
   Let the Church with gladness
   hymns of triumph sing,
   for her Lord now liveth;
   death hast lost its sting.

3. No more we doubt thee,
   glorious Prince of life;
   life is nought without thee:
   aid us in our strife.
   Make us more than conqu'rors
   through thy deathless love;
   bring us safe through Jordan
   to thy home above.

   Edmond L. Budry (1854-1932),
   tr. Richard B. Hoyle (1875-1939)

4. Rising, I thank you,
   mighty and strong One,
   King of creation,
   giver of rest,
   firmly confessing
   Threeness of persons,
   Oneness of Godhead,
   Trinity blest.

   Ascribed to St Patrick (372-466),
   adapted by James Quinn (b. 1919)

416

1. This day God gives me
   strength of high heaven,
   sun and moon shining,
   flame in my hearth,
   flashing of lightning,
   wind in its swiftness,
   deeps of the ocean,
   firmness of earth.

2. This day God sends me
   strength as my steersman,
   might to uphold me,
   wisdom as guide.
   Your eyes are watchful,
   your ears are list'ning,
   your lips are speaking,
   friend at my side.

3. God's way is my way,
   God's shield is round me,
   God's host defends me,
   saving from ill.
   Angel of heaven,
   drive from me always
   all that would harm me,
   stand by me still.

417

1. This is my body, broken for you,
   bringing you wholeness, making
     you free.
   Take it and eat it, and when you do,
   do it in love for me.

2. This is my blood, poured out for you,
   bringing forgiveness, making you free.
   Take it and drink it, and when you do,
   do it in love for me.

3. Back to my Father soon I shall go.
   Do not forget me; then you will see
   I am still with you, and you will know
   you're very close to me.

4. Filled with my Spirit, how you
     will grow!
   You are my branches; I am the tree.
   If you are faithful, others will know
   you are alive in me.

5. Love one another: I have loved you,
   and I have shown you how to be free;
   serve one another, and when you do,
   do it in love for me.

   Vv 1 and 2 Jimmy Owens, vv 3-5 Damian Lundy
   Vv 1 and 2 © 1978 Bud John Songs Inc/CopyCare Ltd

418

1. This is my will, my one command,
   that love should dwell among you all.
   This is my will that you should love
   as I have shown that I love you.

2. No greater love a man can have
   than that he die to save his friends.
   You are my friends if you obey
   all I command that you should do.

3. I call you now no longer slaves;
   no slave knows all his master does.
   I call you friends, for all I hear
   my Father say, you hear from me.

4. You chose not me, but I chose you,
   that you should go and bear much fruit.
   I called you out that you in me
   should bear much fruit that will abide.

5. All that you ask my Father dear
   for my name's sake you shall receive.
   This is my will, my one command,
   that love should dwell in each, in all.

James Quinn (b. 1919)

419

1. This is the day, this is the day
   that the Lord has made,
   that the Lord has made;
   we will rejoice, we will rejoice
   and be glad in it, and be glad in it.
   This is the day that the Lord has made;
   we will rejoice and be glad in it.
   This is the day, this is the day
   that the Lord has made.

2. This is the day, this is the day
   when he rose again,
   when he rose again;
   We will rejoice, we will rejoice,
   and be glad in it, and be glad in it.
   This is the day when he rose again;
   we wil rejoice and be glad in it.
   This is the day, this is the day
   when he rose again.

3. This is the day, this is the day
   when the Spirit came,
   when the Spirit came;
   We will rejoice, we will rejoice,
   and be glad in it, and be glad in it.
   This is the day when the Spirit came;
   we will rejoice and be glad in it.
   This is the day, this is the day
   when the Spirit came.

Les Garrett (b. 1944), based on Psalm 118
© 1967 Scripture in Song/CopyCare Ltd

420

1. This is the image of the queen
   who reigns in bliss above;
   of her who is the hope of men,
   whom men and angels love.
   Most holy Mary, at thy feet
   I bend a suppliant knee;
   in this thy own sweet month of May,
   do thou remember me.

2. The homage offered at the feet
   of Mary's image here
   to Mary's self at once ascends
   above the starry sphere.
   Most holy Mary, at thy feet
   I bend a suppliant knee;
   in all my joy, in all my pain,
   do thou remember me.

3. How fair soever be the form
which here your eyes behold,
its beauty is by Mary's self
excelled a thousandfold.
Most holy Mary, at thy feet,
I bend a suppliant knee;
in my temptations each and all,
do thou remember me.

Edward Caswall (1814-1878)

421

1. This joyful Eastertide,
away with sin and sorrow,
my love, the Crucified,
hath sprung to life this morrow.

Had Christ, that once was slain,
ne'er burst his three-day prison,
our faith had been in vain:
but now hath Christ arisen,
arisen, arisen, arisen.

2. My flesh in hope shall rest,
and for a season slumber:
till trump from east to west
shall wake the dead in number.

3. Death's flood hath lost his chill,
since Jesus crossed the river:
lover of souls, from ill
my passing soul deliver.

George Ratcliffe Woodward (1848-1934)

422

This little light of mine,
I'm gonna let it shine.
This little light of mine,
I'm gonna let it shine.
This little light of mine,
I'm gonna let it shine,
let it shine, let it shine,
let it shine.

1. The light that shines
is the light of love,
lights the darkness
from above,
it shines on me
and it shines on you,
and shows what the
power of love can do.
I'm gonna shine my light
both far and near,
I'm gonna shine my light
both bright and clear.
Where there's a dark
corner in this land,
I'm gonna let my
little light shine.

2. On Monday he gave
me the gift of love,
Tuesday peace came
from above.
On Wednesday he told me
to have more faith,
on Thursday he gave me
a little more grace.
Friday he told me
to watch and pray,
Saturday he told me
just what to say,
on Sunday he gave me
the power divine
to let my
little light shine.

Traditional

423

This, then, is my prayer,
falling on my knees before God
who is Father and source of all life.
May he in his love,
through the Spirit of Christ,
give you pow'r to grow strong
in your innermost self.

1. May Christ live in your hearts
   and may your lives, rooted in love,
   grow strong in him.

2. May you, with all the saints,
   grow in the pow'r to understand
   how he loves you.

3. O how can I explain
   in all its depth and all its scope
   his love, God's love!

   The chorus is not sung after verse 3.

4. For his love is so full,
   it is beyond all we can dream:
   his love, in Christ!

5. And so, glory to him
   working in us, who can do more
   than we can pray!
   Damian Lundy (b. 1944), based on Eph. 3:14-21

424

Thou art worthy, thou art worthy,
thou art worthy, O Lord,
to receive glory, glory and honour,
glory and honour and power.
For thou hast created,
hast all things created,
for thou hast created all things.
And for thy pleasure
they are created,
thou art worthy, O Lord.
Pauline Michael Mills (1898-1992)

425

1. Thou, whose almighty word
   chaos and darkness heard,
   and took their flight;
   hear us, we humbly pray,
   and where the Gospel day
   sheds not its glorious ray,
   let there be light.

2. Thou, who didst come to bring,
   on thy redeeming wing,
   healing and sight,
   health to the sick in mind,
   sight to the inly blind,
   O now to all mankind
   let there be light.

3. Spirit of truth and love,
   life-giving, holy Dove,
   speed forth thy flight;
   move on the water's face,
   bearing the lamp of grace,
   and in earth's darkest place
   let there be light.

4. Holy and blessèd Three,
   glorious Trinity,
   Wisdom, Love, Might;
   boundless as ocean's tide
   rolling in fullest pride,
   through the earth far and wide
   let there be light.
   John Marriott (1780-1825)

426

Though the mountains may fall
and the hills turn to dust,
yet the love of the Lord will stand
as a shelter for all
who will call on his name.
Sing the praise and the glory of God.

1. Could the Lord ever leave you?
   Could the Lord forget his love?
   Though the mother forsake her child,
   he will not abandon you.

2. Should you turn and forsake him,
   he will gently call your name.
   Should you wander away from him,
   he will always take you back.

3. Go to him when you're weary;
   he will give you eagle's wings.
   You will run, never tire,
   for your God will be your strength.

4. As he swore to your fathers,
   when the flood destroyed the land,
   he will never forsake you;
   he will swear to you again.

Dan Schutte, based on Isaiah
© 1975 New Dawn Music

427

1. Thy hand, O God, has guided
   thy flock from age to age;
   the wondrous tale is written,
   full clear, on ev'ry page;
   our forebears owned thy goodness,
   and we their deeds record;
   and both of this bear witness:
   one Church, one Faith, one Lord.

2. Thy heralds brought glad tidings
   to greatest, as to least;
   they bade them rise, and hasten
   to share the great King's feast;
   and this was all their teaching,
   in ev'ry deed and word,
   to all alike proclaiming:
   one Church, one Faith, one Lord.

3. Through many a day of darkness,
   through many a scene of strife,
   the faithful few fought bravely,
   to guard the nation's life.
   Their gospel of redemption,
   sin pardoned, hope restored,
   was all in this enfolded:
   one Church, one Faith, one Lord.

4. And we, shall we be faithless?
   Shall hearts fail, hands hang down?
   Shall we evade the conflict,
   and cast away our crown?
   Not so: in God's deep counsels
   some better thing is stored:
   we will maintain, unflinching,
   one Church, one Faith, one Lord.

5. Thy mercy will not fail us,
   nor leave thy work undone;
   with thy right hand to help us,
   the vict'ry shall be won;
   and then by all creation,
   thy name shall be adored.
   And this shall be their anthem:
   one Church, one Faith, one Lord.

Edward Plumtre (1821-1891), alt.

428

1. To Christ, the Prince of peace,
   and Son of God most high,
   the Father of the world to come,
   sing we with holy joy.

2. Deep in his heart for us
   the wound of love he bore;
   that love wherewith he still inflames
   the hearts that him adore.

3. O Jesu, victim blest,
   what else but love divine
   could thee constrain to open thus
   that sacred heart of thine?

Continued overleaf

4. O fount of endless life,
   O spring of water clear,
   O flame celestial, cleansing all
   who unto thee draw near!

5. Hide us in thy dear heart,
   for thither we do fly;
   where seek thy grace through life,
      in death
   thine immortality.

6. Praise to the Father be,
   and sole-begotten Son;
   praise, holy Paraclete, to thee,
   while endless ages run.

   Catholic Hymnologium Germanicum (1587)
   tr. Edward Caswall (1814-1878)

429

1. To Jesus' heart, all burning
   with fervent love for men,
   my heart with fondest yearning
   shall raise its joyful strain.

   While ages course along,
   blest be with loudest song
   the sacred heart of Jesus
   by ev'ry heart and tongue,
   the sacred heart of Jesus
   by ev'ry heart and tongue.

2. O heart, for me on fire
   with love that none can speak,
   my yet untold desire
   God gives me for thy sake.

3. Too true, I have forsaken
   thy love for wilful sin;
   yet now let me be taken
   back by thy grace again.

4. As thou art meek and lowly,
   and ever pure of heart,
   so may my heart be wholly
   of thine the counterpart.

5. When life away is flying,
   and earth's false glare is done:
   still, Sacred Heart, in dying,
   I'll say I'm all thine own.

   Aloys Schlör (1805-1852),
   tr. A. J. Christie (1817-1891), alt.

430

1. Trust is in the eyes of a tiny babe
   leaning on his mother's breast.
   In the eager beat of a young bird's wings
   on the day it leaves the nest.

   It is the living Spirit
   filling the earth, bringing to birth
   a world of love and laughter,
   joy in the light of the Lord.

2. Hope is in the rain that makes
      crystal streams
   tumble down a mountain side,
   and in ev'ry man who repairs his nets,
   waiting for the rising tide.

3. Love is in the hearts of all those
      who seek
   freedom for the human race.
   Love is in the touch of the hand
      that heals,
   and the smile that lights a face.

4. Strength is in the wind as it bends
      the trees,
   warmth is in the bright red flame,
   light is in the sun and the candle-glow,
   cleansing are the ocean's waves.

   Estelle White (b. 1925)

431

Turn to me, O turn and be saved,
says the Lord, for I am God;
there is no other, none beside me.
I call your name.

1. I am he that comforts you;
   who are you to be afraid
   of flesh that fades,
   is made like the grass of the field,
   soon to wither.

2. Listen to me, my people,
   give ear to me, my nation:
   a law will go forth from me,
   and my justice for a light
   to the people.

3. Lift up your eyes to the heavens,
   and look at the earth down below.
   The heavens will vanish like smoke,
   and the earth will wear out
   like a garment.

John Foley, based on Isaiah 45 and 51
© 1975 New Dawn Music

432

Ubi caritas et amor.
Ubi caritas Deus ibi est.

1. Your love, O Jesus Christ,
   has gathered us together.

2. May your love, O Jesus Christ,
   be foremost in our lives.

3. Let us love one another
   as God has loved us.

4. Let us be one in love together
   in the one bread of Christ.

5. The love of God in Jesus Christ
   bears eternal joy.

6. The love of God in Jesus Christ
   will never have an end.

Taizé Community

433

1. Unto us a boy is born!
   King of all creation;
   came he to a world forlorn,
   the Lord of ev'ry nation,
   the Lord of ev'ry nation.

2. Cradled in a stall was he,
   watched by cows and asses;
   but the very beasts could see
   that he the world surpasses,
   that he the world surpasses.

3. Then the fearful Herod cried,
   'Pow'r is mine in Jewry!'
   So the blameless children died
   the victims of his fury,
   the victims of his fury.

4. Now may Mary's Son, who came
   long ago to love us;
   lead us all with hearts aflame
   unto the joys above us,
   unto the joys above us.

5. Alpha and Omega he!
   Let the organ thunder,
   while the choir with peals of glee
   shall rend the air asunder,
   shall rend the air asunder.

15th century, tr. Percy Dearmer
(1867-1936), alt.

434

1. Upon thy table, Lord, we place
   these symbols of our work and thine,
   life's food won only by thy grace,
   who giv'st to all the bread and wine.

Continued overleaf

2. Within these simple things there lie
   the height and depth of human life,
   the thought of all, our tears and toil,
   our hopes and fears, our joy and strife.

3. Accept them, Lord; from thee
      they come:
   we take them humbly at thy hand.
   These gifts of thine for higher use
   we offer, as thou dost command.

   M. F. C. Wilson (1884-1944), alt.

435

1. Vaster far than any ocean,
   deeper than the deepest sea
   is the love of Christ my Saviour,
   reaching through eternity.

2. But my sins are truly many,
   is God's grace so vast, so deep?
   Yes, there's grace o'er sin abounding,
   grace to pardon, grace to keep.

3. Can he quench my thirst for ever?
   Will his Spirit strength impart?
   Yes, he gives me living water,
   springing up within my heart.

   Unknown

436

1. Veni, Creator Spiritus,
   mentes tuorum visita,
   imple superna gratia,
   quæ tu creasti pectora.

2. Qui diceris Paraclitus,
   Altissimi donum Dei,
   fons vivus, ignis, caritas,
   et spiritalis unctio.

3. Tu septiformis munere,
   digitus paternæ dexteræ,
   tu rite promissum Patris,
   sermone ditans guttura.

4. Accende lumen sensibus,
   infunde amorem cordibus,
   infirma nostri corporis
   virtute firmans perpeti.

5. Hostem repellas longius,
   pacemque dones protinus:
   ductore sic te prævio,
   vitemus omne noxium.

6. Per te sciamus da Patrem,
   noscamus atque Filium,
   teque utriusque Spiritum
   credamus omni tempore.

7. Deo Patri sit gloria,
   et Filio, qui, a mortuis
   surrexit, ac Paraclito,
   in sæculorum sæcula. Amen.

   Ascribed to Rabanus Maurus (776-856)

437

1. Veni, Sancte Spiritus,
   et emitte coelitus
   lucis tuæ radium.

2. Veni, pater pauperum,
   veni, dator munerum,
   veni, lumen cordium.

3. Consolator optime,
   dulcis hospes animæ,
   dulce refrigerium.

4. In labore requies,
   in æstu temperies,
   in fletu solatium.

5. O lux beatissima
reple cordis intima
tuorum fidelium.

6. Sine tuo numine,
nihil est in homine,
nihil est innoxium.

7. Lava quod est sordidum,
riga quod est aridum,
sana quod est saucium.

8. Flecte quod est rigidum,
fove quod est frigidum,
rege quod est devium.

9. Da tuis fidelibus,
in te confidentibus,
sacrum septenarium.

10. Da virtutis meritum,
da salutis exitum,
da perenne gaudium.
Amen.

Ascribed to Stephen Langton (d. 1228)

438

Veni, veni, veni Sancte Spiritus.

1. Spirit, whose name is love,
sent to us as a dove,
breeze from the heavens,
stirring our hearts anew,
come in power to fill our life.

2. Spirit, with healing wings,
whose name creation sings,
comfort our sorrow,
bind up the broken heart,
bless and gladden each chosen soul.

3. Spirit, eternal truth,
both source and living proof,
sent from the Father,
through his belovèd Son,
loosen our bonds, set your people free.

Kevin Mayhew (b. 1942)

439

Wait for the Lord, his day is near.
Wait for the Lord: be strong, take heart!

1. Prepare the way for the Lord.
Make a straight path for him.

2. The glory of the Lord
shall be revealed.

3. All the earth will see the Lord.

4. Rejoice in the Lord always:
he is at hand.

5. Seek first the kingdom of God,
seek and you shall find.

6. Joy and gladness for all
who seek the Lord.

7. I waited for the Lord:
he heard my cry.

8. Our eyes are fixed
on the Lord our God.

9. O Lord, show us your way.
Guide us in your truth.

10. Prepare the way of the Lord.

Taizé Community, based on Scripture

440

Wake up, O people,
the Lord is very near!
Wake up and stand for the Lord.
Wake up, O people,
the Lord is very near!
Wake up and stand for the Lord.

1. Your saving Lord is near. Wake up!
   His glory will appear. Wake up!
   Your hour of grace is nearer
   than it ever was.

2. The night of sin has passed. Wake up!
   The light is near at last. Wake up!
   The day star, Christ,
   the Son of God will soon appear.

3. To live in love and peace. Wake up!
   To let all quarrels cease. Wake up!
   To live that all you do
   may stand the light of day.

4. That Christ may be your shield.
   Wake up!
   That death to life may yield. Wake up!
   That heaven's gate be
   opened wide again for you.
   Marie Lydia Pereira (b. 1920), from Rom 13:11-14

441

Walk with me, O my Lord,
through the darkest night
and brightest day.
Be at my side, O Lord,
hold my hand and guide me
on my way.

1. Sometimes the road seems long,
   my energy is spent.
   Then, Lord, I think of you
   and I am given strength.

2. Stones often bar my path
   and there are times I fall,
   but you are always there
   to help me when I call.

3. Just as you calmed the wind
   and walked upon the sea,
   conquer, my living Lord,
   the storms that threaten me.

4. Help me to pierce the mists
   that cloud my heart and mind,
   so that I shall not fear
   the steepest mountain-side.

5. As once you healed the lame
   and gave sight to the blind,
   help me when I'm downcast
   to hold my head up high.
   Estelle White (b. 1925)

442

1. We are gathering together unto him.
   We are gathering together unto him.
   Unto him shall the gath'ring
   of the people be,
   we are gathering together unto him.

2. We are offering together unto him.
   We are offering together unto him.
   Unto him shall the off'ring
   of the people be,
   we are offering together unto him.

3. We are singing together unto him.
   We are singing together unto him.
   Unto him shall the singing
   of the people be,
   we are singing together unto him.

4. We are praying together unto him.
   We are praying together unto him.
   Unto him shall the praying
   of the people be,
   we are praying together unto him.

   Unknown

443

We are the Easter people:
'Alleluia' is our song.
Let us rejoice!
Let us sing out:
'Jesus is risen!
Alleluia, alleluia, alleluia'.

1. He died for us:
   now he is risen.
   We share his life:
   Jesus is Lord!

2. His light shines out,
   dispelling the darkness.
   Tell the whole world:
   Jesus is Lord!

3. Proclaim his glory:
   Christ is the Saviour.
   He dies no more:
   Jesus is Lord!

4. God's people sing!
   You share his victory.
   Have no more fear:
   Jesus is Lord!

   Tom Leigh (b. 1942)

444

We behold the splendour of God
shining on the face of Jesus.
We behold the splendour of God
shining on the face of the Son.

1. And O how his beauty transforms us,
   the wonder of Presence abiding.
   Transparent hearts give reflection
   of Tabor's light within,
   of Tabor's light within.

2. Jesus, Lord of glory,
   Jesus belovèd Son.
   O how good to be with you;
   how good to share your light,
   how good to share your light.

   Carey Landry

445

1. We have a gospel to proclaim,
   good news for all throughout the earth;
   the gospel of a Saviour's name:
   we sing his glory, tell his worth.

2. Tell of his birth at Bethlehem,
   not in a royal house or hall
   but in a stable dark and dim:
   the Word made flesh, a light for all.

3. Tell of his death at Calvary,
   hated by those he came to save;
   in lonely suff'ring on the cross
   for all he loved, his life he gave.

4. Tell of that glorious Easter morn:
   empty the tomb, for he was free;
   he broke the pow'r of death and hell
   that we might share his victory.

Continued overleaf

5. Tell of his reign at God's right hand,
   by all creation glorified
   he sends his Spirit on his church
   to live for him, the Lamb who died.

6. Now we rejoice to name him King:
   Jesus is Lord of all the earth,
   this gospel-message we proclaim:
   we sing his glory, tell his worth.

   Edward Burns (b. 1938)

446

*We hold a treasure, not made of gold,
in earthen vessels, wealth untold;
one treasure only: the Lord, the Christ,
in earthen vessels.*

1. Light has shone in our darkness;
   God has shone in our heart,
   with the light of the glory
   of Jesus, the Lord.

2. He has chosen the lowly,
   who are small in this world;
   in his weakness is glory,
   in Jesus the Lord.

   John Foley, based on 2 Cor. 4 and 1 Cor . 1
   © 1975 New Dawn Music

447

1. We three kings of Orient are;
   bearing gifts we traverse afar;
   field and fountain, moor and mountain,
   following yonder star.

   *O star of wonder, star of night,
   star with royal beauty bright,
   westward leading, still proceeding,
   guide us to thy perfect light.*

2. Born a King on Bethlehem plain,
   gold I bring, to crown him again,
   King for ever, ceasing never,
   over us all to reign.

3. Frankincense to offer have I,
   incense owns a Deity nigh.
   Prayer and praising, gladly raising,
   worship him, God most high.

4. Myrrh is mine, its bitter perfume
   breathes a life of gathering gloom;
   sorrowing, sighing, bleeding, dying,
   sealed in the stone-cold tomb.

5. Glorious now behold him arise,
   King and God and sacrifice;
   alleluia, alleluia,
   earth to heav'n replies.

   John Henry Hopkins (1820-1891), alt.

448

1. Welcome all you noble saints of old,
   as now before your very eyes unfold
   the wonders all so long ago foretold.

   *In Christ there is a table set for all,
   in Christ there is a table set for all.*

2. Elders, martyrs, all are falling down;
   prophets, patriarchs are
       gath'ring round,
   what angels longed to see now we
       have found.

3. Beggars, lame and harlots also here;
   repentant publicans are drawing near;
   wayward ones come home without
       a fear.

4. Who is this who spreads the
      vict'ry feast?
   Who is this who makes our
      warring cease?
   Jesus risen Saviour, Prince of peace.

5. Here he gives himself to us as bread;
   here, as wine, we drink the blood
      he shed.
   Born to die, we eat and live instead.

6. Worship in the presence of the Lord,
   with joyful songs and hearts in
      one accord,
   and let our host at table be adored.

7. When at last this earth shall
      pass away,
   when Jesus and his bride are one
      to stay,
   the feast of love is just begun that day.

Robert J. Stamps
© 1977 Dawn Treader Music/CopyCare Ltd

449

1. Were you there when
   they crucified my Lord?
   Were you there when
   they crucified my Lord?
   O, sometimes it causes me
   to tremble, tremble, tremble.
   Were you there when
   they crucified my Lord?

2. Were you there when
   they nailed him to a tree?
   Were you there when
   they nailed him to a tree?
   O, sometimes it causes me
   to tremble, tremble, tremble.
   Were you there when
   they nailed him to a tree?

3. Were you there when
   they pierced him in the side?
   Were you there when
   they pierced him in the side?
   O, sometimes it causes me
   to tremble, tremble, tremble.
   Were you there when
   they pierced him in the side?

4. Were you there when
   the sun refused to shine?
   Were you there when
   the sun refused to shine?
   O, sometimes it causes me
   to tremble, tremble, tremble.
   Were you there when
   the sun refused to shine?

5. Were you there when
   they laid him in the tomb?
   Were you there when
   they laid him in the tomb?
   O, sometimes it causes me
   to tremble, tremble, tremble.
   Were you there when
   they laid him in the tomb?

6. Were you there when
   he rose from out the tomb?
   Were you there when
   he rose from out the tomb?
   O, sometimes it causes me
   to tremble, tremble, tremble.
   Were you there when
   he rose from out the tomb?

Spiritual

450

1. What can we offer you,
   Lord our God?
   How can we worship you
   as you deserve?
   We can only offer
   what our lips do proclaim.
   We can only offer you
   humble acts of praise.
   But we offer this
   with Jesus, our brother,
   Jesus, your Son.
   We join with him,
   glory to you, O God!
   We join with him,
   glory to you, O God!

2. What can we offer you,
   Lord our God?
   How can we thank you
   for all that you've done?
   We can only say it,
   Lord God, we thank you so.
   We can only try to live
   grateful lives, O Lord.
   But we offer this
   with Jesus, our brother,
   Jesus, your Son.
   We join with him,
   our thanks to you, O God.
   We join with him,
   our thanks to you, O God.

3. What can we offer you,
   Lord our God?
   How do we prove
   we are truly sorry, Lord?
   We can say it often,
   God, sorry that we are.
   We can try to prove it,
   Lord, by the way we live.

And we offer this
with Jesus, our brother,
Jesus, your Son.
We join with him,
forgive our sins, O God.
We join with him,
forgive our sins, O God.

4. What can we offer you,
   Lord our God?
   Dare we present you
   with another call for help?
   We just have to say it,
   Lord God, we need you so.
   We just have to beg you,
   Lord, take us by the hand.
   And we offer this
   with Jesus, our brother,
   Jesus, your Son.
   We join with him,
   Lord, we need you so.
   We join with him,
   Lord, we need you so.
   Tom Shelley

451

1. What child is this who, laid to rest,
   on Mary's lap is sleeping?
   Whom angels greet with anthems sweet,
   while shepherds watch are keeping?
   This, this is Christ the King,
   whom shepherds guard and angels sing:
   come greet the infant Lord,
   the babe, the Son of Mary!

2. Why lies he in such mean estate,
   where ox and ass are feeding?
   Good Christians, fear: for sinners here
   the silent Word is pleading.
   Nails, spear, shall pierce him through,
   the cross be borne for me, for you:
   hail, hail the Word made flesh,
   the babe, the Son of Mary!

3. So bring him incense, gold and myrrh,
come peasant, king, to own him.
The King of kings salvation brings,
let loving hearts enthrone him.
Raise, raise the song on high,
the virgin sings her lullaby:
joy, joy for Christ is born,
the babe, the Son of Mary!

William Chatterton Dix (1837-1898)

452

*Whatsoever you do
to the least of my brothers,
that you do unto me.*

1. When I was hungry
you gave me to eat.
When I was thirsty
you gave me to drink.
Now enter into
the home of my Father.

2. When I was homeless
you opened your door.
When I was naked
you gave me your coat.
Now enter into
the home of my Father.

3. When I was weary
you helped me find rest.
When I was anxious
you calmed all my fears.
Now enter into
the home of my Father.

4. When in a prison
you came to my cell.
When on a sick-bed
you cared for my needs.
Now enter into
the home of my Father.

5. When I was aged
you bothered to smile.
When I was restless
you listened and cared.
Now enter into
the home of my Father.

6. When I was laughed at
you stood by my side.
When I was happy
you shared in my joy.
Now enter into
the home of my Father.

Willard F. Jabusch (b. 1930)

453

1. When Christ our Lord to
Andrew cried:
'Come, thou and follow me,'
the fisher left his net beside
the Sea of Galilee.
To teach the truth his Master taught,
to tread the path he trod
was all his will, and thus he brought
unnumbered souls to God.

2. When Andrew's hour had come,
and he
was doomed like Christ to die,
he kissed his cross exultingly,
and this his loving cry:
'O noble cross! O precious wood!
I long have yearned for thee;
uplift me to my only good
who died on thee for me.'

3. The faith that Andrew taught
once shone
o'er all this kingdom fair;
the cross that Jesus died upon
was honoured ev'rywhere.
But evil men that faith beat down,
reviling Andrew's name; the cross,
though set in kingly crown,
became a sign of shame.

Continued overleaf

4. Saint Andrew, now in bliss above,
   thy fervent prayers renew
   that Scotland yet again may love
   the faith, entire and true;
   that I the cross allotted me
   may bear with patient love!
   'Twill lift me, as it lifted thee,
   to reign with Christ above.

   E. M. Barrett

454

1. When I survey the wondrous cross
   on which the Prince of Glory died,
   my richest gain I count but loss,
   and pour contempt on all my pride.

2. Forbid it, Lord, that I should boast,
   save in the death of Christ, my God:
   all the vain things that charm me most,
   I sacrifice them to his blood.

3. See from his head, his hands, his feet,
   sorrow and love flow mingled down:
   did e'er such love and sorrow meet,
   or thorns compose so rich a crown?

4. Were the whole realm of nature mine,
   that were an off'ring far too small;
   love so amazing, so divine,
   demands my soul, my life, my all.

   Isaac Watts (1674-1748)

455

1. When is he coming,
   when, O when is he coming,
   the Redeemer?
   When will we see him,
   when, O when will we see him,
   the Redeemer?

Come, O come,
from your kingdom up there,
from your kingdom up there above!
Come, O come,
to your people on earth,
to your people on earth bring love!
Emmanuel! Emmanuel! Emmanuel!

2. Long years a-waiting,
   many years here a-waiting
   the Redeemer!
   Ready to greet him,
   always ready to meet him,
   the Redeemer!

3. Spare us from evil,
   from the clutches of evil,
   O Redeemer!
   Though we are sinners
   we have known your forgiveness,
   O Redeemer!

   David Palmer (b. 1933)

456

1. When morning gilds the skies
   my heart awakening cries,
   may Jesus Christ be praised.
   Alike at work and prayer
   to Jesus I repair;
   may Jesus Christ be praised.

2. The night becomes as day,
   when from the heart we say:
   may Jesus Christ be praised.
   The pow'rs of darkness fear,
   when this sweet chant they hear:
   may Jesus Christ be praised.

3. In heav'n's eternal bliss
   the loveliest strain is this:
   may Jesus Christ be praised.
   Let air, and sea, and sky
   from depth to height reply:
   may Jesus Christ be praised.

4. Be this, while life is mine,
   my canticle divine:
   may Jesus Christ be praised.
   Be this th' eternal song
   through all the ages on:
   may Jesus Christ be praised.

   German (19th century),
   tr. Edward Caswall (1814-1878)

457

1. When our Lord's loving mind
   thought to save lost mankind,
   only one could he find
   pure and free of sinning,
   grace and favour winning.

   O the night is day:
   sin is turned away!
   Glory's dawn: love is born,
   Jesus Christ our Saviour!

2. For in God's chosen time,
   Mary saw heav'n sublime
   light a way from the crime
   Eve and Adam's thieving
   did to true believing.

3. What may tell more of grace
   than this pure mother's face,
   shining clear on our race,
   Light of Light reflecting,
   God of God protecting?

4. Wrong and ill shall be right
   when her Son comes in sight.
   Nations all, ending fight,
   bowed in peace before him
   will, like her, adore him.

   Mark Woodruff (b. 1959)

458

1. While shepherds watched their flocks
         by night,
   all seated on the ground,
   the angel of the Lord came down,
   and glory shone around.

2. 'Fear not,' said he, (for mighty dread
   had seized their troubled mind)
   'glad tidings of great joy I bring
   to you and all mankind.

3. 'To you in David's town this day
   is born of David's line
   a Saviour, who is Christ the Lord;
   and this shall be the sign:

4. 'The heav'nly babe you there
         shall find
   to human view displayed,
   all meanly wrapped in
         swathing bands,
   and in a manger laid.'

5. Thus spake the seraph, and forthwith
   appeared a shining throng
   of angels praising God, who thus
   addressed their joyful song:

6. 'All glory be to God on high,
   and on the earth be peace,
   goodwill henceforth from heav'n
         to men
   begin and never cease.'

   Nahum Tate (1652-1715)

459

1. Will you come and follow me
   if I but call your name?
   Will you go where you don't know,
   and never be the same?
   Will you let my love be shown,
   will you let my name be known,
   will you let my life be grown
   in you, and you in me?

2. Will you leave yourself behind
   if I but call your name?
   Will you care for cruel and kind,
   and never be the same?
   Will you risk the hostile stare
   should your life attract or scare,
   will you let me answer prayer
   in you, and you in me?

3. Will you let the blinded see
   if I but call your name?
   Will you set the pris'ners free,
   and never be the same?
   Will you kiss the leper clean
   and do such as this unseen,
   and admit to what I mean
   in you, and you in me?

4. Will you love the 'you' you hide
   if I but call your name?
   Will you quell the fear inside,
   and never be the same?
   Will you use the faith you've found
   to reshape the world around
   through my sight and touch and sound
   in you, and you in me?

5. Lord, your summons echoes true
   when you but call my name.
   Let me turn and follow you,
   and never be the same.
   In your company I'll go
   where your love and footsteps show.
   Thus I'll move and live and grow
   in you, and you in me.

John Bell (b. 1949) and Graham Maule (b. 1958)

460

Within our darkest night,
you kindle the fire
that never dies away,
that never dies away.
Within our darkest night,
you kindle the fire
that never dies away,
that never dies away.

Taizé Community

461

1. Word made flesh,
   Son of God.

   Come, Lord Jesus,
   come again.
   Come, Lord Jesus,
   come again.

2. Lord and Saviour,
   Son of God.

3. Prince of peace,
   Son of God.

4. Alleluia,
   Son of God.

5. Bread of Life,
   Son of God.

6. Light of the World,
   Son of God.

7. Jesus Christ,
   Son of God.

Virginia Vissing

462

Yahweh, I know you are near,
standing always at my side.
You guard me from the foe
and you lead me in ways everlasting.

1. Lord, you have searched my heart,
   and you know when I sit
   and when I stand.
   Your hand is upon me,
   protecting me from death,
   keeping me from harm.

2. Where can I run from your love?
   If I climb to the heavens,
   you are there.
   If I fly to the sunrise
   or sail beyond the sea,
   still I'd find you there.

3. You know my heart and its ways,
   you who formed me
   before I was born,
   in secret of darkness,
   before I saw the sun,
   in my mother's womb.

4. Marvellous to me are your works;
   how profound are your thoughts,
   my Lord!
   Even if I could count them,
   they number as the stars,
   you would still be there.

Dan Schutte, based on Psalm 139
© 1971, 1974 New Dawn Music

463

1. Ye choirs of new Jerusalem,
   your sweetest notes employ,
   the Paschal victory to hymn
   in strains of holy joy.

2. How Judah's Lion burst his chains,
   and crushed the serpent's head;
   and brought with him,
       from death's domain,
   the long-imprisoned dead.

3. From hell's devouring jaws the prey
   alone our leader bore;
   his ransomed hosts pursue their way
   where he hath gone before.

4. Triumphant in his glory now
   his sceptre ruleth all:
   earth, heav'n and hell before him bow
   and at his footstool fall.

5. While joyful thus his praise we sing,
   his mercy we implore,
   into his palace bright to bring,
   and keep us evermore.

6. All glory to the Father be,
   all glory to the Son,
   all glory, Holy Ghost, to thee,
   while endless ages run.

St Fulbert of Chartres (c. 1000),
tr. Robert Campbell (1814-1868)

464

1. Ye holy angels bright,
   who wait at God's right hand,
   or through the realms of light
   stream at your Lord's command,
   assist our song,
   for else the theme
   too high doth seem
   for mortal tongue.

Continued overleaf

2. Ye blessèd souls at rest,
   who ran this earthly race,
   and now, from care released,
   behold the Saviour's face,
   God's praises sound,
   as in his sight
   with sweet delight
   ye do abound.

3. Ye saints, who toil below,
   adore your heav'nly King,
   and onward as ye go
   some joyful anthem sing;
   take what he gives
   and praise him still,
   through good or ill,
   who ever lives.

4. My soul, bear thou thy part,
   triumph in God above:
   and with a well-tuned heart
   sing thou the songs of love;
   let all thy days
   till life shall end,
   whate'er he send,
   be filled with praise.

   Richard Baxter (1615-1591) and others

465

Alleluia, alleluia, alleluia.

1. Ye sons and daughters of the Lord,
   the King of glory, King adored,
   this day himself from death restored.
   Alleluia.

2. All in the early morning grey
   went holy women on their way
   to see the tomb where Jesus lay.
   Alleluia.

3. Then straightway one in white they see,
   who saith, 'Ye seek the Lord; but he
   is risen, and gone to Galilee.'
   Alleluia.

4. That self-same night, while out of fear
   the doors were shut, their Lord
       most dear
   to his apostles did appear.
   Alleluia.

5. But Thomas, when of this he heard,
   was doubtful of his brethren's word;
   wherefore again there comes the Lord.
   Alleluia.

6. 'Thomas, behold my side,' saith he;
   'my hands, my feet, my body see,
   and doubt not, but believe in me.'
   Alleluia.

7. When Thomas saw that wounded side,
   the truth no longer he denied:
   'Thou art my Lord and God!' he cried.
   Alleluia.

8. Now let us praise the Lord most high,
   and strive his name to magnify
   on this great day, through earth
       and sky.
   Alleluia.

   Jean Tisserand (d. 1494),
   tr. Edward Caswall (1814-1878)

466

1. You shall cross the barren desert,
   but you shall not die of thirst.
   You shall wander far in safety
   though you do not know the way.
   You shall speak your words in
       foreign lands
   and they will understand.
   You shall see the face of God and live.

Be not afraid.
I go before you always.
Come, follow me,
and I will give you rest.

2. If you pass through raging waters
   in the sea, you shall not drown.
   If you walk amid the burning flames,
   you shall not be harmed.
   If you stand before the pow'r of hell
   and death is at your side,
   know that I am with you through it all.

3. Blessèd are the poor,
   for the kingdom shall be theirs.
   Blest are you that weep and mourn,
   for one day you shall laugh.
   And if wicked men insult and
     hate you
   all because of me,
   blessèd, blessèd are you!

Bob Dufford, based on Isaiah 43:2-3, Luke 6:20
© 1975, 1978 New Dawn Music

467

You shall go out with joy
and be led forth with peace,
and the mountains and the hills
shall break forth before you.
There'll be shouts of joy
and the trees of the field
shall clap, shall clap their hands.
And the trees of the field
shall clap their hands,
and the trees of the field
shall clap their hands,
and the trees of the field
shall clap their hands,
and you'll go out with joy.

Stuart Dauermann (b. 1944), based on Isaiah 55:12
© 1975 Lillenas Publishing Co/Kingsway's Thankyou Music

468

1. You who dwell in the shelter of
     the Lord,
   who abide in his shadow for life,
   say to the Lord: 'My refuge,
   my rock in whom I trust!'

And he will raise you up
on eagle's wings,
bear you on the breath of dawn,
make you to shine like the sun,
and hold you in the palm of his hand.

2. The snare of the fowler will never
     capture you,
   and famine will bring you no fear.
   Under his wings your refuge,
   his faithfulness your shield.

3. You need not fear the terror of
     the night,
   nor the arrow that flies by day;
   though thousands fall about you,
   near you it shall not come.

4. For to his angels he's given a command
   to guard you in all of your ways;
   upon their hands they will bear you up,
   lest you dash your foot against a stone.

Michael Joncas (b. 1951), based on Psalm 90 (91)
© 1979, 1991 New Dawn Music

469

1st Sunday of Advent: Year A

1. Waken, O sleeper, wake and rise,
   salvation's day is near,
   and let the dawn of light and truth
   dispel the night of fear.

2. Let us prepare to face the day
   of judgement and of grace,
   to live as people of the light,
   and perfect truth embrace.

3. Watch then and pray, we cannot know
   the moment or the hour,
   when Christ, unheralded, will come
   with life-renewing power.

4. Then shall the nations gather round
   to learn his ways of peace,
   when spears to pruning-hooks are turned,
   and all our conflicts cease.

470

2nd Sunday of Advent: Year A

1. Behold, the Saviour of the nations
   shall spring from David's royal line,
   to rule with mercy all the peoples,
   and judge with righteousness divine!

2. He shall delight in truth and wisdom,
   with justice for the meek and poor,
   and reconcile his whole creation,
   where beasts of prey shall hunt no more.

3. Here may his word, with
      hope abounding,
   unite us all in peace and love,
   to live as one with all creation,
   redeemed by mercy from above.

4. Prepare the way with awe and wonder;
   salvation comes on judgement's wing,
   for God will purify his people,
   and 'Glory!' all the earth shall sing.

471

3rd Sunday of Advent: Year A

1. The Saviour will come,
   resplendent in joy;
   the lame and the sick
   new strength will enjoy.
   The desert, rejoicing,
   shall burst into flower,
   the deaf and the speechless
   will sing in that hour!

2. The Saviour will come,
   like rain on the earth,
   to harvest at last
   his crop of great worth.
   In patience await him,
   with firmness of mind;
   both mercy and judgement
   his people will find.

3. The Saviour will come,
   his truth we shall see:
   where lepers are cleansed
   and captives set free.
   No finely-clad princeling
   in palace of gold,
   but Christ with his people,
   O wonder untold!

472

4th Sunday of Advent: Year A

1. The sign of hope, creation's joy,
   is born of purest beauty:
   the virgin's womb, now glorified,
   where grace unites with duty.

2. Emmanuel shall be his name,
   a title pure and holy,
   for God with us will truly be
   among the poor and lowly.

3. Where love divine concurs with trust
   to share redemption's story,
   Emmanuel in hope is born,
   and earth exults in glory.

4. Now we, by grace and duty called,
   proclaim to ev'ry nation
   the Sign of hope which Mary bore,
   and promise of salvation.

473

1st Sunday of Advent: Year B

1. Return, Redeemer God,
   with judgement and with healing:
   our wayward hearts restore,
   your light and truth revealing.
   O leave us not alone,
   nor let us go astray,
   but open ev'ry heart
   to know your perfect way.

2. Here let us wait and pray
   to greet the Lord returning,
   as watchers in the night
   with beacons ever burning:
   for none can know the hour
   his people long to see,
   when Christ, with justice, comes
   to set creation free.

3. May grace and peace be ours,
   from God the Father flowing,
   through Jesus Christ, our Lord,
   his perfect truth bestowing.
   This Fellowship we share,
   the Father and the Son,
   who with the Spirit, Three,
   eternally are One.

474

2nd Sunday of Advent: Year B

1. Hark, a voice is calling,
   clear and triumphant:
   'Make, across the desert,
   a highway for the Lord.
   Ev'ry hill and valley,
   level out before him:
   God comes in glory
   – hear his holy word!'

2. Gospel of redemption,
   word of forgiveness!
   God, in endless mercy,
   his people has restored.
   Sanctified by water,
   hallowed by the Spirit,
   life in abundance,
   Christ on us has poured!

3. God so long awaited,
   righteous in judgement,
   all creation trembles
   to see your holy face.
   Come in grace and glory,
   rule with truth and justice,
   holding creation
   in your love's embrace.

475

3rd Sunday of Advent: Year B

1. Sing and rejoice, the Lord is near;
   his saving grace proclaim,
   and let the whole creation show
   the glory of his name.

2. We, by the Spirit's pow'r, proclaim
   good news for all the poor:
   our God will set the captive free,
   the broken heart restore.

Continued overleaf

3. Here in the light of Christ alone,
   redeemed by grace, we stand,
   and treasure ev'ry perfect gift
   of his unfailing hand.

4. Freedom and truth,
      like garden flowers,
   upon the earth shall grow,
   and all the nations, lost in praise,
   his perfect peace will know.

476

4th Sunday of Advent: Year B

1. The Saviour of the nations
   is born of David's line,
   from humble service lifted
   to majesty divine.
   He comes with peace and justice,
   in judgement ever sure;
   and, founded on compassion,
   his reign shall be secure.

2. The Spirit is rejoicing
   in bringing hope to birth,
   and life in all its fullness
   he breathes upon the earth.
   The humble and the lowly
   his promise have received:
   the virgin's womb has flowered,
   the barren have conceived!

3. The mystery of ages,
   the secret long-concealed,
   of full and free salvation,
   at last has been revealed.
   The Father's name we honour,
   through Jesus Christ, our Lord,
   who, in the Spirit's power,
   will ever be adored.

477

1st Sunday of Advent: Year C

1. Holy God, our great Redeemer,
   give us grace to watch and pray,
   till the sun and stars bear witness
   to the long-awaited day,
   when triumphant,
   when triumphant,
   truth and freedom come to stay,
   truth and freedom come to stay!

2. See, the day is surely coming,
   promised by divine decree;
   joyous day of truth and virtue,
   justice and integrity!
   God has spoken!
   God has spoken!
   All the world will wholeness see,
   all the world will wholeness see!

3. Come, O God, in liberation;
   from ourselves we would be free,
   filled with love for one another,
   and for all humanity;
   all creation,
   all creation,
   one in holy liberty,
   one in holy liberty.

478

2nd Sunday of Advent: Year C

1. Let all creation now rejoice,
   a song of freedom singing,
   proclaiming peace and liberty
   from truth and justice springing.

2. We still can hear the prophet's voice
   in barren places crying,
   'Repent and seek the way of truth,
   on God alone relying!'

3. The exiles shall rejoicing come,
   from east and west returning,
   and God will be their guiding light,
   with hope and justice burning.

4. Our God began, and will complete,
   the drama of salvation,
   as knowledge, hope and love increase,
   uniting all creation.

479

3rd Sunday of Advent: Year C

1. As people of God,
   let us sing and rejoice,
   for God our Redeemer
   is giving us voice.
   The terror of evil
   is falling away,
   and God joins the dance
   on the festival day!

2. God gives us our goods
   and resources to share,
   and bids us in commerce
   and dealings be fair.
   In calling the people
   these ways to embrace,
   the prophet announces
   both judgement and grace.

3. Then let us in patient
   forbearance abound,
   for there may the truest
   contentment be found;
   from fear and resentment
   our minds will be freed,
   and peace yet unknown
   will fulfil ev'ry need.

480

4th Sunday of Advent: Year C

1. From the humblest of the cities,
   Bethlehem, the very least,
   comes the Saviour of the nations,
   born to rule in truth and peace.
   There, among the poor and humble,
   justice will be brought to birth;
   see the pow'r of love eternal
   manifest throughout the earth.

2. Needing not the gifts and praises
   our poor worship may afford,
   God prepares the perfect off'ring
   of the co-eternal Word:
   Word of wholeness and perfection,
   now in flesh and blood revealed;
   Christ the one, the true oblation,
   ev'ry sacrifice has sealed.

3. See the hope of liberation,
   by the humble poor received,
   by the virgin and the barren,
   with such holy joy conceived!
   Mary, mother of salvation,
   full of unexpected grace,
   all our hopes and longings quicken
   by the joy of your embrace.

481

Christmas: Midnight Mass: Year ABC

1. Those who walked in
      deepest darkness
   see a great and splendid light,
   heralding a Son now given,
   born of God to human sight.
   He will reign in peace for ever,
   all injustice put to flight.

Continued overleaf

2. Shepherds hear the angels calling,
   telling of a new-born King
   lying in a straw-filled manger;
   O the mystery they sing!
   'Glory in the highest heaven!'
   All the world with joy will ring!

3. Now, the work of grace completed,
   all creation reconciled,
   let us live in Godly freedom,
   not as slaves by sin defiled;
   seek again the greater glory
   once revealed in Mary's child.

482

Christmas: Daytime Mass: Year ABC

1. Lovely feet upon the mountains
   bring the distant runner near,
   with the message of salvation,
   set to gladden ev'ry ear.
   Sing for joy, you ransomed people,
   God has made the vision clear.

2. Now in even greater glory
   comes the co-eternal Word,
   he through whom, in primal darkness,
   first creation's breath was stirred.
   All the glory of the Godhead
   in his form is seen and heard.

3. He, the Father's very image,
   came to save and justify,
   then, the full atonement finished,
   took his proper place on high.
   Now his name, with awe and wonder,
   all the angels glorify.

483

The Holy Family: Year A

1. Holy Jesus, in our likeness
   born, a human home to share,
   you who knew a father's kindness
   and a loving mother's care,
   by your ever-present mercy,
   may we catch this vision fair,
   may we catch this vision fair!

2. Look with kindness and compassion
   on each mortal family.
   Give us joy in one another,
   touching here eternity!
   Saviour, hold your many people
   in the sweetest harmony,
   in the sweetest harmony.

3. May we live for one another,
   growing through life's ev'ry stage,
   with protection for the youngest
   and respect for greater age;
   all a common value sharing,
   what a holy heritage,
   what a holy heritage!

484

The Holy Family: Year B

1. O God of Abraham,
   your promises we own,
   that through the human family
   your glory will be shown.

2. Then give us faith to know
   your word will never fail:
   the troubles of the present day
   a brighter future veil.

3. The temple prophet speaks,
   and we his vision see,
   of pain and blessings both to come
   in ev'ry family.

4. May Mary's faith be found
   in ev'ry human heart,
   to wonder at the mystery
   and play our humble part.

485

The Holy Family: Year C

1. O God, whose love for all we see
   in that most holy family,
   show us the mystery of grace,
   as freedom flow'rs in love's embrace!

2. Your gift of life, we now confess,
   is ours to love but not possess.
   Then help us all, in faith and prayer,
   to trust each other to your care.

3. Help us to hear and own the truth,
   when spoken by the lips of youth,
   to welcome their disturbing voice,
   and in your mystery rejoice!

4. O God, whose love for all we see
   most clearly in the Trinity,
   let your mysterious pow'r be known
   to set us free, yet make us one.

486

Solemnity of Mary, Mother of God: Year ABC

1. O Christ, incarnate God,
   and author of salvation,
   by God of woman born,
   to liberate creation;
   your Spirit we receive,
   who comes to set us free,
   and 'Abba! Father!' cry,
   as now his face we see!

2. Now with the virgin pure,
   we stand in awe and wonder,
   this great mysterious word
   to treasure and to ponder;
   the word of perfect grace
   by simple shepherds told,
   yet ever more profound
   than scholar's mind can hold!

3. O Abba! Father! God!
   Your children seek your blessing,
   who stand before your throne,
   imperfect praise expressing.
   O bless us with your peace,
   preserve us by your grace,
   and let us here behold
   the radiance of your face!

487

2nd Sunday after Christmas: Year ABC

1. Word made flesh, eternal Wisdom,
   born from above,
   light and life of all creation,
   perfect in love;
   faithful to the Father's sending,
   perfectly our nature blending
   by the Spirit's pow'r, attending
   as holy Dove.

2. Spread through all the world
   your presence,
   fragrant with grace;
   let eternal truth enlighten
   all time and space!
   Come, the Father's love revealing,
   to our wayward souls appealing,
   till within his presence kneeling,
   we see his face.

Continued overleaf

3. Blessèd be our God and Father,
   Saviour and Lord,
   calling us to be his children
   sending his Word,
   who before the world's foundation
   planned our undeserved salvation;
   hail him God of all creation,
   ever adored!

488

The Epiphany of the Lord: Year ABC

1. Arise to greet the Lord of light,
   you people of his choice.
   In uncreated glory bright,
   he bursts upon our inward sight,
   and bids the heart rejoice,
   and bids the heart rejoice!

2. Towards his light shall kings be drawn
   this majesty to see;
   and in the brightness of the dawn
   shall see the world in hope reborn,
   in justice full and free,
   in justice full and free.

3. The holy light in Judah's skies
   calls sages from afar.
   The hope of kings they recognise
   which, in the virgin mother's eyes,
   outshines the guiding star,
   outshines the guiding star!

4. This majesty for long concealed
   from longing human sight,
   in Jesus Christ is now revealed,
   and God's eternal promise sealed
   in love's unending light,
   in love's unending light.

489

The Baptism of the Lord: Year A

1. Behold the Servant of the Lord,
   the chosen one, his soul's delight,
   within whose heart the Spirit dwells
   of faith and justice, truth and light.

2. He will not raise his voice aloud,
   nor do to death the struggling flame,
   but bring forth justice on the earth,
   and nations all shall own his name.

3. The great baptismal act is o'er,
   now hear the thunder from above,
   and see the co-eternal Son,
   resplendent in the Father's love.

4. So now to all the world proclaim
   the news of universal grace,
   and let the name of Christ be known
   in ev'ry nation, tribe and race.

490

The Baptism of the Lord: Year B

1. God, whose thoughts and ways exalted,
   human wisdom cannot know,
   pour on us your Holy Spirit,
   let your goodness overflow.
   Alleluia! Alleluia!
   Truth and justice here may grow!

2. Thoughts of truth and ways of freedom
   your incarnate Word revealed,
   with authority of heaven
   in the Holy Spirit sealed.
   Alleluia! Alleluia!
   Here our mortal wounds are healed.

3. Spirit of the risen Saviour,
   bearer still of life divine:
   by the signs of blood and water,
   faith and hope in us refine.
   Alleluia! Alleluia!
   Feed our souls with bread and wine.

491

The Baptism of the Lord: Year C

1. All the glory of the heavens
   is to humankind revealed,
   with the news of sin forgiven,
   hungry fed and broken healed.
   See it here in sign and symbol,
   by the Holy Spirit sealed.

2. We have seen God's love in action,
   hope reborn and life restored
   by the power of the Spirit,
   and the cleansing water poured.
   Christ, the Word of life abundant,
   be by all the world adored!

3. Not baptised in water only,
   but in Spirit and in fire,
   looking for the consummation
   of the great divine desire,
   let us live in expectation,
   and to higher truth aspire.

492

Ash Wednesday: Year ABC

1. Holy God, of righteous glory,
   see your people gathered here,
   in a solemn congregation,
   your forgiving word to hear.
   God of love and slow to anger,
   gracious, longing to restore,
   hear your priests and people calling,
   give us grace to sin no more.

2. We confess the pride we suffer,
   needs which none can satisfy;
   how we love the praise of mortals,
   swift to flow'r and quick to die.
   Let us find rewards eternal
   as we quietly seek your face,
   and our open, public living
   witness only to your grace.

3. Free us from our self-bound living,
   better witnesses to be,
   to the world by grace appealing,
   telling forth the mystery:
   how creation's pure Redeemer
   walked among us undefiled,
   by his deathless love proclaiming,
   God with us is reconciled.

493

1st Sunday of Lent: Year A

1. Lord of creation,
   forgive us we pray
   for following Adam's
   rebellious way;
   subdue our ambitions
   and restless desires,
   and open our hearing
   to the Word who inspires.

2. Sad and bereft,
   O what beauty we lose,
   in seeking creation
   to own and abuse!
   O how we exploit her
   for profit and gain,
   not hearing her protest,
   nor aware of her pain!

3. Keep our religion
   from poison and stain,
   and let us not use it
   for glory or gain;
   in truer perspective
   our vision restore
   as you and you only
   we exalt and adore.

Continued overleaf

4. Point us to Christ,
   in whose passion we see
   forgiveness and mercy
   both priceless and free.
   At last may we stand
   in the light of his face,
   in kinship created,
   and forgiven by grace.

494

2nd Sunday of Lent: Year A

1. Here in this holy time and place,
   transfigured Lord,
   grant us to know your perfect grace
   by sign and word.

2. Then let us on our journey move,
   leaving behind
   passions and cares which
     hindrance prove,
   for heart and mind.

3. Let us not seek for cheap relief
   from loss and shame,
   but tread the holy path of grief,
   Christ, in your name.

4. Here may we celebrate the grace
   so long concealed,
   now in the glory of your face
   fully revealed.

495

3rd Sunday Of Lent: Year A

1. O God of all truth,
   our doubting forgive,
   our caution remove,
   and teach us to live.
   Renew by your mercy
   the spirit within,
   and flood with submission
   the dryness of sin.

2. This gospel of grace
   is ours to proclaim:
   Christ Jesus restores
   from sin and from shame.
   The water of freedom
   the sinner may share,
   the broken find healing
   and love past compare!

3. O mercy profound,
   ineffable grace!
   The fullness of love
   is seen in his face.
   He died for us sinners
   while sinful we stood,
   who, saved by his passion,
   are counted as good.

496

4th Sunday of Lent: Year A

1. Holy Shepherd, King divine,
   meet us in this holy place;
   gather all our wayward hearts
   in the warmth of your embrace.
   Here accept the praise we sing,
   and the humble gifts we bring.

2. God who chose and crowned as King
   one who played the shepherd's part,
   unimpressive to the eye,
   but of true and faithful heart,
   look on ev'ry upturned face
   with the knowing eye of grace.

3. Holy Shepherd, set us free
   from the terrors of the night;
   open now our sightless eyes;
   let us see creation's Light,
   and with all the world rejoice
   as the Spirit gives us voice!

497

5th Sunday of Lent: Year A

1. O God of our fathers,
   almighty to save,
   come rescue our spirits
   from sin's early grave.
   Enliven our souls
   with the promise of grace,
   and give us the courage
   new life to embrace.

2. Though deeply entombed
   in the cavern of shame,
   we thrill to the Saviour
   who calls us by name!
   Released from despair
   and assured of our worth,
   we welcome with rapture
   the call to come forth!

3. Now, freed from enslavement
   to sin and to death,
   we sing of this grace as
   the Spirit gives breath,
   and order our lives,
   both in action and word,
   as those who are sharing
   the joy of the Lord.

4. All honour and glory
   to Father and Son,
   and life-giving Spirit,
   eternally one,
   whose promise of perfect
   salvation we know,
   and from whose abundance
   true justice will flow.

498

1st Sunday of Lent: Year B

1. O God of truth, your dreadful might,
   in judgement's flood was shown;
   yet to our undeserving sight,
   in gracious arcs of dancing light,
   your promises are known,
   your promises are known.

2. By light and water, still you bring
   your people to your side,
   who drink from hope's eternal Spring,
   and joyful songs of freedom sing
   with Christ, now glorified,
   with Christ, now glorified.

3. The way of truth shall be our choice,
   with all its doubt and fear;
   let us not heed the tempter's voice,
   but in the gospel word rejoice:
   'Behold the kingdom near!
   Behold the kingdom near!'

499

2nd Sunday of Lent: Year B

1. Remember, O God,
   your mercies of old;
   come quickly to save,
   to heal and to hold.
   Our spirits are prompted
   to seek for your face,
   and find in your presence
   compassion and grace.

2. You suffered to save
   the broken and lost,
   not shirking the pain,
   nor counting the cost.
   The hopes we most cherish
   we lay at your throne,
   and trust for our future
   your goodness alone.

Continued overleaf

3. Your promise of hope
   now dawns on our sight,
   as Christ is revealed,
   resplendent in light.
   The past and the present
   transfigured we see,
   foretelling the future
   untainted and free.

500

3rd Sunday of Lent: Year B

1. The wisdom of the living God
   is seen in Jesus crucified;
   such weakness can unite and heal
   where human pow'r and
       strength divide.

2. The ancient books contain the law
   of love for God and humankind;
   the Word incarnate lives and breathes
   with grace and mercy unconfined!

3. Both grace and judgement here
       are found,
   his body is the perfect sign:
   though once by human
       hands destroyed,
   now raised, and filled with life divine.

4. Redeemer God, O give us grace
   to find new life in one who died,
   and call the world to rise and share
   the wisdom of the Crucified.

501

4th Sunday of Lent: Year B

1. From death to life restored,
   from sin to hope reborn,
   we see the light of judgement's fire
   become salvation's dawn.

2. God's work of art we are,
   in Christ for wholeness made,
   though dead in sin, now brought to life,
   by grace and mercy saved.

3. For God so loved the world
   that Christ, incarnate, came
   confronting evil, fear and death
   with love's eternal claim.

4. Then let the world rejoice
   to see salvation's dawn,
   when all creation is at peace,
   by grace and faith reborn.

502

5th Sunday of Lent: Year B

1. See, the promised time is coming,
   when the covenant of grace,
   in unbroken truth and freedom,
   all creation will embrace.
   Then shall God be known
       and worshipped
   by the greatest and the least,
   in the light of perfect justice,
   at the royal kingdom's feast.

2. To a life of prayer and passion,
   Christ, the Word eternal came;
   found perfection in obedience,
   and received the highest name.
   Author of the world's salvation,
   teach us humbly to obey,
   sharing in the pain and sorrow
   of redemption's costly way.

3. Saviour Christ, eternal Victim,
   seed of hope who fell and died,
   with the pow'rless and exploited
   may the church be glorified.
   Let our lives be freely scattered
   in the dark, oppressive ground,
   till the day when peace and justice,
   God's great harvest, will abound.

503

1. God, we call upon you;
   hear us and answer;
   rescue us from evil,
   for grace and pow'r are yours.
   From our long enslavement,
   lead us out to freedom
   and, in compassion,
   all our lives restore.

2. On the desert journey,
   tested and tempted,
   give us grace and courage,
   your sacrifice to share,
   not for easy glory,
   comfort or advantage,
   seeking to profit
   from the faith we bear.

3. Keep us ever faithful,
   always confessing,
   both by word and action,
   the truth our hearts believe.
   Then, in love, embracing
   all without distinction,
   life in abundance
   call us to receive.

504

2nd Sunday of Lent: Year C

1. God of eternal light,
   your promises we claim;
   as Abram's heirs, we recognise
   the honour of your name.
   Our sacrifice accept,
   our lives of faith inspire,
   and ev'ry fearful heart transform
   with purifying fire.

2. High on the mountain side
   your glory was revealed,
   and yet, that great mysterious light
   a deeper truth concealed!
   What fearful shadows still
   those sights and sounds portray:
   a dreadful kind of majesty
   that words cannot convey!

3. Christ, from the heav'ns descend,
   eternal life make known,
   and all our mortal bodies change
   to copies of your own.
   Your great and glorious light
   creation then shall see,
   when truth and peace are all around,
   and justice flowing free!

505

3rd Sunday of Lent: Year C

1. The fire of grace and judgement
   burns brightly on the plain,
   and calls your pilgrim people
   to journey once again.
   From forced and futile labour
   you long to set us free;
   a God of hope and freedom
   is what you choose to be!

2. We follow in the footsteps
   of Moses' ancient race,
   who, in the Red Sea waters,
   received baptismal grace.
   The rock provided water
   to nourish mind and soul,
   yet many, still rebellious,
   would fail to reach their goal.

Continued overleaf

3. We stand as equal sinners,
   dependent on your grace;
   we come in true repentance
   to seek your saving face.
   O God of hope, release us
   to walk the kingdom's ways,
   till justice joins with freedom
   to offer perfect praise.

506

4th Sunday of Lent: Year C

1. We celebrate the new creation,
   to God, in Christ, now reconciled,
   and recognise our full salvation
   in him whom people once reviled.

2. In token of our liberation,
   within God's presence now we stand,
   to share the banquet of salvation,
   the harvest of the promised land.

3. The news of reconciliation
   is now entrusted to our care;
   so spread the word throughout creation,
   the feast is here for all to share.

4. Begin the joyful celebration:
   the lost return, the dead arise,
   to see the light of exultation
   which shines from God's forgiving eyes.

507

5th Sunday of Lent: Year C

1. Great God, who opened up the sea,
   and led your ransomed people through,
   help us to leave the past behind,
   and let your grace our lives renew.

2. You are our refuge and our strength;
   the cause of justice you defend.
   In place of death you give us hope,
   and promise life that has no end.

3. In Christ the life renewed we find,
   who comes the sinner to restore;
   who sets the guilty spirit free
   to live again, and sin no more.

4. O help us leave, with willing hearts,
   the worldly wealth we count as dross,
   for life in all its glory shines
   beyond the shadow of the cross.

508

Passion (Palm) Sunday: Year ABC

1. What dreadful sight is this,
   by fear and envy wrought;
   the faithful servant of the Lord
   in pain and death distraught!

2. But God will give him strength,
   with patience to endure,
   and bring him through this time of trial
   in word and action pure.

3. And now, before our eyes,
   a myst'ry so divine;
   redemption's wondrous story, told
   in broken bread and wine!

4. The co-eternal Son,
   in splendour bright arrayed,
   for us his glory set aside
   and unto death obeyed.

5. Exalted now above,
   and giv'n the highest name,
   him shall all nations, kings and powers
   eternally acclaim.

509

Holy Thursday: Year ABC

1. God of the Passover,
   Author and Lord of salvation,
   gladly we gather to bring you
   our hearts' adoration;
   ransomed and free,
   called and commissioned to be
   signs of your love for creation.

2. Here we remember that
   evening of wonder enthralling,
   myst'ry of passion divine,
   and betrayal appalling.
   Breaking the bread,
   'This is my body,' he said,
   'do this, my passion recalling.'

3. God of the Eucharist,
   humbly we gather before you,
   and, at your table,
   for pardon and grace we implore you.
   Under the cross,
   counting as profit our loss,
   safe in its shade, we adore you.

510

Good Friday: Year ABC

1. Day of wrath and day of wonder,
   whence hope has fled!
   See the body torn asunder,
   blood freely shed.
   Stripped of majesty we saw him,
   human sight recoiled before him,
   yet it was our sorrows tore him;
   for us he bled.

2. Day of hope and day of glory,
   though unperceived!
   See redemption's dreadful story,
   long, long conceived.
   Evil pow'rs, in downfall lying,
   knowing death itself is dying,
   hear the voice triumphant crying,
   'All is achieved!'

3. Day of majesty and splendour,
   here ends the race!
   Christ, our Priest, our souls' defender,
   us will embrace.
   He who walked this earth before us,
   tried and tempted, yet victorious,
   calls us to the kingdom glorious,
   O perfect grace!

511

Easter Sunday: Year ABC

1. To him who died is now restored
   the life he gladly gave.
   We worship here the Lord of life,
   now risen, risen, risen,
   risen from the grave!

2. The misty light of early dawn
   reveals an empty cave.
   How vain to search the tomb for one
   now risen, risen, risen,
   risen from the grave!

3. His were the hands that healed
      the sick,
   and made the fearful brave.
   Though once despised, his pow'r
      we see
   now risen, risen, risen,
   risen from the grave!

Continued overleaf

4. The pleasures of this passing age
   cannot our souls enslave;
   for true contentment rests with him,
   now risen, risen, risen,
   risen from the grave!

5. To all the nations we proclaim,
   'The pow'r to heal and save
   is vested in the living Lord
   now risen, risen, risen,
   risen from the grave!'

512

2nd Sunday of Easter: Year A

1. Blest be the God and Father
   of Jesus Christ our Lord,
   for hope to sinners given,
   through his unfailing word;
   the promise of redemption
   eternally is sealed,
   and Christ in deathless glory
   by broken tomb revealed.

2. Here let the bread be broken
   of fellowship and peace,
   and in our blest communion
   the anxious find release.
   Our life of common sharing
   foretells the life to come,
   where truth and justice flower
   in heav'n's eternal home.

3. Although we have not seen it,
   his promise we believe;
   what minds can never capture
   our hearts by faith receive.
   Our spirits thirst with longing,
   like infants at the breast,
   to see the Saviour's glory,
   and in his presence rest.

513

3rd Sunday of Easter: Year A

1. The risen Lord we now confess
   as him the world has once denied.
   His deeds of uncreated power
   to Godly nature testified.

2. Though scorned, betrayed and done
      to death,
   the grave his life could not confine;
   he scorned its pow'r and burst its seal,
   and meets us here in bread and wine.

3. The Lord has walked our lonely road,
   and shared the fear we all have known.
   He breaks with us the bread of life,
   whereby his presence still is shown.

4. Forsaking all our vain desires,
   the saving blood of Christ we claim.
   In rev'rent fear and holy joy,
   we call upon the Father's name.

514

4th Sunday of Easter: Year A

1. Let the world in concert name him,
   Jesus Christ, the one who died,
   by the Father now exalted,
   as Messiah glorified.
   O creation, seek salvation
   in an outcast crucified!

2. Patiently for us he suffered;
   all the lost are his concern.
   Innocent, he bears our sorrow;
   his forbearance we may learn.
   Now confiding, nothing hiding,
   to the Shepherd we return.

3. Still the risen Saviour calls us;
   we for him must make our choice.
   Gladly will we rise and follow,
   knowing well the Shepherd's voice,
   calling, leading, for us pleading,
   where the saints in light rejoice.

515

5th Sunday of Easter: Year A

1. The temple of the living God
   is built of living stones,
   a holy people, called to live
   by light of Christ alone.
   With special joy we celebrate
   the word the psalmist said:
   'The stone the builders cast aside
   is now the corner's head!'

2. The temple of the living God
   is set secure above,
   where Christ invites the world
     to share
   his perfect reign of love.
   And we who seek the Father's face
   are summoned to obey,
   and follow where he goes before,
   the Life, the Truth, the Way.

3. The temple of the living God
   upon the earth must grow,
   and those of ev'ry race and class
   his true compassion know.
   The widow and the fatherless
   receive a special care,
   till all creation, just and free,
   his perfect peace will share.

516

6th Sunday of Easter: Year A

1. Let all the world exultant sing,
   in holy harmony,
   and constant alleluias ring
   to God who sets us free.

2. We own the name of Christ, who died
   in agony and shame,
   now by the Spirit glorified
   with heaven's highest name.

3. His is the name by which we live;
   his passion we embrace,
   and glory to the Saviour give
   for his abundant grace.

4. O Holy Spirit, come in power
   to liberate and save;
   bring life to all whose spirits cower
   in fear's unholy grave.

5. Let all the world exultant sing,
   in holy harmony,
   by word and action honouring
   the blessèd Trinity.

517

The Ascension of the Lord: Year A

1. Hail the risen Lord, ascending
   to his holy Father's side,
   angels lost in awe and wonder
   now acclaim the Lord who died.
   Alleluia, alleluia,
   Christ triumphant, glorified!

2. He who once, from royal splendour,
   came to share our state of blame,
   now ascends in clouds of glory
   to the heights from which he came.
   Alleluia, alleluia,
   Christ for evermore the same!

3. He will grant his praying servants,
   from the riches of his power,
   grace to live as risen people
   in this present watching hour.
   Alleluia, alleluia,
   God on us his blessings shower.

Continued overleaf

4. Now he bids us tell his story,
   where the lost and fearful roam:
   he will come again triumphant,
   and will lead his people home.
   Alleluia, alleluia.
   Maranatha! Come, Lord, come!

518

7th Sunday of Easter: Year A

1. Father, bless your people,
   that we may be one,
   sharing in the glory
   of your only Son;
   held and forgiven,
   reconciled by grace,
   knowing life eternal,
   here in time and space.

2. In these special moments,
   lightly we may pray;
   but in humbler service
   faithful let us stay;
   and, when we gather
   in the simplest place,
   show us in each other
   your incarnate face.

3. When we face injustice
   for the faith we claim,
   let us know we suffer
   in the Saviour's name.
   Victims forgotten,
   innocents accused,
   know the silent protest
   of their Christ abused.

4. Praise the blessèd Father,
   and eternal Son,
   praise the Holy Spirit,
   ever Three-in-One.
   Perfect Communion,
   rich diversity,
   essence of creation,
   blessèd Trinity!

519

2nd Sunday of Easter: Year B

1. 'We have not seen the risen Saviour
   in flesh and blood before our eyes!'
   The frailty of our mortal senses
   for proof, unveiled and certain, cries.

2. But Christ, the Word of God incarnate,
   has overcome the world's desires,
   and in the Spirit's life abundant
   a surer faith in us inspires.

3. The risen Christ we now acknowledge,
   who meets us here in bread and wine,
   and calls us into close communion
   to share the fellowship divine.

4. Now in the homeless, poor and lonely,
   his face we learn to recognise.
   There may we see the risen Saviour
   in flesh and blood before our eyes!

520

3rd Sunday of Easter: Year B

1. The 'justice' of this fallen world
   in all its shame we see,
   when innocents are crucified
   to keep the brutal free.
   But greater is the God of truth,
   who raised the Crucified,
   and calls us all to life and hope
   in Christ, now glorified.

2. He shows his wounded hands and feet
   to all who live in fear,
   and both in word and sacrament
   reveals the kingdom near.
   And still, in places dark with death,
   he calls us to his side
   as witnesses of living hope
   to people crucified.

3. The Word of life reveals the way
   of sacrificial love,
   encompassed by the God of hope,
   in whom we live and move.
   In Christ, the perfect Sacrifice,
   is full atonement found;
   then let the earth, from pole to pole,
   with joyful praise resound!

521

4th Sunday of Easter: Year B

1. The pow'r of God throughout
      the world
   is gloriously displayed,
   and in the breathing of the word
   the universe was made.

2. The Word is breathed with
      living power
   to heal and to restore;
   the name of Christ brings health
      and hope
   and justice to the poor.

3. As children of the living God
   we take our proper place;
   by love redeemed, yet still to learn
   the full extent of grace.

4. Then praise the God of perfect love,
   who longs to save the lost;
   and praise the Word whose life reveals
   the glory and the cost.

522

5th Sunday of Easter: Year B

Sing a new and joyful song
to God who makes us one;
he the nations' hope reveals
by pow'r of love alone.

1. God's presence is around us,
   and yet we have no fear;
   we find no accusation
   nor condemnation here.

2. On Christ alone depending
   the life divine we share,
   and fruits of peace and justice
   the healthy vine will bear.

3. God give us grace and courage
   this gospel to proclaim:
   the word of perfect freedom
   and justice, in his name.

523

6th Sunday of Easter: Year B

1. Come, let us live by love
   which flows from God alone,
   whose life and truth in Christ we see,
   in radiant beauty shown.
   The Spirit gives us grace
   to follow where Christ trod,
   and know that ev'ryone who loves
   is born and known of God.

2. God is the only source
   of love that knows no end;
   which, open to another's pain,
   itself will gladly spend.
   This is the great command,
   to live the life of heav'n
   where ev'rything we own is shared
   and love is freely giv'n.

3. Wake to the Spirit's voice,
   proclaiming from outside,
   'In unexpected people, still,
   will God be glorified,
   whose love embraces all,
   of ev'ry creed and race;
   so praise, with them, love's
      only Source,
   the God of truth and grace!'

524

1. Christ, in risen pow'r ascended,
   promise of the life to be;
   from our fears and narrow vision
   set our earth-bound spirits free.
   For your kingdom, for your kingdom,
   keep us watching constantly,
   keep us watching constantly.

2. Where our earthly kings and empires
   over all their subjects tower,
   may your rule of peace and justice
   truer splendour bring to flower.
   Give us wisdom, give us wisdom
   to perceive a humbler power,
   to perceive a humbler power.

3. Christ, in risen pow'r ascended,
   given now the highest name,
   let us speak of truth and wholeness,
   and injustice put to shame.
   Alleluia! Alleluia!
   Grace and judgement we proclaim,
   grace and judgement we proclaim!

525

1. Hear us, O God, when we
   call on your name;
   your mercy and justice
   are ever the same.
   Our hearts prompt us daily
   to look for your face,
   O do not hide from us
   the abundance of grace.

2. Saviour, you call us
   new life to proclaim,
   with hope for the fearful
   and strength for the lame;
   your spirit unites us
   as witnesses all,
   who live in your presence
   and respond to your call.

3. You we acknowledge,
   your love we have known;
   within you our spirits
   have quickened and grown.
   We share in your Spirit
   of freedom divine;
   let love and love only
   be our token and sign.

4. Call us, unite us
   and send us by grace
   the broken and guilty
   to heal and embrace;
   to love may we witness,
   with common accord,
   in truth consecrated,
   by the pow'r of the word.

526

1. Come, Holy Spirit,
   the Breath in the Word of salvation,
   breathe in the church,
   with the promise of life for creation.
   Grace is revealed,
   bodies and spirits are healed,
   joining the great celebration!

2. Give us the faith
   to believe without touching and seeing;
   open our hearts and enliven
   the depths of our being.
   Give us your peace,
   calling our doubting to cease,
   hope and creativeness freeing.

3. Alpha and Omega,
   Christ the beginning and ending,
   come in the glory of heaven,
   your servants befriending:
   one who had died,
   now over all glorified,
   death and its terrors transcending.

527

3rd Sunday of Easter: Year C

1. O God of hope and justice,
   let us not be dismayed
   when Godless opposition
   demands to be obeyed.
   You claim our first allegiance,
   our honour you command,
   for Christ to risen glory
   was lifted by your hand.

2. You meet us in the presence
   of failure and regret,
   to mortal eyes revealing
   a greater glory yet;
   and those who once have fallen
   to wholeness you restore;
   the word of pardon lifts us
   to life for evermore.

3. Then, 'To the Lamb be glory!'
   the shining hosts proclaim,
   and all creation honours
   the life-renewing name.
   Ten thousand times ten thousand,
   and countless thousands more,
   the great 'Amen!' re-echo
   and joyfully adore.

528

4th Sunday of Easter: Year C

1. Sing the gospel of salvation,
   tell it out to all the earth;
   to the ones so long excluded,
   speak of hope and human worth.
   All the darkness of injustice
   cannot dim salvation's light,
   for the outcast and exploited
   count as worthy in God's sight.

2. Christ, the one eternal Shepherd,
   calls creation to rejoice,
   and the victims of oppression
   thrill to hear salvation's voice.
   All who recognise the Saviour
   take their place within the fold,
   there, in perfect truth and freedom,
   life's eternal joys to hold.

3. See, the host that none can number
   gathers in from ev'ry side,
   once the victims of injustice,
   now redeemed and glorified.
   Fear and weeping here are ended,
   hunger and oppression cease.
   Now the Lamb becomes
     the Shepherd!
   Now begins the reign of peace!

529

5th Sunday of Easter: Year C

1. 'As I have loved you,
   love one another;
   this is the moment,
   this is the place.'
   Jesus has spoken
   his new commandment,
   making us holy,
   giving us grace.

Continued overleaf

2. Gospel of wholeness
   tell to the nations;
   into the kingdom
   open the door.
   Help and encourage
   in perseverance;
   conflicts and hardships
   gladly endure.

3. Earth and the heavens
   long for renewal,
   just as the bridegroom
   waits for the bride.
   Pain will be ended,
   death non-existent,
   God in creation
   be glorified.

530

6th Sunday of Easter: Year C

1. Holy Spirit, give us peace
   and our burdened souls release;
   liberate the hearts confined
   by the legalistic mind.
   On the law's unyielding face
   shine the living light of grace.

2. Call to mind the way preferred
   by the true incarnate Word,
   in whose perfect life is shown
   grace abundant, love unknown;
   lead us into truth divine,
   signified in bread and wine.

3. Let us now the vision see
   of the city fair and free,
   built on apostolic ground,
   with eternal glory crowned,
   sunless, yet for ever bright,
   with the Lamb its only light.

531

The Ascension of the Lord: Year C

1. The risen Saviour now ascends
   towards the highest place,
   and offers broken human flesh
   before the throne of grace!

2. His blood has opened up the way,
   salvation is secure,
   and we may stand within the veil
   in mind and body pure.

3. Through pain and death to life
      and hope,
   Christ trod the way of love,
   and he will clothe the church below
   with glory from above.

532

7th Sunday of Easter: Year C

1. Heaven is open wide,
   and Christ in glory stands,
   with all authority endowed
   and set at God's right hand.
   Above the world of noise
   extends his reign of peace,
   and all the blood of martyrs calls
   our angry ways to cease.

2. Heaven is open wide,
   and perfect love we see
   in God's eternal self revealed:
   the blessèd Trinity.
   Christ for the church has prayed,
   that we may all be one,
   and share the triune grace whereby
   creation was begun.

3. Heaven is open wide,
   and Christ in glory stands:
   the Source and End, the First and Last,
   with justice in his hands.
   Let all the thirsty come
   where life is flowing free,
   and Christ, in splendour yet unknown,
   our morning star will be.

533

Pentecost Sunday: Year A

1. Holy Spirit, to us given
   at the Pentecostal feast,
   breath of God and fire of heaven,
   promise of our great High Priest,
   fill our hearts with joy and wonder
   in this special Sabbath hour,
   burst the locks of fear asunder,
   send us out with risen power.

2. Holy Spirit, love undying,
   promise of the risen Lord,
   be your power unifying
   breathed in his eternal word.
   Pour on us your special blessing,
   members many, body one,
   Jesus Christ as Lord confessing,
   he the co-eternal Son.

3. Holy Spirit, in us living,
   vigour of the risen Lord,
   to our mortal bodies giving
   life, by sacrament and word,
   send us to the warring nations,
   to a world by sin defiled,
   with the gospel of salvation:
   all creation reconciled.

534

Pentecost Sunday: Year B

1. The Spirit of the living God
   upon the earth is poured,
   inspiring humankind with love
   God only can afford.

2. O Spirit, come to all who wait,
   in longing or in fear,
   and send us out to speak of hope
   in word and action clear.

3. You lead us from our darkest fears
   and self-indulgent ways,
   to where the light of truth and peace
   upon our vision plays.

4. Great Advocate, in ways of truth
   our wand'ring spirits guide,
   and in the giving of our lives
   may God be glorified.

535

Pentecost Sunday: Year C

1. Come, Spirit of our God,
   our lives with truth inspire,
   and burn within our fearful hearts
   like purifying fire.

2. Fill ev'ry heart with love;
   the word we would obey.
   O teach us all we need to know
   of your most holy way.

3. Come with the gift of life,
   our nature to refine;
   as sons and daughters let us live,
   the heirs of love divine.

Continued overleaf

4. Give us a willing voice
   to speak in ev'ry place,
   wherever doubts and fears confine,
   of liberating grace.

536

1. Behold the glory long concealed,
   though to the prophet shown;
   in dark mysterious cloud once sealed,
   this majesty is now revealed,
   to mortal sight made known,
   to mortal sight made known!

2. The Father of eternal love
   his Son incarnate gave,
   with grace and glory from above,
   death's final curtain to remove,
   and Adam's children save,
   and Adam's children save.

3. With joy and praise, eternally,
   creation will resound,
   to Father, Son and Spirit, three,
   one undivided Trinity,
   O Mystery profound,
   O Mystery profound!

537

1. Lead us to freedom,
   God of liberty;
   Father, Son and Spirit,
   holy One-in-Three.
   Still, in grace and judgement,
   we may hear your voice;
   freedom and obedience
   both shall be your choice.

   Lead us to freedom,
   God of liberty;
   Father, Son and Spirit,
   holy One-in-Three.

2. We, by the Spirit,
   'Abba! Father!' cry;
   now to hope and freedom
   let us testify.
   Both in joy and sorrow,
   heirs, with Christ, of God,
   let us dare to follow
   where his feet have trod.

3. Christ, lead us onward,
   in your glorious power,
   calling all to freedom
   in the present hour.
   Give us faith and courage,
   born of hope sublime,
   knowing you are with us
   to the end of time.

538

1. O holy wisdom, found at play
   before the world was born,
   you danced in light's first dawning ray,
   delighting in the primal day
   which saw creation's dawn,
   which saw creation's dawn.

2. Come, Holy Spirit, gift divine
   of Father and of Son;
   reveal the truth by word and sign,
   and celebrate in bread and wine
   the life in God begun,
   the life in God begun.

3. Eternal God of time and space,
   create, sustain, restore.
   Through Jesus Christ, by faith
      and grace,
   let us your patient hope embrace,
   and let the world adore,
   and let the world adore!

539

Corpus Christi: Year A

1. Holy God, your pilgrim people
   by you were fed,
   through the vast and dreadful desert
   guided and led;
   water from the rock-face pouring,
   hope to ev'ry heart restoring,
   sets the failing spirit soaring,
   life from the dead!

2. Living bread for mortals broken,
   gift from above,
   live in us the life eternal,
   perfect in love.
   Come, the word of
      wholeness bringing,
   where our fearful souls are clinging;
   and of life abundant singing,
   all fear remove.

3. One the bread and one the chalice,
   one work of grace;
   one the church of Christ, united
   in his embrace.
   One the gospel of salvation,
   for the wholeness of creation:
   Christ is poured in ev'ry nation,
   and ev'ry race.

540

Corpus Christi: Year B

1. God of the covenant,
   yours is the word of salvation,
   moving the heart to repentance
   and true adoration.
   Blood is the seal,
   pow'rful to cleanse and to heal,
   sprinkled on all your creation.

2. God of the covenant,
   known in the breaking and pouring,
   body and blood of the Saviour,
   creation restoring:
   here we prepare,
   Christ, in your passion to share,
   humbly your presence adoring.

3. God of the covenant,
   yours is the Word of salvation
   bearing the terrible cost
   of the world's liberation.
   Freedom at last!
   Christ through the curtain has passed.
   God is at one with creation!

541

Corpus Christi: Year C

1. See the holy table,
   spread for our healing;
   hear the invitation
   to share in bread and wine.
   Catch the scent of goodness,
   taste and touch salvation;
   all mortal senses
   tell of love divine!

Continued overleaf

2. As the bread is broken,
   Christ is remembered;
   as the wine is flowing,
   his passion we recall;
   as redemption's story
   opens up before us,
   hope is triumphant,
   Christ is all in all.

3. Tell again the story,
   wonder of wonders:
   Christ, by grace eternal,
   transforms the simplest food!
   Sign of hope and glory,
   life in all its fullness,
   God's whole creation
   ransomed and renewed!

542

2nd Sunday in Ordinary Time: Year A

1. Thus says the Lord of hosts
   to his belov'd creation,
   'My servant I commend,
   a light for ev'ry nation.
   My people he will call
   from ev'ry time and place,
   and wholeness, my desire,
   this broken world embrace.'

2. Behold, the Lamb of God,
   our sinful souls befriending.
   The Spirit is his sign,
   in pow'r and grace descending.
   Of higher nature he
   than all who went before,
   to lost and guilty come,
   with perfect grace in store.

3. Now may the Father's grace,
   to all the world be given,
   through his eternal Son,
   with perfect peace of heaven.
   O fellowship divine,
   and love's eternal spring,
   your never-ending praise
   let all creation sing!

543

3rd Sunday in Ordinary Time: Year A

1. Sing to God a song of gladness,
   tell his glory, all the earth;
   robed in truth and full of beauty,
   he who wrought creation's birth!
   Alleluia! Alleluia!
   Laud and honour are his worth,
   laud and honour are his worth!

2. Once in deepest darkness living,
   we have seen a wondrous light;
   all the brightness of salvation
   bursts upon our waiting sight!
   Alleluia! Alleluia!
   See the darkness put to flight,
   see the darkness put to flight!

3. From the pride and predilections
   which the holy church divide,
   we are called to true communion
   in the light of him who died.
   Alleluia! Alleluia!
   To the Saviour crucified,
   to the Saviour crucified!

544

4th Sunday in Ordinary Time: Year A

1. O God of hope, your people save
   who cry for justice in your name.
   The poor and humble glorify,
   and put the pow'r of might to shame.

2. In perfect wisdom you have called
   the 'nothings' whom the
      proud despise,
   and those we count of little worth
   you use to shame the worldly-wise.

3. O let us see in those who weep
   the image of the Saviour's tears,
   and, in his likeness, cultivate
   the eye that sees, the ear that hears.

4. So may our only wisdom be
   the folly of the Crucified;
   let justice be our one desire
   and Christ himself our only pride.

545

5th Sunday in Ordinary Time: Year A

1. Come, let us worship
   the Lord of our birth,
   who stretched out the heavens
   and founded the earth;
   his love never falters,
   his mercy is sure;
   in hope ever faithful
   shall his kingdom endure.

2. Christ bids us serve him
   as salt and as light,
   to make of creation
   a feast of delight;
   for justice and mercy
   should flavour the earth,
   but salt bland and tasteless
   is devoid of all worth.

3. Wholeness and health
   in creation restore,
   give bread to the hungry
   and shelter the poor;
   find clothes for the naked,
   relieve the oppressed,
   and thereby discover,
   he who blesses is blessed!

4. O may the gospel
   so simply be told,
   no artful philosophy
   here to unfold!
   We nothing need know
   but the death of the Lord,
   and trust not in words,
   but in the pow'r of the Word!

546

6th Sunday in Ordinary Time: Year A

1. O holy wisdom, gracious offer
   of fire or water, life or death!
   We choose the joy of holy living,
   enlivened by the Spirit's breath.

2. But now behold, with woe
      and wonder,
   the wisdom of the dying Lord,
   from chosen death his
      world redeeming
   at cost we never could afford!

3. This wisdom, ev'ry law surpassing,
   comes not to cancel or replace,
   but breathes into those
      lifeless strictures
   the unrestricted life of grace.

4. Praise Father, Son and Holy Spirit,
   eternal, blessèd One-in-Three;
   our strength, our guide,
      our pure salvation,
   the wisdom of the Trinity.

547

7th Sunday in Ordinary Time: Year A

1. Holy God, eternal Father,
   we, your church, would holy be.
   As your temple, here we gather;
   keep us from all malice free.
   Alleluia! Alleluia!
   Grant us here your face to see.

Continued overleaf

2. In your saving pow'r rejoicing,
   we would sing eternal praise,
   all our hope and homage voicing,
   holy God of endless days.
   Alleluia! Alleluia!
   Truth and mercy are your ways.

3. Holy Wisdom, now transcending
   all the strictures of the law,
   from the legal code unbending
   set us free to love you more!
   Alleluia! Alleluia!
   Perfect fellowship restore.

4. Holy God, eternal Father,
   we, your church, would holy be.
   As your temple, here we gather,
   now by grace and faith set free.
   Alleluia! Alleluia!
   Let us live abundantly!

548

8th Sunday in Ordinary Time: Year A

1. God is our strength from days of old,
   and now our hope will be.
   He loves us with a love profound,
   and longs to set us free.

2. Just as a mother loves and holds
   the baby at the breast,
   so God will hold his people close,
   and we in him may rest.

3. He clothes the flow'rs in glory bright,
   he sees the sparrow fall,
   and overflows with saving love
   for us who 'Abba!' call.

4. So, with no fear or vain reproach,
   his saving grace we own,
   and trusting only him, prepare
   to stand before his throne.

549

9th Sunday in Ordinary Time: Year A

1. O look upon us, Lord,
   be merciful and kind,
   and may our sin and poverty
   your true compassion find.

2. We long to keep the law,
   in which your love is known,
   to follow in the way of truth
   and trust in you alone.

3. And yet this truth we know:
   the law cannot atone;
   the sinner will be justified
   by grace and faith alone.

4. So on this rock we stand,
   and to it make appeal:
   our faith in Jesus crucified,
   and him our sign and seal.

5. O give us grace to know
   the Saviour's faithful ways,
   to live in sacrificial love
   and offer worthy praise.

550

10th Sunday in Ordinary Time: Year A

1. Come, O God, like morning light,
   bringing judgement clear and bright;
   come like water on the earth,
   calling life and hope to birth;
   come to bless the humble poor,
   and the sinner to restore.

2. God, whose promise was received
   when the patriarch believed,
   now your waiting people bless,
   counting faith as righteousness,
   sinners only justified
   by the blood of one who died.

3. Now, our faith professed to prove,
   fill our hearts with holy love;
   may we hold, with special grace,
   those the world will not embrace,
   in the people most denied,
   let us serve the Crucified.

551

11th Sunday in Ordinary Time: Year A

1. O God of the wilderness,
   mountain and plain,
   who rescued your people
   from slav'ry and pain,
   your goodness and grace
   in our hearts are made known,
   a kingdom and priesthood
   you choose as your own.

2. This gospel of joy to the world
   we proclaim:
   the grace of the Saviour
   is ever the same.
   The sick he will heal
   and the dead he will raise,
   and all of creation
   resound to his praise.

3. O wonder! O glory!
   O myst'ry unknown!
   What merciful goodness
   the Saviour has shown!
   He suffered for us,
   who by sin were defiled,
   and now counts us good,
   by his death reconciled.

4. O God of the exodus,
   God of the cross,
   you rescue your people
   at measureless cost!
   Through death and through desert
   you travel before;
   in faith let us follow,
   to praise and adore!

552

12th Sunday in Ordinary Time: Year A

1. Sing to God, praise the Lord!
   O what grace in his word!
   Hope of peace he affords,
   lifting up the lowly,
   bringing judgement holy.

   God is good, good, good,
   God is good, good, good,
   God our strength,
   God our song,
   God our guide for ever.

2. Jesus came, full of grace,
   light and truth in his face,
   to redeem Adam's race,
   conquered death in dying,
   perfect grace supplying.

3. He will come, have no fear,
   all that's hid will be clear,
   trust his love ever near,
   grace and truth abounding.
   Hear his praise resounding:

553

13th Sunday in Ordinary Time: Year A

1. O come, all nations, celebrate
   the promise of the Lord most high,
   that love will find its true reward,
   and hope itself will never die.

2. In Christ we have the promise sealed,
   who broke the tomb's appalling power;
   through water, fear and death
     he leads,
   and brings eternal life to flower.

Continued overleaf

3. We meet him in the stranger's face,
   when simple care and love are shown,
   and in the giving of his peace,
   the perfect grace of Christ is known.

4. Then let the nations shout with joy
   and, with a voice of singing, praise
   the one from whom all goodness flows,
   the holy God of endless days.

554

14th Sunday in Ordinary Time: Year A

1. O let us rejoice
   and welcome our King!
   Triumphant he comes,
   true justice to bring.
   No war-horse or chariot,
   no weapons or pride,
   but humbly he chooses
   a donkey to ride!

2. O let us rejoice
   in things of true worth,
   inverting by grace
   the values of earth.
   The things of the Spirit
   will ever endure,
   for life is his favour
   and mercy his cure.

3. O let us rejoice
   this myst'ry to know,
   which God in his love
   has chosen to show.
   Unspeakable wonder,
   unreachable prize,
   his gift to his children,
   yet veiled from the wise!

555

15th Sunday in Ordinary Time: Year A

1. The word of God, like seed, is sown
   upon the waiting land,
   and life-renewing water flows
   from God's attentive hand.
   His word can never fruitless be,
   his purpose will succeed,
   for grace abundant will fulfil
   the deepest human need.

2. Whatever pains we now endure
   can never be compared
   with all the glory yet to come,
   by Providence prepared.
   The Spirit joins with us, to share
   the groaning of the earth,
   which, by the grace of God, will be
   the pains of joyful birth.

3. The seed of life is freely spent
   on good and barren ground,
   and in the plenitude of grace
   the harvest will abound.
   In justice and in liberty,
   the Lord will show his face,
   revealing his abundant love
   to all the human race.

556

16th Sunday in Ordinary Time: Year A

1. To you, O Lord, our only help,
   our life in love upholding,
   we bring a willing sacrifice,
   our constant praise unfolding.

2. For you alone are Lord Most High,
   in light eternal living,
   and from the greatness of your power
   a gentle judgement giving.

3. O Holy Spirit, love divine,
   our halting tongues enlighten,
   and by your wordless sighs of grace
   our sense of glory heighten.

4. O Holy Reaper, come with grace
   to us, whose hearts adore you,
   who long to see your kingdom come
   and stand in joy before you.

557

17th Sunday in Ordinary Time: Year A

God is in his holy place,
his reign shall never cease.
He will give the poor a home
and bring his people peace.

1. To him for countless ages
   have kings and beggars prayed
   for faith and perfect wisdom,
   which cannot fail and fade.

2. He works with those who love him
   to see his purpose done,
   in faithful hearts perfecting
   the image of the Son.

3. This priceless pearl we long for:
   the faith that sets us free,
   to call both Lord and Brother
   the Christ of Calvary!

558

18th Sunday in Ordinary Time: Year A

1. O God of hope, your people hear;
   give peace to all who hurt or fear,
   with help and comfort ever near.

2. O you who give, with open hand,
   the produce of the sea and land,
   be bread for us who waiting stand.

3. There is no pow'r in time or space
   can keep us from this saving grace,
   now fully known in Jesus' face.

4. O risen Lord, our sense refine,
   to recognise the truth divine:
   yourself revealed in bread and wine!

5. In lonely places long ignored,
   we hear your voice, O serving Lord:
   'Give them the food that I afford.'

6. Then let us see the hungry fed,
   with truth and justice, wine and bread,
   and honour Christ, our living head.

559

19th Sunday in Ordinary Time: Year A

1. O God of truth and justice,
   defender of the poor,
   we trust your promise faithful,
   your mercy ever sure.
   Come not in fire or earthquake,
   or sign of worldly power,
   but let your gentle whisper
   announce the hallowed hour!

2. When storms of life around us
   condemn our hearts to fear,
   then let the voice of stillness
   compose the anxious ear,
   and from our fears remake us
   with faithful hearts and brave
   who, fixing on the Saviour,
   may ride the threatening wave.

3. O give us grace to follow
   where Christ himself has trod,
   with gentle voice proclaiming
   the perfect peace of God:
   the promise of redemption
   which first the fathers heard,
   in Jesus Christ made perfect,
   the co-eternal Word.

560

20th Sunday in Ordinary Time: Year A

1. Protector God, your people's strength,
   defender of the earth,
   a single day within your courts
   a thousand lost is worth!

2. You call for justice and for truth
   from all who bear your name;
   your perfect grace is known of old,
   and ever stays the same.

3. O let the nations come to know
   how steadfast is your love,
   who ev'ry promise will fulfil
   and ever faithful prove.

4. Then shall your all-sufficient grace
   throughout the world be spread,
   and all creation come to share
   your children's special bread.

561

21st Sunday in Ordinary Time: Year A

1. Great Father of light,
   in glory above,
   all wisdom and pow'r
   are gifts of your love.
   O look on all people
   of notable place,
   and let all their judgements
   be ruled by your grace.

2. Authority pure
   in Jesus we see,
   who humbled himself
   to set people free.
   The keys of the kingdom
   to Peter he gave,
   with pow'r and dominion
   to heal and to save.

3. O wonder untold!
   O mystery great;
   no art can design,
   nor mind penetrate!
   His infinite wisdom
   no author may pen.
   To him be all glory
   forever, amen!

562

22nd Sunday in Ordinary Time: Year A

1. God of prophecy and promise,
   give us grace to bear your name;
   in the place of structured evil
   let us light redemption's flame.
   O the fire prophetic, burning
   with a passion none can tame!

2. Let us not, for easy ransom,
   seek a cheaper price to pay;
   nor by faithless good intention
   bar the suff'ring Saviour's way.
   Lead us through the night of sorrow
   into glad salvation's day.

3. Grant us, in our life and worship,
   you alone to glorify;
   not afraid of truly living
   nor, for you, afraid to die.
   When the world, for fear, rejects us,
   'Alleluia!' may we cry!

563

23rd Sunday in Ordinary Time: Year A

1. O God of justice, righteous judge,
   what light your word imparts!
   Give us a clear prophetic voice
   and ever-gentle hearts.

2. May we on your transforming word
   our hearts for ever set;
   let peace our obligation be,
   and love our only debt.

3. May we, throughout our common life,
   the love of Christ reveal,
   by speaking truth in charity,
   and all our conflicts heal.

4. Then to the holy triune God
   let perfect praise ascend,
   when all the nations, bound in peace,
   bring conflict to an end.

564

24th Sunday in Ordinary Time: Year A

1. O all-forgiving God,
   your faithful people save,
   and hear the longing prayers of all
   who your compassion crave.

2. Give us forgiving hearts
   when others' rage we know,
   and let us not fan anger's flames
   but costly mercy show.

3. Of countless debts forgiven,
   such mercies we receive;
   but others' paltry debts recall,
   and make the Saviour grieve.

4. O high eternal Lord,
   who shared our mortal shame,
   the living and the dead shall own
   your all-redeeming name.

565

25th Sunday in Ordinary Time: Year A

1. Look to the Lord of life,
   and seek his way to learn;
   abandon ev'ry harmful thought
   and from all evil turn.
   O wonder unrevealed,
   so far our thoughts above,
   as far from us as heav'n from earth,
   his perfect way of love.

2. Here may we live by grace,
   from work's obsession freed,
   and reckon not with wages earned
   but only human need.
   It is his sov'reign right
   his mercies to bestow,
   with justice ever more profound
   than mortal mind can know.

3. O, for the life above
   incessantly we long;
   a life of unremitting joy
   and sweet angelic song.
   Yet higher thought demands
   we call this world our home,
   and share in all its joys and woes
   until his kingdom come.

566

26th Sunday in Ordinary Time: Year A

1. God of truth and justice,
   seated in splendour,
   freely we confess that
   our hearts have disobeyed.
   Father all-forgiving,
   merciful and tender,
   favour your people,
   let your hand be stayed.

Continued overleaf

2. O with wonder hear it:
   word all astounding!
   Now to saints and sinners
   is heaven open wide!
   See the risen Saviour,
   grace and truth abounding,
   welcome the people
   others have denied.

3. Christ from highest heaven,
   humbly descending,
   chose to set his glory
   and majesty aside;
   death in death defeating,
   hell's dominion ending,
   then by the Father
   fully glorified!

4. So shall ev'ry nation,
   kneeling before him,
   full of truth and beauty
   the Christ in glory see;
   ev'ry tongue confess him,
   ev'ry heart adore him,
   splendid in grace and
   endless mystery!

567

27th Sunday in Ordinary Time: Year A

1. God, the great Creator,
   sets the world in place,
   tenderly creating
   works of love and grace.
   Father of beauty,
   ev'rything you own,
   earth and stars and heaven
   are your royal throne.

2. Like a fertile vineyard,
   tilled with loving care,
   fruits of truth and justice
   should have flowered there.
   O shame indeed!
   When came the reaping hour,
   though with passion tended,
   ev'ry fruit was sour.

3. So our heav'nly Father
   sent his royal Son,
   into his creation,
   trusting grace alone.
   Faithful to death,
   he poured the blood divine,
   made the vineyard ready
   for a sweeter wine!

4. God of peace, be with us
   in our deepest need;
   may we love and honour
   all you have decreed,
   trusting in truth,
   all other things above
   and, in grace abundant,
   loving only love!

568

28th Sunday in Ordinary Time: Year A

*God is longing to forgive
the sins we cannot face.
In his love we all may live,
O perfect work of grace!*

1. Upon his holy mountain
   a banquet he prepares,
   removes all bitter poison
   and life eternal shares.

2. Those chosen and invited
   disdainfully decline,
   so to the poor and humble
   goes out the call divine!

3. And O what love eternal,
   in grace, he offers still:
   in palace or in prison,
   our needs he will fulfil!

569

29th Sunday in Ordinary Time: Year A

1. O God, through all the nations' life,
   in truth and justice move,
   and breathe into the world's affairs
   the politics of love.

2. When in their fear, the voice of hate
   the warring nations raise,
   in unexpected people work,
   and unexpected ways.

3. Let not the duties commonplace
   ungraced and Godless be,
   but in the coinage of our lives
   your image may we see.

4. To God the Father, glory be,
   through Christ the risen Lord,
   whose Spirit breathes in all our prayers
   the power of the Word!

570

30th Sunday in Ordinary Time: Year A

1. Let us rejoice in God our strength,
   seeking his face,
   and in the fullness of his love
   his truth embrace.

2. He is the Lord we recognise
   as God alone,
   and one another's joy and pain
   gladly we own.

3. Then, with the voice of holy love,
   help us to speak;
   let us not profit from the poor
   or hurt the weak.

4. All that we own and hold as ours,
   gladly we share,
   and for the naked and the cold,
   we seek to care.

5. Now let our life in church and world
   stand as a sign,
   pointing to Christ our risen Lord,
   Servant divine!

571

31st Sunday in Ordinary Time: Year A

1. Great Father of us all,
   come to our help we pray;
   recall us to your holy word
   and keep us in your way.

2. O let us not aspire
   to cheap and tawdry fame;
   the trappings which the world adores
   we recognise as shame.

3. A greater glory this,
   and our much higher throne:
   to serve with such a humble love
   as his whose name we own.

4. Good News is this indeed,
   no simple mortal word,
   but living in the risen life
   of our eternal Lord!

5. Great Father of us all,
   your word we would obey.
   We glorify your holy name
   and seek your perfect way.

572

1. Wisdom is ever bright,
   the light by which we see,
   revealed to our expectant sight,
   the depths of mystery!
   We seek this truth to know,
   this holy path to take,
   and so in understanding grow
   and anxious fears forsake.

2. Now in the waiting night,
   O let us watchful be,
   preparing for the blessèd sight
   of Wisdom full and free;
   when all shall be at rest,
   and peace and justice flow,
   and ev'ryone by fear oppressed
   his perfect love will know.

3. Joy of the aching heart,
   O wondrous vision fair,
   that those by death now kept apart
   that glorious day will share!
   O for the angel's voice,
   the trumpet's ringing sound,
   when all the saints in light rejoice
   in mystery profound!

573

1. God of peace and order,
   all life enfolding,
   call us by your mercy,
   within your courts to live,
   faithful in your service,
   poor and needy holding,
   knowing the peace that
   you alone can give.

2. Master, all-perceiving,
   all weakness knowing,
   yet to us entrusting
   resources rich and rare,
   O return in glory,
   grace and love bestowing,
   call us your kingdom's
   promises to share.

3. O in faith await him,
   humbly adoring,
   moving from the darkness
   to resurrection's light,
   till the day appointed when,
   all life restoring,
   Christ's perfect peace,
   creation will unite!

574

1. Lord Christ, triumphant,
   universal King,
   let redeemed creation
   praise and glory sing!
   Seek the lost and scattered,
   lead the wand'rers home,
   then in truth triumphant
   let your kingdom come!

   Lord Christ, triumphant,
   universal King,
   let redeemed creation
   praise and glory sing!

2. O perfect judgement,
   grace awaited long!
   Heal the sick and broken,
   bid the weak be strong!
   Those who recognised you
   in the last and least,
   now invite to join you
   in the kingdom's feast.

3. O Word immortal,
   co-eternal Son,
   in the Father's glory,
   by the Spirit, one,
   Adam's great redeemer,
   first-fruits from the dead,
   call us all to follow
   where your feet have led.

575

2nd Sunday in Ordinary Time: Year B

1. Let all creation worship you,
   O God most high,
   break into songs of joyous praise,
   and 'Holy' cry.

2. Come to us at our place of rest,
   calling our name,
   and by the righteous word you speak
   set us aflame.

3. Body of Christ, for glory raised,
   hope's greatest sign,
   here let us rise to share your life
   in bread and wine.

4. Then on the living rock of faith,
   held firm by grace,
   we would acclaim your living Word,
   and see your face.

576

3rd Sunday in Ordinary Time: Year B

1. The voice of redemption
   repeatedly cries,
   and calls us from futile
   indulgence to rise.
   Our ways we must change,
   not a moment delay,
   the call to repentance
   must move us today!

2. The voice of the present,
   the voice of the past,
   recall us from things which
   we know cannot last.
   Our pain and our pleasures
   are passing away;
   so follow the hope which
   will never decay.

3. Where daily concerns
   and obsessions enslave,
   the voice of redemption
   is pow'rful to save.
   The call of the Saviour
   our souls can release,
   to share in his mission
   of justice and peace.

577

4th Sunday in Ordinary Time: Year B

1. God has raised a prophet
   from among our own,
   who, in word and action,
   perfect truth has shown;
   speaking in judgement,
   yet the voice of grace,
   hope eternal springing,
   here in time and space!

2. On the kingdom's journey,
   let us travel light,
   and be single-minded,
   clear in thought and sight;
   holy in body,
   pure in mind and soul,
   signs that Christ is making
   all creation whole.

Continued overleaf

3. Christ as you empow'r us,
   let us clearly speak,
   hush the voice of evil
   and uphold the weak;
   end all oppression,
   set the captives free,
   till the world rejoices,
   grace and truth to see.

578

5th Sunday in Ordinary Time: Year B

'Freedom! Freedom!' let us cry
for all who are oppressed;
'Freedom!' cries the God of hope
from furthest east and west.

1. For those whose life is joyless,
   no better than a slave,
   who wish away their life-span
   in longing for the grave:

2. For those confined by illness,
   or gripped by guilty fear,
   whose cries, though here unheeded,
   have reached the Saviour's ear:

3. For those obsessed with duties,
   or seeking for rewards,
   who lose the joy and freedom
   which selfless love affords:

579

6th Sunday in Ordinary Time: Year B

1. God of salvation,
   cleanse us and cure us,
   come, reassure us,
   speaking in grace,
   prejudice healing,
   goodness revealing,
   holding creation
   in your embrace.

2. Humble in glory,
   healing and holding,
   warmly enfolding
   all who were lost,
   you re-create us,
   and reinstate us,
   sharing the story,
   bearing the cost.

3. Christ as our brother,
   loving and living,
   ever-forgiving,
   fullness of grace;
   come to inspire us,
   fill us and fire us,
   and in each other
   show us your face.

580

7th Sunday in Ordinary Time: Year B

1. O holy God, our sins forgive,
   and let us not the past recall;
   you open up the way of hope,
   renewing life within us all.

2. We bring you our disabling fears,
   our sightless eyes, our narrow minds
   and, in the presence of your Word,
   a greater strength and vision find.

3. Your holy word, we now proclaim;
   the promises in Christ revealed,
   remembered here in bread and wine,
   and in the Holy Spirit sealed.

4. In you our only hope is found,
   and so we come before your face
   to sing your everlasting praise,
   and glory in your perfect grace.

581

8th Sunday in Ordinary Time: Year B

1. In love, O God, you gently call us,
as speaks the bridegroom to the bride
and, with integrity and justice,
you long to hold us at your side.

2. This is the time for celebration
of hope eternal and divine;
we glory in your presence, sharing
the kingdom's effervescent wine!

3. Your covenant of love is written
in words of love upon our hearts;
the Spirit celebrates the union
which even death can never part.

4. Eternal God, our great Creator,
who in the Word of life we see,
we praise you as the Spirit moves us,
most holy One, for ever Three.

582

9th Sunday in Ordinary Time: Year B

1. God of redemptive power,
you set your people free,
and move us from oppression's death
to life and liberty;
this day you set aside,
a sign of love's release,
to call a world enslaved by greed
to value rest and peace.

2. Word of eternal life,
through streets and fields you trod
and, to the narrow, legal mind,
revealed the way of God:
no soul-enslaving law,
but liberating grace
to make, within our crowded lives,
a light and open space.

3. Light of the waiting world,
in darkest places shine,
and open to our awe-struck hearts
the mystery divine.
These earthen vessels fill
with over-flowing grace,
till all creation comes to rest
in liberty's embrace.

583

10th Sunday in Ordinary Time: Year B

1. O Source of goodness,
truth and light,
forgive us our unholy ways,
and show us how to make our lives
a fitting sacrifice of praise.

2. Help us to hear and recognise
your word of healing for our shame,
and not, through jealousy or fear,
the very Word of life defame.

3. Our common hope and faith is found
in you who raised the Crucified;
then be your life within us shown
and grace among us multiplied.

4. We praise you, great Creator God,
in whose redeeming Word we see
the fullness of the Spirit's power,
the wholeness of the Trinity.

584

11th Sunday in Ordinary Time: Year B

1. See the kingdom grow and flourish
from the smallest shoot or seed;
on its spreading branches bearing
fruit to meet creation's need.
Here the destitute find shelter,
sick are healed and captives freed.

Continued overleaf

2. Constantly, through light and darkness,
   will the fruitful kingdom grow,
   spreading peace and bearing justice,
   giving further seeds to sow;
   from God's hand, in rich abundance,
   grace and goodness overflow.

3. Let us now in perfect freedom
   take our place within its shade,
   looking forward to the promise
   by this parable displayed,
   when injustice shall be ended,
   burdens lifted, debts repaid.

585

12th Sunday in Ordinary Time: Year B

1. God of love, whose voice we hear
   speaking at the heart of fear,
   bidding rampant chaos cease,
   calling justice forth with peace;
   love's amazing story tell,
   and our selfish pride dispel.

2. Speak, our anxious fear to still,
   and with trust our spirits fill.
   Let us for each other live,
   and to fearful people give
   rising hope for falling tears,
   selfless love for selfish fear.

3. Jesus Christ, the one who died,
   risen now and glorified,
   may your death in us be shown,
   may we live for you alone.
   Bid our raging anger cease,
   give your new creation peace.

586

13th Sunday in Ordinary Time: Year B

1. God, the source of life eternal,
   in whose image we are made,
   in the goodness of creation
   is your pow'r and love displayed.
   Let us live the life of wholeness,
   in your presence, unafraid.

2. Christ, enthroned in heav'nly splendour,
   bless us by your poverty;
   in the use of our possessions,
   help us signs of grace to be.
   Let us live the life of heaven,
   glorious in simplicity!

3. Those who touch life's outer edges
   to its heart are now restored
   and, in place of dereliction,
   life abundant you have poured;
   where the pow'r of death oppresses,
   breathe your liberating Word.

587

14th Sunday in Ordinary Time: Year B

1. The Spirit is upon us,
   and calls us all to stand
   for faithfulness and justice,
   in this rebellious land;
   though openly rejected
   and stubbornly ignored,
   we lay before the nations
   the true prophetic word.

2. The carpenter we follow,
   though not of noble birth,
   with bleeding hands re-modelled
   the structures of the earth.
   By those he loves rejected,
   his Spirit never dies,
   but calls the new creation
   in glorious hope to rise.

3. His is the only power
   we dare to recognise,
   for in our human weakness
   his great potential lies.
   So let the church, rejoicing,
   the world's contempt embrace,
   with greater joy proclaiming
   the saving pow'r of grace.

588

15th Sunday in Ordinary Time: Year B

1. Called from safer pastures,
   lifestyles of our choice,
   challenging injustice
   with the prophet's voice,
   firm may we stand,
   the message to proclaim,
   when the world would send us
   back from whence we came!

2. On the kingdom's journey,
   may we travel light,
   let the sick find healing,
   and the blind their sight.
   Judgement and mercy
   travel side by side;
   in their proclamation,
   God is glorified.

3. Glory to the Father,
   and the holy Son,
   by whose grace and passion
   is our freedom won;
   Spirit of promise,
   pledge of things to be,
   let the world sing
   'Glory to the Trinity!'

589

16th Sunday in Ordinary Time: Year B

1. Listen to the voice of judgement,
   all who cause the poor to weep;
   leaders who exploit the people,
   shepherds who neglect the sheep;
   God will call the lost and scattered,
   give the silent poor a voice,
   and in perfect truth and justice
   all the pow'rless shall rejoice.

2. See the Word of grace and judgement;
   to the world, in Christ, revealed;
   those who hear, in faith responding,
   find their broken spirits healed.
   Here, the victims of oppression
   learn of mercy, truth and peace;
   death is faced with life abundant,
   and the captives find release.

3. Christ, our reconciling Saviour,
   all hostility destroy;
   by the Spirit's gracious presence,
   make us one in peace and joy.
   Let us praise your triune glory,
   great Creator, holy Word,
   in the unifying Spirit
   ever worshipped and adored!

590

17th Sunday in Ordinary Time: Year B

1. In hopeful trust, O God, we come
   to hear your promise spoken,
   that you will give the poor a home,
   and heal the lost and broken.

2. The harvest of the sea and land
   to us is freely given
   and, in your outstretched, open hand,
   portrays the feast of heaven.

Continued overleaf

3. You call us, in the world, to show
   the presence of salvation,
   to offer life on ev'ry hand,
   and hope for all creation.

4. So may our lives in faith be spent,
   this word of wholeness giving;
   one Lord, one faith, one sacrament,
   one God in all things living.

591

18th Sunday in Ordinary Time: Year B

1. Holy manna, bread of heaven,
   given by the God of grace;
   sign of life and hope eternal,
   in the world of time and space;
   in your presence, in your presence
   life and wholeness we embrace,
   life and wholeness we embrace.

2. Christ, the bread of life, once broken,
   be yourself our only sign;
   give us strength of mind and purpose
   for the work of love divine.
   By your Spirit, by your Spirit,
   meet us here in bread and wine,
   meet us here in bread and wine.

3. God of light and hope, transform us,
   heart and mind, by grace, renew.
   Let us seek, by your example,
   all that's holy, good and true.
   Alleluia! Alleluia!
   Let us worship only you,
   let us worship only you.

592

19th Sunday in Ordinary Time: Year B

1. In ev'ry heart, O God,
   your covenant restore;
   arise in glorious life and hope,
   defender of the poor.

2. Despairing spirits heal,
   and see your people fed;
   sustain the broken and oppressed
   with eucharistic bread.

3. In Christ, the bread of life,
   rejected by his own,
   we see the highest work of grace
   the world has ever known.

4. O Holy Spirit, come,
   our selfishness remove,
   and make of all our broken lives
   a sacrifice of love.

593

20th Sunday in Ordinary Time: Year B

1. Here, upon a holy table,
   Wisdom has her feast prepared;
   at her call the bread is broken,
   wine is freely poured and shared.
   From our folly still she calls us;
   life and vision are her fare.

2. Here the Bread of Life is broken,
   wine recalls the lifeblood shed,
   sign of hope from sorrow springing,
   life eternal from the dead.
   So mysterious, yet so simple,
   flowing wine and broken bread!

3. Spirit of the risen Saviour,
   call us now to Wisdom's feast;
   fill us with the joy of living,
   from our foolishness released.
   Then to God, through Christ,
     be offered
   thanks and praise that never cease.

594

1. God of life and God of freedom,
   lead your wand'ring people home;
   let our anxious hearts be strengthened
   and our idols overthrown.
   You alone can liberate us
   from the chains to which we cling;
   you alone the word have spoken
   whence eternal life will spring.

2. Word of life, our hearts disturbing,
   calling us in faith to move
   from our safe and selfish present,
   through the wilderness of love,
   may our sacrificial living
   show how firmly we believe:
   those who take the risk of dying
   shall eternal life receive.

3. Spirit of our God, transform us;
   ev'ry selfish thought remove;
   let us offer one another
   true respect as well as love.
   Let us live the life of heaven,
   minds and bodies fully free,
   sharing in the perfect wholeness
   of the blessèd Trinity.

595

1. Holy and unchanging,
   God ever-faithful,
   Source of all perfection
   and uncreated light.
   In the law, you give us
   truth and understanding;
   may our obedience
   bring your love to sight.

2. Not in words and tokens
   lies our obedience,
   nor in our obsession
   with mere external signs.
   By your word, disturb us,
   challenge and confront us;
   let your compassion
   all our lives refine.

3. Give us true religion,
   hearing and active,
   faithful in our service
   of all who are oppressed;
   till, in hope rejoicing,
   humble are exalted,
   captives are freed and
   all the poor are blessed.

596

1. 'Be not afraid, your God will come,'
   we hear the prophet sing,
   'and living waters, at his word,
   shall from the desert spring!'

2. 'Then shall the sightless people see,
   the deaf rejoice to hear;
   the voiceless poor shall sing for joy,
   the lame shall leap like deer!'

3. Come then, O Christ, the Word
      of life,
   our senses to befriend,
   and to our opened ears proclaim
   the love that has no end.

4. Then no distinction let us make
   of gender, class or race,
   but to the world, in hope, proclaim
   the openness of grace.

597

1. The servant of the living God
   is found among the humble poor;
   in their oppression he will share,
   and human dignity restore.

2. The Servant now we recognise
   as Son of man and Son of God;
   then let us follow, not obstruct,
   the painful path of hope he trod.

3. He calls us to a living faith,
   to costly love in action shown;
   for faith itself is counted dead,
   unless in caring works made known.

4. O give us faith, eternal God,
   among the poor to take our place,
   and let our words and actions show
   the presence of undying grace.

598

1. Human wisdom has no measure
   for the foolishness of grace:
   false ideas of pow'r and pleasure
   crucify the human race.
   Who would dare to voice a protest?
   Who would take the victim's case?

2. Higher Wisdom God can offer;
   Christ, in death, has pow'r to save,
   loving both the saint and scoffer
   in the shadow of the grave!
   Let us, then, with child-like wonder,
   live the life he gladly gave.

3. In a life of true compassion,
   let us work for hope and peace,
   showing love in costly action,
   bidding exploitation cease;
   constantly for wisdom praying,
   that the kingdom may increase.

599

1. Help us, O God, to hear your word,
   your promises believe,
   as in the unexpected voice
   your challenge we receive.

2. Through voices we have never known,
   of unfamiliar name,
   in faith and culture far apart,
   your purpose you proclaim.

3. So save us from religious pride
   and narrowness of mind,
   that we may recognise your love
   in all of humankind.

4. Call us, with openness, to hear
   the voices of the poor,
   then let us of our greed repent
   and righteousness restore.

600

1. God, who man and woman made,
   that your love might be displayed,
   make us stewards of the earth,
   bringing life and hope to birth;
   cover all the human race
   with the glory of your grace.

2. As we take the risk of love
   may we ever faithful prove,
   joy and sorrow gladly share,
   faults and disappointments bear.
   In the life of church and home
   may we let your kingdom come.

3. Christ, in homes most humble found,
   and with highest glory crowned,
   come and fill each painful place
   with your all-perfecting grace;
   in our homes be glorified,
   and creation sanctified.

601

28th Sunday in Ordinary Time: Year B

1. The spirit of wisdom
   is brighter than gold;
   her riches and splendour
   no coffers can hold.
   So flawless her beauty,
   no wealth can compare;
   no sceptre so noble,
   no silver so rare!

2. The wisdom of God is
   the gospel of grace,
   which all who love riches
   find hard to embrace.
   His challenge to goodness
   let no-one ignore,
   for wholeness is found in
   the hands of the poor.

3. The secret desires of
   our hearts will be known,
   when all that is hidden
   is opened and shown;
   when all of the humble
   to glory are raised,
   and God in creation
   eternally praised.

602

29th Sunday in Ordinary Time: Year B

1. The Servant, crushed with pain,
      we see,
   his body bruised and broken,
   and yet his suff'ring will fulfil
   the promise God has spoken.

2. His broken body yet reveals
   the glory of salvation;
   his humble majesty outshines
   the leaders of the nations.

3. For earthly kings and queens
      are found
   in regal splendour living,
   but God reveals the perfect rule:
   a life of humble giving.

4. In Christ, eternal life is shown,
   who suffered our temptation,
   but sinless rose our great high priest,
   redeeming all creation.

603

30th Sunday in Ordinary Time: Year B

1. Sing for joy, all the earth,
   God has brought hope to birth,
   and affirms human worth,
   liberation bringing,
   songs of freedom singing!

   Come and see our God,
   come and see our God,
   life and light,
   health and sight,
   justice overflowing!

Continued overleaf

2. Jesus calls us to see
   what a world this could be,
   full of truth, just and free,
   life abundant knowing,
   into wholeness growing.

   Come and see our God,
   come and see our God,
   life and light,
   health and sight,
   justice overflowing!

3. Christ, our priest, goes before,
   life and hope to restore;
   let the world all adore,
   and the whole creation
   hear the invitation:

604

31st Sunday in Ordinary Time: Year B

1. The great command we would obey,
   our God to know and love;
   with heart and mind and soul
       and strength,
   our true devotion prove.

2. The love which we for God declare
   is to each other shown;
   we share our neighbours' hopes
       and joys,
   their sorrows as our own.

3. And yet, since mortal flesh is weak,
   our love cannot suffice,
   for loving others as ourselves
   demands too high a price.

4. For this our great High Priest has come,
   the sacrifice to make,
   and all our broken, selfish lives
   by costly love remake.

5. His sacrifice, made once for all,
   is perfect and complete;
   in him creation's finest hopes
   for health and wholeness meet.

605

32nd Sunday in Ordinary Time: Year B

1. Lord, from the greatness of our wealth
   teach us to give,
   and in the smallness of our need
   call us to live.

2. Here from the humble and the poor
   help us to learn,
   and with compassion for their need
   cause us to burn.

3. Value in ev'ry human face
   help us to see,
   and in the place of greatest need
   call us to be.

4. Christ, by your final sacrifice,
   all has been done.
   Now, in the fullness of your grace,
   make all things one.

606

33rd Sunday in Ordinary Time: Year B

1. In fear and in hope
   the great day will dawn,
   when out of the grave
   new life will be born;
   when judgement and mercy
   creation refine,
   and wisdom and beauty
   eternally shine.

2. The earth and the heav'ns
   shall all pass away,
   though none can foretell
   the hour or the day.
   Through fear and through darkness
   the word will endure,
   in pow'r and great glory
   eternally sure.

3. Christ's work is unique,
   his sacrifice one;
   the life he has giv'n
   for sin will atone.
   Eternal perfection
   his dying achieves,
   and Christ from the Father
   his glory receives.

607

Our Lord Jesus Christ, Universal King: Year B

1. Christ, come in glory,
   with your reign of peace;
   let all pain be ended,
   all injustice cease.
   Come in clouds of heaven,
   as the prophet saw
   and, in truth abounding,
   let the world adore!

   Christ, come in glory,
   with your reign of peace;
   let all pain be ended,
   all injustice cease.

2. Lifted in glory,
   reigning from the cross,
   give us life abundant
   from your bitter loss;
   for no earthly kingship
   can with yours compare;
   painful truth you witness,
   thorns and nails you bear!

3. O perfect witness,
   first-born from the dead,
   purify creation
   by the blood you shed.
   Alpha and Omega,
   all our lives embrace,
   in the truth and justice
   of your reign of grace.

608

2nd Sunday in Ordinary Time: Year C

You we praise, O God most high,
your glory we proclaim;
hear the joyful song we sing
in worship to your name.

1. To your unfaithful people,
   you came with grace divine,
   turned life into a wedding,
   and water into wine!

2. The people once rejected,
   unworthy in your sight,
   by grace are now accepted
   to share in your delight!

3. Your one uniting Spirit
   so many gifts has given,
   through all the church expressing
   the promises of heaven.

609

3rd Sunday in Ordinary Time: Year C

1. We have heard the prophet speaking
   through the pages of the law,
   calling us to celebration
   in the service of the poor.
   Amen, amen! Amen, amen!
   Justice to the world restore!

Continued overleaf

2. Now, with holy pow'r anointed,
   we would set the captive free,
   to the poor, good news proclaiming,
   crying hope and liberty.
   Amen, amen! Amen, amen!
   Glory ev'ry eye shall see.

3. Holy Spirit, here unite us,
   our diversity embrace,
   many members, yet one body,
   joined in sacramental grace.
   Amen, amen! Amen, amen!
   Speaking peace to ev'ry race.

3. Christ comes to save us
   from our racial pride;
   all our class distinctions
   love can sweep aside.
   Now proclaim salvation,
   free to ev'ry race;
   welcome all creation
   into love's embrace!

611

5th Sunday in Ordinary Time: Year C

1. O God of grace, in glorious state,
   whom seraphim attend,
   here your unworthy servants wait
   for you to call and send.

2. The burning heat of love divine
   can cleanse the faithless heart,
   and by the gifts of bread and wine,
   your healing you impart.

3. Within the world of time and space,
   eternal love is known;
   the sheer abundance of your grace
   in Jesus Christ is shown.

4. Our firm belief we now declare
   in one who died and lives,
   who calls the world your love to share
   and life eternal gives.

610

4th Sunday in Ordinary Time: Year C

1. Love's great endeavour
   praise and glorify:
   faith endures for ever,
   hope will never die.
   Known before created,
   called before conceived,
   owned and consecrated,
   and in love received.

   Love's great endeavour
   praise and glorify:
   faith endures for ever,
   hope will never die.

2. Love, all-enduring,
   keeps no count of slights;
   all resentment curing,
   love in truth delights.
   Words of judgement voicing,
   prophets rise and fall,
   love remains, rejoicing,
   faithful to her call.

612

6th Sunday in Ordinary Time: Year C

1. Happy are those who trust in you,
   all else above.
   Help us, O God, to praise your name;
   lead us in love.

2. Just as the tree beside the stream
   fears not the heat,
   so on your love may we rely,
   faith be complete.

3. Since, from the darkness of the grave,
   Christ has been raised,
   we who have died with him arise
   and sing your praise.

4. Call us, with you, to raise the poor,
   hungry to feed,
   till, in a world from greed released,
   Christ reigns indeed.

613

7th Sunday in Ordinary Time: Year C

1. 'As you give to others,
   so you will receive,'
   this is scripture's promise;
   help us to believe.
   God of compassion,
   teach us how to live;
   out of your abundance,
   let us freely give.

2. Adam, in creation,
   mortal life was given,
   but the second Adam
   knew the life of heaven.
   God of compassion,
   Adam's children take,
   fill us with your Spirit,
   and our lives re-make.

3. Let us not, in anger,
   spiteful vengeance seek,
   rather, words of kindness
   and forgiveness speak.
   God of compassion,
   fill us with your grace,
   seeking only goodness
   in each other's face.

4. Greater joy in giving
   help us all to learn,
   sharing our resources,
   asking no return.
   God of compassion,
   and of liberty,
   from possessions' burdens
   set our spirits free.

614

8th Sunday in Ordinary Time: Year C

1. O God, refine our faith,
   let all our words be true;
   then shall our daily lives proclaim
   the love for ever new.

2. Let truth and peace be found
   in each believer's heart,
   and ev'ry word your servants speak,
   a greater word impart.

3. From all our eyes remove
   our sight-impairing pride,
   for only when our sight is clear,
   each other may we guide.

4. Then help our tongues describe
   the vision that we see:
   the whole creation clothed, at last,
   in immortality.

615

9th Sunday in Ordinary Time: Year C

1. Christ, in ev'ry mortal language,
   let your name be glorified;
   give the church the grace to listen
   to the voices from outside.
   Alleluia! Alleluia!
   Shame our narrow-minded pride!

Continued overleaf

2. To the pagan Roman soldier,
   your authority was known;
   to his voice, your ears were open,
   to his servant, healing shown.
   Alleluia! Alleluia!
   For our prejudice, atone.

3. Let us not confine our vision,
   seeking worthless human praise;
   help us risk ourselves to freedom,
   in your kingdom's open ways.
   Alleluia! Alleluia!
   Ev'ry nation tribute pays.

616

10th Sunday in Ordinary Time: Year C

1. God of old, who sent the prophet,
   with the life-renewing word,
   charged with fury and compassion,
   which the poor and humble heard;
   where the tears of grief are falling,
   hear the church's angry cry,
   with abundant life responding
   to the great resounding 'Why?'

2. God of life, in hope resplendent,
   greet us at the final gate;
   meet the threat of dereliction
   with the pow'r to re-create.
   Feel again the prophet's anger,
   hear again the widow's cries;
   speak at last the word of healing,
   calling us from death to rise.

3. God of hope, you chose and called us
   from the darkness of the womb,
   to the joy of life abundant,
   stronger even than the tomb.
   Harness all our hope and anger
   with the energy of grace,
   joy in life renewed proclaiming,
   forcing open death's embrace.

617

11th Sunday in Ordinary Time: Year C

1. Christ, at your table we present
   all that we are.
   Close to your feet, we worship you,
   not from afar.

2. All of the things that bring us shame
   here we outpour,
   knowing that penitential hearts
   you will restore.

3. Where, by our use of wealth and power,
   we harm the weak,
   call us by your revealing word,
   pardon to seek.

4. Help us to find your saving grace
   through love and law,
   and by the faith which you impart,
   our lives restore.

618

12th Sunday in Ordinary Time: Year C

1. O the myst'ry of salvation
   by the pierced redeemer shown!
   In his blood is life eternal,
   in his dying, love unknown.
   Holy Saviour, holy Saviour,
   call us back to Calvary's throne,
   call us back to Calvary's throne.

2. For the healing of creation
   Christ is called to suffer pain.
   By his own, abused, rejected,
   he must die and rise again.
   Let us follow! Let us follow!
   Then shall life not be in vain,
   then shall life not be in vain!

3. By our faith in Christ united,
   no distinctions now we see,
   here uniting all the races,
   male and female, slave and free.
   By his passion, by his passion,
   he has won our liberty,
   he has won our liberty.

619

13th Sunday in Ordinary Time: Year C

Holy God, we hear your call,
and follow where you lead.
From our self-indulgent lives
our spirits you have freed.

1. Elisha, at the furrow,
   Elijah's summons heard,
   and sacrificed his future,
   responding to your word.

2. In Christ, you stand before us,
   and call us to decide;
   the challenge of the kingdom
   all else must override.

3. The Spirit calls and guides us
   our selfish ways to leave
   and, loving one another,
   the highest joy receive.

620

14th Sunday in Ordinary Time: Year C

1. Holy God, give us peace,
   let hope flow'r, love increase;
   grace and truth now release,
   like a river flowing,
   through the nations growing.

   Give us peace and joy,
   give us peace and joy,
   God of truth,
   God of hope,
   God of love eternal.

2. Send us out to proclaim
   peace and truth in your name,
   still the word is the same:
   'God in mercy sends us,
   and in hope befriends us.'

3. In the cross is our pride,
   to the world crucified,
   sing of grace far and wide,
   Christ is our salvation;
   join the new creation!

621

15th Sunday in Ordinary Time: Year C

1. Creator of all,
   your word we acclaim,
   and seek, in our lives,
   to honour your name.
   Not distant or hidden,
   but close as the heart,
   the word all-revealing
   its truth will impart.

2. Your statute of love
   in Jesus we see,
   and neighbours to all
   he calls us to be.
   In places of danger,
   the broken we seek,
   and risk our resources
   defending the weak.

3. Give glory to Christ,
   and honour and worth,
   who all things unites
   in heaven and earth.
   From death he has risen,
   our souls to release;
   his reign shall be endless,
   in justice and peace.

622

16th Sunday in Ordinary Time: Year C

1. Heal us, O God, our only help;
   our lives' foundation prove,
   and let us bring, with willing hearts,
   a sacrifice of love.

2. Call us to open up our lives
   to be a sign of grace,
   and in the ones who seek our help
   to recognise your face.

3. Come and be welcome in our homes,
   as our most honoured guest,
   and in life's bustle give us grace
   to listen and to rest.

4. O what a mystery of love
   your scars, O Christ, reveal!
   You send us out in glorious hope,
   creation's wounds to heal.

623

17th Sunday in Ordinary Time: Year C

1. O God, within this special place,
   we pray for strength, for hope and grace,
   the weak and homeless to embrace.

2. Like Abraham, we dare to plead
   for people in their special need,
   as for the world we intercede.

3. O hear our long, persistent cry
   for all who in oppression die,
   where greed and envy crucify.

4. As sons and daughters, may we pray,
   through Christ who died,
      our debts to pay,
   and now to life has led the way.

5. O Christ, perfect your gift of grace,
   transcend the bounds of time and space,
   uniting ev'ry tribe and race.

624

18th Sunday in Ordinary Time: Year C

1. Wisdom of the ages,
   help us and save us
   from the stress and straining
   that fill our waking hours.
   Vanity ensnares us,
   fame and wealth enslave us,
   futile injustice
   drains our vital powers.

2. Greater, ever greater,
   grows our ambition,
   larger, ever larger,
   our warehouses and stores.
   How we love possessions,
   long for recognition!
   Greed, in its blindness,
   deeper needs ignores.

3. Let us follow Jesus,
   share in his dying,
   crucify the longings
   which hinder and enthral,
   peace and justice loving,
   wholeness glorifying,
   till, in perfection,
   Christ is all in all.

625

19th Sunday in Ordinary Time: Year C

1. God of liberation,
   let us hear your cry,
   banish all oppression,
   freedom glorify.
   Ready and waiting
   may we ever be,
   singing songs of justice
   and of liberty.

2. Keep your servants watchful,
   waiting your return;
   when the night is darkest,
   brightest lamps must burn;
   ready and waiting,
   knowing not the hour,
   longing for the kingdom's
   liberating power.

3. Only faith sustains us
   in the hope we hold,
   waiting for the promised
   blessings to unfold.
   Ready and waiting,
   help us to believe,
   old and poor and barren
   will your gifts conceive.

4. Strangers, nomads, pilgrims,
   on the earth we roam,
   while our hearts are longing
   for a better home;
   ready and waiting,
   confident to see
   all injustice righted,
   and creation free.

626

20th Sunday in Ordinary Time: Year C

1. O God, renew our vision,
   and clear our sight to see
   the figure of the Saviour,
   enthroned at Calvary.
   O what a confrontation!
   He disregards the shame;
   meets evil with compassion,
   and stakes the kingdom's claim.

2. When kings and politicians
   abuse their earthly power;
   where greed and exploitation
   make all the world seem sour,
   then with a better vision,
   let us with Jesus stand,
   confronting hostile forces
   with your most just demand.

3. When opposition rises,
   let us not seek to hide,
   or shirk the confrontation
   which Jesus glorified.
   He takes his place in glory
   by God's eternal throne,
   his perfect grace disposing
   to make creation one.

627

21st Sunday in Ordinary Time: Year C

1. From east and west, from north
      and south,
   the nations come to join the feast,
   but those who count themselves
      as best
   are placed among the last and least!

2. Not all who say the 'proper' words
   are guaranteed a kingdom place,
   but those who do the will of God
   in ev'ry nation, faith and race.

3. And many, of a humble mind,
   will find their special place prepared,
   who took the risk of pain and scorn,
   and for the lost and broken cared.

4. In pain and sorrow let us share,
   and never seek for swift release,
   for there God's children are prepared
   to share the reign of truth and peace.

628

1. God of true humility,
   humble servants we would be.
   Save us then from vain conceit;
   make the work of grace complete.
   Open each attentive ear
   your eternal truth to hear.

2. Let us share your royal feast
   with the poorest and the least,
   who cannot our gifts return;
   let them be our chief concern,
   giving them a higher place
   in the order of your grace.

3. O what majesty is found!
   Here we stand on holy ground,
   welcomed in at heaven's gate,
   where the angels celebrate.
   Name of names, let us adore,
   with the outcast and the poor.

629

1. God eternal, cosmic wisdom,
   move our hearts to sing your praise.
   Who can understand your nature,
   fathom your mysterious ways?
   Send on us your Holy Spirit,
   who such deeper truth conveys.

2. Shame the world's possessive madness
   by the wisdom of the cross;
   from the prisons which 'secure' us,
   set us free to suffer loss.
   Give us grace to be disciples,
   and the strength to bear the cost.

3. Let us learn to live together
   as your people, not as slaves,
   holding, helping and releasing
   ev'ryone who freedom craves,
   looking to the risen Saviour,
   whose compassion heals and saves.

630

1. God of forgiveness,
   your people you freed,
   and saw them return
   to idolatrous greed;
   with anger against them,
   you righteously burned,
   but then to compassion
   and forgiveness you turned.

2. God of forgiveness,
   the Saviour you sent,
   proclaiming good news,
   with the call to repent.
   With merciful love
   and forgiveness he came,
   the lost and the headstrong
   to embrace and reclaim.

3. God of forgiveness,
   your pow'r we implore,
   with mercy and wholeness,
   our lives to restore.
   Perverse and misguided,
   our souls we deprave;
   O come, full of healing,
   with compassion to save.

631

25th Sunday in Ordinary Time: Year C

1. The word of God rings harsh
   and clear:
   the judgement will be great
   on those who trade dishonestly,
   and tamper with the weight.
   'You wish the sabbath day were gone,
   its spirit you ignore;
   you long to prey upon the weak
   and buy and sell the poor.'

2. The Saviour said, 'You cannot serve
   both God and money, too;
   you will be faithless to the one,
   and to the other true.'
   Then let us all, for God alone,
   in freedom make our choice,
   and in the things of greatest worth
   eternally rejoice.

3. Now to the God who loves the poor
   let praise and prayers ascend,
   for justice in the present world
   and mercy at the end.
   For people in authority,
   your wisdom we implore,
   who stewards of your love must be,
   defenders of the poor.

632

26th Sunday in Ordinary Time: Year C

1. The rich in splendid castle homes,
   the poor ones at the gate,
   God has created equally,
   and hates their current state.

2. The word of warning comes to all
   who others' needs ignore,
   who live in luxury untold,
   provided by the poor!

3. The prophets all proclaimed the word
   of judgement, grace and fear,
   but those for whom the word is meant
   are not inclined to hear.

4. The saintly life which God commands
   resources would release,
   and hasten in the glorious time
   of justice and of peace.

633

27th Sunday in Ordinary Time: Year C

1. 'How long, O God,' the people cry,
   'must poverty prevail,
   while wars and famines come and go
   and all our efforts fail?'

2. The world we see appears devoid
   of reason and of rhyme,
   but faith will keep the vision bright,
   till comes the promised time.

3. We see our faith as small and weak,
   and long for it to grow,
   yet even such a tiny seed
   may great achievements know.

4. So kindle here the gift of faith,
   and fan it to a flame,
   then justice, truth and liberty
   will glorify God's name.

634

28th Sunday in Ordinary Time: Year C

1. God of creation, with what joy
   your goodness we proclaim!
   Your love is freely shown to all
   who do not know your name.

Continued overleaf

2. Those whom the world has
   called unclean
   you gladly touch and hold;
   and all, who from a distance cry,
   your open arms enfold.

3. Nothing you ask of us but love;
   your grace we cannot earn.
   You freely give to even those
   who never thanks return.

4. Let us this gospel now declare,
   but not for worldly gain;
   we look towards the promised time
   of love's unhindered reign.

635

29th Sunday in Ordinary Time: Year C

1. Eternal God, you cry for justice,
   and call the church that cry to share;
   so some engage in mortal combat,
   and some in agonising prayer.

2. The human judge, for peace and quiet,
   will heed the widow's constant cry,
   but you, O God, for pure compassion,
   to our petition will reply.

3. Then give us grace, when all
      seems futile,
   in hopeful prayer to persevere,
   our hopes, our dreams, our
      failures bringing
   to you, who all our prayers will hear.

4. So may we call the world to freedom,
   confronting all who would oppose,
   with courage firm,
      the truth proclaiming,
   till justice through creation flows.

636

30th Sunday in Ordinary Time: Year C

1. Come, holy God, our spirits cleanse
   of ev'ry trace of pride,
   and in humility of heart
   may you be glorified.

2. The humble poor, in ev'ry age,
   to you present their case;
   you listen to the widow's prayer,
   the orphan you embrace.

3. The sinner to your presence comes,
   with penitential plea,
   and finds in your redeeming word
   forgiveness flowing free.

4. So by your pow'r, eternal God,
   the gospel we proclaim
   and, from the depths of humble hearts,
   your saving love acclaim.

637

31st Sunday in Ordinary Time: Year C

1. God of salvation, loving and longing,
   holding and healing people who fall,
   come in compassion, caring and calling,
   help us to hear and answer your call.

2. Christ, our redeemer, sinners restoring,
   giving the guilty hope and respect,
   move us and melt us, love us and lift us,
   giving us grace we dare not expect.

3. God, we adore you, worship
      and wonder,
   praise and repentance lay at your feet.
   Seek us and save us, rest and redeem us,
   grace us with goodness,
      make us complete.

638

1. O listen to our prayer,
   great God of all who live,
   and to the pleading of our hearts
   a timely answer give.

2. When evil forces rage,
   then let us faithful stay,
   for from oppression's darkest night
   comes resurrection's day.

3. You are the source of life,
   the God of Abraham,
   to Jacob and to Isaac known,
   and Moses' great 'I am'.

4. Let all the world rejoice,
   for Christ has set us free
   from paralysing fear of death,
   for life and liberty.

639

1. The dreaded day will surely dawn,
   in judgement awesome and divine,
   and at its heart, with healing rays,
   the sun of righteousness will shine.

2. The gracious judgement of our God
   will set oppression's victims free,
   and all who patiently endure
   will live for all eternity.

3. The pow'rs and rulers of this world
   will call on us to make our case;
   on God alone we will rely,
   and trust the all-sufficient grace.

4. So let us fully play our part,
   for wholeness and for liberty,
   till Christ is known throughout
      the world,
   and all creation glad and free.

640

1. Christ reigns triumphant,
   worldly splendour pales!
   See the throne of glory,
   made from wood and nails!
   Let the pow'rful mock him,
   let the thief deride;
   hist'ry will remember
   Jesus glorified!

   Christ reigns triumphant,
   worldly splendour pales!
   See the throne of glory,
   made from wood and nails!

2. Christ, Son of David,
   Shepherd of the sheep,
   in this glorious shadow
   all your people keep.
   By the pain you suffer,
   bring creation peace,
   and from fear and malice
   ev'ry heart release.

3. Likeness and image
   of the God of light,
   robed in scarlet splendour,
   awesome to our sight;
   first-born of creation,
   first-born from the grave,
   from the pow'rs of darkness
   all creation save!

641

St David, Patron of Wales March 1

1. Christ to humble service calls us,
   pours us out as salt and light,
   flavouring the whole creation,
   bringing hope and truth to sight.
   In Saint David's footsteps treading,
   we proclaim a promise bright.

2. For a life of selfless giving,
   we are sanctified by grace;
   with this patron saint before us,
   let us gladly run the race.
   Christ eternal life is granting,
   through the saints, in time and space.

3. In the hope that springs eternal
   great Saint David lived and died,
   and the promise of the Saviour
   in his life is glorified;
   peace and justice, truth and wholeness,
   in an ever-flowing tide.

642

St Patrick, Patron of Ireland March 17

1. O God, you inspired
   Saint Patrick to speak
   of hope for the poor
   and strength for the weak.
   Though humble the language
   which mortals can frame,
   his faith and compassion
   brought praise to your name.

2. The harvest is great,
   the labourers few;
   O God, by your grace,
   our vigour renew;
   his trust and commitment
   upon us bestow,
   inspire us and send us
   your glory to show.

3. Like Patrick, we hear
   your voice with delight;
   with justice and hope,
   creation is bright.
   The word of salvation
   we gladly receive;
   your promise of wholeness
   we truly believe.

643

St George, Patron of England April 23

1. With gladness we commemorate
   Saint George, who set his life aside,
   and bravely faced the martyr's death
   for following the Crucified.

2. The special majesty of Christ
   confronts the world of selfish pride,
   and those who choose the saintly way
   are called to suffer at his side.

3. The order of the present world
   is threatened by his Godly claim,
   as evil pow'rs are overcome
   and poor exalted in his name.

4. Then let us choose, in faith and trust,
   to follow where Saint George has trod
   and, in the world of conflict, share
   the sorrow and the joy of God.

644

The Birth of St John the Baptist June 24

1. Commissioned and anointed,
   the holy prophet came,
   to brighten all the nations
   with hope's eternal flame.
   The word, which filled and quickened
   the darkness of the womb,
   from primal days foreshadowed
   the breaching of the tomb.

2. The poor with joy are singing,
   the barren have conceived,
   who heard the gracious promise
   and, full of hope, believed.
   In desert places sounding,
   the voice of judgement cries,
   by God's own word commissioned
   to challenge and baptise.

3. The prophet still announces
   the coming of the Word,
   whose message of salvation
   the centuries have heard.
   From David's line descended,
   Christ comes to reign in peace;
   the poor shall be exalted,
   and justice never cease.

645

Ss Peter and Paul, Apostles June 29

1. Let us set our feet to follow
   where the feet of Peter trod
   and, with Paul, in pain and hardship,
   trust the perfect grace of God.
   Where the forces of oppression
   seek to mute your people's voice,
   come, O God of liberation,
   call the captives to rejoice.

2. Christ, the long-awaited Saviour,
   joyfully we recognise,
   holy Word of God incarnate,
   open to our mortal eyes.
   On the faith of these apostles,
   you have made the church secure:
   in the face of greed and hatred,
   love and mercy will endure.

3. By Saint Peter's faith sustain us,
   with Saint Paul to run the race.
   Let our lives like yours be broken,
   pouring out the wine of grace.
   Then at last, the task completed,
   in your presence may we stand,
   crowned with mercy and compassion,
   with the saints on every hand.

646

The Transfiguration of the Lord August 6

1. Holy Christ, in light transfigured,
   shining hope upon the earth,
   brighten ev'ry place of darkness,
   bring the age of truth to birth.
   Point us to the great awakening,
   when the world in hope shall rise:
   fear and exploitation ended,
   perfect peace shall be the prize.

2. Let us share the special vision,
   hear the great affirming voice;
   in the glorious revelation,
   call creation to rejoice.
   Through the darkness of oppression
   let the prophets light the way,
   pointing to the peace and justice
   promised on the final day.

3. Come, O Christ, in clouds of glory,
   set our fervent hopes ablaze!
   Offer up the new creation
   to the God of ancient days.
   From a thousand thousand voices
   songs of praise and joy release,
   when the ending of oppression
   heralds everlasting peace.

647

1. Holy, universal Mother,
   crying in the pains of earth,
   where the face of evil threatens,
   bring the child of hope to birth.
   Full of holy grace and glory,
   sing a song of human worth.

2. Sing to us of hope and freedom:
   how the mighty are brought down,
   while the humble are exalted,
   and the poor receive the crown.
   Full of holy grace and glory,
   sing a song of high renown.

3. Now to heights unknown exalted,
   sing of joy that will not cease:
   Christ has burst oppression's darkness,
   life abundant to release.
   Full of holy grace and glory,
   sing a song of lasting peace.

648

1. Firm in the faith of God,
   the saints have lived and died,
   who now with Christ in glory stand,
   redeemed and purified.
   This is the glorious hope
   in which our hearts abound,
   to look upon the face of God
   with love eternal crowned.

2. Blessèd are those who thirst
   for freedom, love and peace,
   who long to see the truth prevail
   and all injustice cease.
   The humble and the poor,
   and all who weep or mourn,
   shall rise with all the saints to see
   the new creation's dawn.

3. 'Glory to God,' we sing,
   'and to the Lamb on high,'
   whom, in the Spirit ever one,
   we praise and glorify.
   You hold in one embrace
   the saints in heav'n and earth,
   who praise your triune majesty
   and sing creation's worth.

649

1. Jesus, when you call us,
   let our hearts be stirred,
   open, with Saint Andrew,
   to your saving word.
   Call us and save us,
   put us not to shame,
   let our faith and service
   glorify your name.

2. In our trade and commerce,
   let us hear your voice,
   and the kingdom's values
   be our willing choice.
   Call us and save us,
   give us grace to move,
   pilgrims on a journey,
   saved by faith and love.

3. Jesus, still you call us,
   give us ears to hear;
   let this saint's example
   overcome our fear.
   Call us and save us,
   send us to proclaim,
   to the poor and captive,
   freedom in your name.

650

1. O salutaris hostia,
   quae cæli pandis ostium,
   bella premunt hostilia,
   da robur, fer auxilium.

2. Uni trinoque Domino
   sit sempiterna gloria,
   qui vitam sine termino
   nobis donet in patria. Amen.

or

1. O saving victim, op'ning wide
   the gate of heav'n to man below;
   our foes press on from ev'ry side;
   thine aid supply, thy strength bestow.

2. To thy great name be endless praise,
   immortal Godhead, One in Three;
   O grant us endless length of days
   in our true native land with thee.
   Amen.

St Thomas Aquinas (1227-1274)
Translation by John Mason Neale (1818-1866)

651

1. Tantum ergo Sacramentum
   veneremur cernui:
   et antiquum documentum
   novo cedat ritui;
   præstet fides supplementum
   sensuum defectui.

2. Genitori, genitoque
   laus et jubilatio,
   salus, honor, virtus, quoque
   sit et benedictio;
   procedenti ab utroque
   compar sit laudatio. Amen.

or

1. Come, adore this wondrous presence,
   bow to Christ, the source of grace.
   Here is kept the ancient promise
   of God's earthly dwelling-place.
   Sight is blind before God's glory,
   faith alone may see his face.

2. Glory be to God the Father,
   praise to his co-equal Son,
   adoration to the Spirit,
   bond of love, in Godhead one.
   Blest be God by all creation
   joyously while ages run. Amen.

St Thomas Aquinas (1227-1274)
Translation by James Quinn (b. 1919)

652

Adoremus in æternum
sanctissimum sacramentum.

1. Laudate Dominum, omnes gentes;
   laudate eum, omnes populi.

2. Quoniam confirmata est super nos
   misericordia ejus;
   et veritas Domini manet in æternum.

3. Gloria Patri et Filio;
   et Spiritui Sancto.

4. Sicut erat in principio et nunc
   et semper;
   et in sæcula sæculorum. Amen.

Psalm 117

653

Kyrie

1. Lord, have mercy; Lord, have mercy;
   on your servants, Lord, have mercy.
   God almighty, just and faithful,
   Lord, have mercy; Lord, have mercy.

2. Christ, have mercy; Christ, have mercy;
   gift from heaven, Christ, have mercy.
   Light of truth and light of justice,
   Christ, have mercy; Christ, have mercy.

3. Lord, have mercy; Lord, have mercy;
   on your servants, Lord, have mercy.
   God almighty, just and faithful,
   Lord, have mercy; Lord, have mercy.

Gospel acclamation

Alleluia, alleluia,
let us praise Christ, our Lord Jesus.
Alleluia, let us praise him,
now among us in his Gospel.

Sanctus

1. Holy, holy, holy, holy,
   Lord of hosts. You fill with glory
   all the earth and all the heavens.
   Sing hosanna, sing hosanna.

2. Blest and holy, blest and holy,
   he who comes now in the Lord's name.
   In the highest sing hosanna,
   in the highest sing hosanna.

Memorial acclamation

When we eat this bread you give us,
and we drink this cup you left us,
we proclaim your death, Lord Jesus,
till you come again in glory.

Agnus Dei

1. Jesus, Lamb of God, have mercy,
   bearer of our sins, have mercy.
   Jesus, Lamb of God, have mercy,
   bearer of our sins, have mercy.

2. Saviour of the world, Lord Jesus,
   may your peace be with us always.
   Saviour of the world, Lord Jesus,
   may your peace be with us always.

The 'American' Eucharist.
Adapted from the Liturgy by Sandra Joan Billington
(b. 1946) and Robert B. Kelly (b. 1948)

654

Kyrie

1. Father of all, O Lord, have mercy.
   Father of all, O Lord, have mercy.
   Father of all, have mercy on us.
   Father of all, be ever near us.

2. Saviour of all, O Christ, have mercy.
   Saviour of all, O Christ, have mercy.
   Saviour of all, have mercy on us.
   Saviour of all, be ever near us.

3. Spirit of all, O Lord, have mercy.
   Spirit of all, O Lord, have mercy.
   Spirit of all, have mercy on us.
   Spirit of all, be ever near us.

Sanctus

1. Holy are you, Lord of creation!
   Holy are you, Lord God of angels!
   Holy are you, God of all people!
   Heaven and earth proclaim your glory.

2. Glory to you! Your name is holy.
   Blessèd is he who comes in your name!
   Glory to him! We sing his praises.
   Heaven and earth proclaim your glory.

Agnus Dei

O Lamb of God, you bore our sinning.
O Lamb of God, you bore our dying.
O Lamb of God, have mercy on us.
O Lamb of God, your peace be
   with us.

The 'Hopwood' Mass
Adapted from the Liturgy
by Terence Collins (b. 1938)

655

Kyrie

1. Lord, have mercy. Lord, have mercy.
   Lord, have mercy on us all.
   Lord, have mercy. Lord, have mercy.
   Lord, have mercy on us all.

2. Christ, have mercy. Christ, have mercy.
   Christ, have mercy on us all.
   Christ, have mercy. Christ, have mercy.
   Christ, have mercy on us all.

3. Lord, have mercy. Lord, have mercy.
   Lord, have mercy on us all.
   Lord, have mercy. Lord, have mercy.
   Lord, have mercy on us all.

Gospel acclamation

Alleluia, alleluia,
this is the Gospel of the Lord!
Alleluia, alleluia,
praise to Christ, who is God's Word.

Sanctus

1. Holy, holy, holy, holy,
   Lord of pow'r, Lord of might.
   Heav'n and earth are filled with glory.
   Sing hosanna evermore.

2. Blest and holy, blest and holy,
   he who comes from God on high.
   Raise your voices, sing his glory,
   praise his name for evermore.

Memorial acclamation

When we eat this bread and drink
   this cup
which you have given us,
we proclaim your death and rising,
till you come again, O Lord.

Agnus Dei

1. Lamb of God, you take away the sin,
   the sin of all the world:
   give us mercy, give us mercy,
   give us mercy, Lamb of God.

2. Lamb of God, you take away the sin,
   the sin of all the world:
   give us mercy, give us mercy,
   give us mercy, Lamb of God.

3. Lamb of God, you take away the sin,
   the sin of all the world:
   grant us peace, Lord;
      grant us peace, Lord;
   grant us peace, O Lamb of God.

The 'Israeli' Mass
Adapted from the Liturgy by Anthony Hamson and
Robert B. Kelly (b. 1948)

656

Kyrie

Kyrie, eleison. Kyrie, eleison.
Christe, eleison. Christe, eleison.
Kyrie, eleison. Kyrie, eleison.

Gloria

Gloria in excelsis Deo,
et in terra pax hominibus
bonæ voluntatis.
Laudamus te,
benedicimus te,
adoramus te,
glorificamus te,
gratias agimus tibi
propter magnam gloriam tuam.
Domine Deus, Rex cælestis,
Deus Pater omnipotens.
Domine Fili unigenite, Jesu Christe.
Domine Deus, Agnus Dei, Filius Patris,
qui tollis peccata mundi,
miserere nobis,
qui tollis peccata mundi,
suscipe deprecationem nostram.
Qui sedes ad dexteram Patris,
miserere nobis.
Quoniam tu solus sanctus,
tu solus Dominus,
tu solus Altissimus,
Jesu Christe,
cum Sancto Spiritu,
in gloria Dei Patris.
Amen.

Sanctus

Sanctus, sanctus, sanctus
Dominus Deus sabaoth.
Pleni sunt cæli et terra gloria tua.
Hosanna in excelsis.
Benedictus qui venit in nomine Domini.
Hosanna in excelsis.

Pater noster

Pater noster, qui es in cælis:
sanctificetur nomen tuum;
adveniat regnum tuum;
fiat voluntas tua,
sicut in cælo, et in terra.
Panem nostrum quotidianum da
   nobis hodie;
et dimitte nobis debita nostra,
sicut et nos dimittimus
   debitoribus nostris;
et ne nos inducas in tentationem;
sed libera nos a malo.

Agnus Dei

Agnus Dei, qui tollis peccata mundi:
miserere nobis.
Agnus Dei, qui tollis peccata mundi:
miserere nobis.
Agnus Dei, qui tollis peccata mundi:
dona nobis pacem.

Dismissal

Minister   Ite, missa est.
All   Deo gratias.

From the Roman Missal

657

Kyrie

Kyrie, eleison. Kyrie, eleison.
Christe, eleison. Christe, eleison.
Kyrie, eleison. Kyrie, eleison.

Sanctus

Sanctus, sanctus, sanctus
Dominus Deus sabaoth.
Pleni sunt cæli et terra gloria tua.
Hosanna in excelsis.
Benedictus qui venit in
   nomine Domini.
Hosanna in excelsis.

Agnus Dei

Agnus Dei, qui tollis peccata mundi:
miserere nobis.
Agnus Dei, qui tollis peccata mundi:
miserere nobis.
Agnus Dei, qui tollis peccata mundi:
dona nobis pacem.

From the Roman Missal

658

Kyrie, eleison.
Christe, eleison.
Kyrie, eleison.

1. Lord Jesus, you come to gather
   the nations
   into the peace of God's kingdom.

2. You come in word and sacrament
   to strengthen us in holiness.

3. You will come in glory
   with salvation for your people.

Adapted from the Liturgy
by Marty Haugen (b. 1950)

659

Kyrie, Christe,
Kyrie, eleison.

From the Roman Missal

660

Kyrie,
Kyrie, eleison.

Taizé Community, from the Roman Missal

661

Gloria, gloria, in excelsis Deo.
Gloria, gloria, in excelsis Deo.

1. Lord God, heavenly King,
   peace you bring to us;
   we worship you, we give you thanks,
   we sing our song of praise.

2. Jesus, Saviour of all,
   Lord God, Lamb of God,
   you take away our sins, O Lord,
   have mercy on us all.

3. At the Father's right hand,
   Lord receive our prayer,
   for you alone are the Holy One,
   and you alone are Lord.

4. Glory, Father and Son,
   glory, Holy Spirit,
   to you we raise our hands up high,
   we glorify your name.

Adapted from the Liturgy
by Mike Anderson (b. 1956)

662

Gloria, gloria in excelsis Deo.
Gloria, gloria in excelsis Deo.

1. **Glory** to **God in** the **high**est,
   and peace to his **peo**ple on **earth**.
   Lord God, heavenly **King**,
   almighty **God** and **Fa**ther,
   we worship you, we give you **thanks**,
   we **praise** you for your **glo**ry.

Continued overleaf

2. **Lord** Jesus **Christ**, only **Son** of
   the **Father**,
   Lord God, Lamb of God,
   you take away the sins of the **world:**
   have **mer**cy on **us;**
   you are seated at the **right** hand
   of the Father:
   re**ceive** our **prayer.**

Gloria, gloria in excelsis Deo.
Gloria, gloria in excelsis Deo.

3. **For** you **alone** are the **Holy One,**
   you alone are the **Lord,**
   you alone are the Most **High,**
   Jesus **Christ,**
   with the Holy **Spirit,**
   in the glory of God the **Father. Amen.**

From the Roman Missal

664

Glory to God in the highest,
and peace to his people on earth.
Lord God, heavenly King,
almighty God and Father,
we worship you,
we give you thanks,
we praise you for your glory.
We praise you for your glory.

Lord Jesus Christ,
only Son of the Father.
Lord God, Lamb of God,
Lord God, Lamb of God,
you take away the sin of the world;
have mercy on us,
have mercy on us.
You who sit at the Father's right hand:
receive our prayer,
receive our prayer.

For you alone are the Holy One,
you alone are the Lord.
You alone are the Most High,
Jesus Christ, Jesus Christ,
with the Holy Spirit,
in the glory of God the Father.
Amen, amen.
Amen, amen.

From the Roman Missal

663

Glory to God in the highest,
and peace to his people on earth.
Lord God, heav'nly King,
almighty God and Father,
we worship you, we give you thanks,
we praise you for your glory.

Lord Jesus Christ, only Son of
   the Father,
Lord God, Lamb of God,
you take away the sin of the world:
have mercy on us;
you are seated at the right hand of
   the Father:
receive our prayer.
For you alone are the Holy One,
you alone are the Lord,
you alone are the Most High,
Jesus Christ,
with the Holy Spirit,
in the glory of God the Father. Amen.

From the Roman Missal

665

Gloria, gloria in excelsis Deo!
Gloria, gloria, alleluia, alleluia!

Taizé Community, from the Roman Missal

666

1. Alleluia, alleluia,
   alleluia, alleluia,
   alleluia, alleluia,
   alleluia, alleluia.

2. Jesus is Lord,
   Jesus is Lord,
   Jesus is Lord,
   Jesus is Lord.

3. And I love him,
   and I love him,
   and I love him,
   and I love him.

4. Christ is risen,
   Christ is risen,
   Christ is risen,
   Christ is risen.

Additional verses may be composed to suit the occasion. For example:

5. Send your Spirit,
   send your Spirit,
   send your Spirit,
   send your Spirit.

6. Abba, Father,
   Abba, Father,
   Abba, Father,
   Abba, Father.

7. Come, Lord Jesus,
   come, Lord Jesus,
   come, Lord Jesus,
   come, Lord Jesus.

Vv 1-4 unknown, vv 5-7 Damian Lundy (b. 1944)

667

Alleluia.

1. Glory to the Father,
   glory to the Son,
   glory to the Spirit,
   God the Three-in-One.

or

2. I call you friends
   because I have told you
   ev'rything I've learnt
   from my Father.

or

3. Open our hearts,
   O Lord,
   to accept the words
   of your Son.

Christopher Walker (b. 1947)
© 1985 OCP Publications

668

Alleluia, alleluia, alleluia.

or during Lent:

*Praise to you, Lord,
praise to you, Lord,
praise to you, Lord.*

1. *For Easter*
   Lord Jesus,
   you are risen from the dead:
   you are our companion
   on the road of life,
   and we know you
   in the breaking of the bread.

Continued overleaf

2. *For Advent and Christmas*
Lord Jesus,
Word of God made man for us,
you reveal your glory
to our broken world,
and we worship you.
Come again in glory!

Alleluia, alleluia, alleluia.

or during Lent:
Praise to you, Lord,
praise to you, Lord,
praise to you, Lord.

3. *For Passiontide*
Lord Jesus,
obedient to the Father's will,
you became a slave,
enduring death for us.
Now you reign as Lord.
Come again in glory!

4. *For Pentecost*
Lord Jesus,
you are at the Father's side:
you have sent your Spirit
to renew our joy,
and we praise you.
Come again in glory!

Damian Lundy (b. 1944)

669

Alleluia.

We will hear your Word, one in love;
we will live your Word, one in love;
we will live your Word, one in love;
we will spread your Word, one in love.

Joe Wise (b. 1939)

670

Halle, halle, hallelujah!
Halle, halle, hallelujah!
Halle, halle, hallelujah!
Hallelujah, hallelujah!

Traditional

671

Credo in unum Deum,
Patrem omnipotentem,
    factorem cæli et terræ,
visibilium omnium, et invisibilium.
Et in unum Dominum Jesum Christum,
Filium Dei unigenitum,
et ex Patre natum ante omnia sæcula.
Deum de Deo, lumen de lumine,
Deum verum de Deo vero,
genitum non factum,
    consubstantialem Patri:
per quem omnia facta sunt.
Qui propter nos homines,
et propter nostram salutem
    descendit de cælis.
Et incarnatus est de Spiritu Sancto
    ex Maria Virgine:
et homo factus est.
Crucifixus etiam pro nobis
    sub Pontio Pilato,
passus et sepultus est.
Et resurrexit tertia die,
    secundum Scripturas,
et ascendit in cælum: sedet
    ad dexteram Patris.
Et iterum venturus est cum gloria,
judicare vivos et mortuos:
cujus regni non erit finis.
Et in Spiritum Sanctum, Dominum,
    et vivificantem:
qui ex Patre Filioque procedit.

Qui cum Patre et Filio simul
   adoratur, et conglorificatur:
qui locutus est per prophetas.
Et unam, sanctam, catholicam
   et apostolicam Ecclesiam.
Confiteor unum baptisma in
   remissionem peccatorum.
Et exspecto resurrectionem
   mortuorum,
et vitam venturi sæculi.
Amen.

From the Roman Missal

672

1. Do you believe in God,
   the Father almighty,
   creator of heav'n and earth?

We believe, we do believe.

2. Do you believe in Jesus Christ,
   his only Son, our Lord,
   who was born of the Virgin Mary,
   was crucified, died and was buried?

3. Do you believe in Jesus Christ,
   who rose from the dead,
   and is now seated at the
   right hand of the Father?

4. Do you believe in the Holy Spirit,
   the holy Catholic Church,
   the communion of saints?

5. Do you believe in the forgiveness
   of sins,
   the resurrection of the body,
   and the life everlasting?

From the Roman Missal

673

1. We believe in one almighty
   God and Father of us all,
   maker of the earth and heaven,
   holding worlds and stars in thrall.
   All things seen and all things unseen
   come to being at his call.

2. We believe in one Redeemer,
   Christ, the Father's only Son.
   Timelessly in love begotten,
   through him all God's work is done.
   Light from Light and God
      from Godhead,
   with the Father's Being, one.

3. All for us and our salvation,
   Christ his glory set aside,
   by the Holy Spirit's power,
   and the womb of virgin bride;
   suffered under Pilate's sentence,
   for our sake was crucified.

4. He has burst the grave asunder,
   rising as the prophets said;
   seated in the Father's presence,
   he is our exalted head.
   He will come again with glory,
   judge the living and the dead.

5. We acclaim the Holy Spirit,
   of all life the source and Lord;
   with the Son and Father worshipped,
   ever honoured and adored;
   speaking through the holy prophets,
   pow'r of sacrament and word.

6. Holy church, and universal,
   apostolic company!
   In one sacrament forgiven,
   signed by water, his to be.
   In the resurrection body
   we shall share eternity.

Michael Forster (b. 1946)

674

Holy, holy, holy Lord,
God of pow'r and might,
heaven and earth
are full of your glory.
Hosanna in the highest.
Blessed is he who comes
in the name of the Lord.
Hosanna in the highest.
Hosanna in the highest.

From the Roman Missal

675

Holy, holy, holy Lord,
God of power and might,
heaven and earth are full of your glory.
Hosanna, hosanna in the highest.

Blessèd is he who comes
in the name of the Lord.
Hosanna in the highest,
hosanna in the highest.

From the Roman Missal

676

Holy, holy, holy Lord,
God of pow'r and might!

1. Full of your glory are heav'n and earth,
   God of pow'r and might.

2. Blessèd is he who comes among us
   in the name of the Lord.

3. Hosanna in the highest!

From the Roman Missal,
adapted by W.R. Lawrence (b. 1925)

677

1. Holy, holy, holy is the Lord,
   holy is the Lord God almighty!
   Holy, holy, holy is the Lord,
   holy is the Lord God almighty!
   Who was and is, and is to come;
   holy, holy, holy is the Lord.

2. Blessèd, blessèd, blest is he who comes,
   blest is he who comes in the
      Lord's name.
   Blessèd, blessèd, blest is he who comes,
   blest is he who comes in the
      Lord's name.
   Hosanna in the heights of heav'n.
   Blessèd, blessèd, blessèd is the Lord.

John Ballantine (b. 1945)

678

Christ has died,
Christ is risen,
Christ will come again,
Christ will come again.

From the Roman Missal

679

Christ has died,
Christ is risen,
Christ will come again.

From the Roman Missal

680

Christ has died, alleluia.
Christ is risen, alleluia.
Christ will come again,
alleluia, alleluia.

From the Roman Missal

681

Dying you destroyed our death.
Rising you restored our life.
Lord Jesus, come in glory.
Lord Jesus, come in glory.

From the Roman Missal

682

Through him, with him, in him,
amen,
in the unity of the Holy Spirit,
amen,
all glory and honour is yours,
almighty Father,
for ever and ever,
amen.

or

Per ipsum, et cum ipso, et in ipso,
amen,
est tibi, Deo Patri omnipotenti,
in unitate Spiritus Sancti,
amen,
omnis honor et gloria,
per omnia sæcula sæculorum,
amen.

From the Roman Missal

683

Through him, with him, in him,
in the unity of the Holy Spirit,
all glory and honour is yours,
almighty Father, for ever and ever.
Amen.

From the Roman Missal

684

Our Father, who art in heaven,
hallowed be thy name;
thy kingdom come;
thy will be done on earth
as it is in heaven.
Give us this day our daily bread;
and forgive us our trespasses
as we forgive those
who trespass against us;
and lead us not into temptation,
but deliver us from evil.

For the kingdom, the pow'r
and the glory are yours,
now and for ever. Amen.

Matthew 6:9-13 and Luke 11:2-4

685

1. Our Father, who art in heaven,
   hallowed be thy name.
   Thy kingdom come, thy will be done,
   hallowed be thy name,
   hallowed be thy name.

2. On earth as it is in heaven.
   hallowed be thy name.
   Give us this day our daily bread,
   hallowed be thy name,
   hallowed be thy name.

3. Forgive us our trespasses,
   hallowed be thy name.
   as we forgive those who trespass
     against us,
   hallowed be thy name,
   hallowed be thy name.

Continued overleaf

4. Lead us not into temptation,
   hallowed be thy name.
   but deliver us from all that is evil,
   hallowed be thy name,
   hallowed be thy name.

5. For thine is the kingdom, the power,
      and the glory,
   hallowed be thy name.
   for ever, and for ever and ever,
   hallowed be thy name,
   hallowed be thy name.

6. Amen, amen, it shall be so.
   hallowed be thy name.
   Amen, amen, it shall be so,
   hallowed be thy name,
   hallowed be thy name.

Traditional Caribbean,
based on Matthew 6:9-13 and Luke 11:2-4

687

Our Father, who art in heaven,
hallowed be thy name;
thy kingdom come;
thy will be done on earth
as it is in heaven.
Give us this day our daily bread;
and forgive us our trespasses
as we forgive those
who trespass against us;
and lead us not into temptation,
but deliver us from all that is evil.

For the kingdom, the pow'r
and the glory are yours,
now and for ever. Amen.

Matthew 6:9-13 and Luke 11:2-4

686

Our Father, who art in heaven,
hallowed be thy name;
thy kingdom come;
thy will be done on earth
as it is in heaven.
Give us this day our daily bread;
and forgive us our trespasses
as we forgive those
who trespass against us;
and lead us not into temptation,
but deliver us from evil.

For the kingdom, the pow'r
and the glory are yours,
now and for ever.

Matthew 6:9-13 and Luke 11:2-4

688

1. Jesus, Lamb of God, the source of life,
   bearer of our sins, renew us in
      your love;
   Holy Lord, Redeemer of the world,
   give us your peace.

2. Lord, we are not worthy to be here
   standing in the presence of the Lamb
      of God;
   but, O Father, if you say the word,
   we shall be healed.

Adapted from the Liturgy
by Christopher Walker (b. 1947)
© 1985 OCP Publications

689

Lamb of God,
you take away the sins of the world:
have mercy on us,
have mercy on us.

Lamb of God,
you take away the sins of the world:
have mercy on us,
have mercy on us.

Lamb of God,
you take away the sins of the world:
grant us peace,
grant us peace.

From the Roman Missal

690

1. Jesus, Lamb of God,
   have mercy on us.
   Jesus, Lamb of God,
   have mercy on us.
   Jesus, Word made flesh,
   bearer of our sins:
   Jesus, Lamb of God,
   have mercy on us.

2. Jesus, Bread of Life,
   have mercy on us.
   Jesus, Bread of Life,
   have mercy on us.
   Jesus, Morning Star;
   Jesus, Prince of Peace:
   Jesus, Bread of Life,
   have mercy on us.

3. Jesus, Lamb of God,
   have mercy on us.
   Jesus, Lamb of God,
   have mercy on us.
   Jesus, King of kings;
   Jesus, Lord of all:
   Jesus, Lamb of God,
   give us your peace.

Adapted from the Liturgy by Paul Inwood (b. 1947)

691

Lamb of God,
you take away the sins of the world,
have mercy on us.

Lamb of God,
you take away the sins of the world,
have mercy on us.

Lamb of God,
you take away the sins of the world,
grant us peace.

From the Roman Missal

Index of Authors

Index of Uses

Scriptural Index

This scriptural index lists all the texts in the Bible which are quoted or referred to in the hymns. This should enable anyone to find appropriate hymns to accompany readings from Scripture, either at Mass or at any other service.

Hymns 469-649 have not been included in this index because they usually only allude to the Bible texts rather than actually quote them. They have this advantage however: each hymn makes some indirect reference to all three Scripture readings at the Mass for which it has been designed, and so provides an apt musical reflection on the theme of the day.

GENESIS
1:2	17, 111, 379, 436
1:3	425
2:7	2, 67
2:9	282
3:14-15	102, 265, 463
8:22	155
15:1	31, 331

EXODUS
3:6	270
3:5	51
3:7	186
14	379
20	290
33:20	177

JOSHUA
3	156

1 KINGS
19:12	104, 238

JOB
38:7	307

PSALMS
2:1	277
4:1	310
4:8	55
5:7	72
15 (16)	126
15 (16):2	53
15 (16):5	31, 53
17 (18):5	370

(Psalms continued)
18 (19):10	40
22 (23)	54, 276, 400, 405, 406
22 (23):1	4, 350
22 (23):4	5, 272
22 (23):6	349
23 (74):7	123, 160
23 (24):7-10	283, 399
24 (25):2	50
26 (27):14	439
30 (31):5	114
33 (34)	402
33 (34):5	199
33 (34): 18	246
35 (36):6	196
41 (42)	40, 237
44 (45):6	394
45 (46):10	49, 50, 51, 52
50 (51):10	24
55 (56):13	59
64 (65)	136
65 (66)	25
67 (68):5	179, 437
69 (70):4	181
70 (71)	174
71 (72)	162
72 (73):1	301
72 (73):26	31
76 (77):20	427
77 (78):24-25	27, 287, 293
77 (78):52	427
85 (86):6-7	310
85 (86):8	9
85 (86):11	439
85 (86):15	345
87 (88):13	177
88 (89)	185
89 (90)	297
90 (91)	65, 468
90 (91):4-5	55, 206, 286
92-99 (93-100)	354
94 (95)	94
94 (95):5	171
95 (96):11	393
97 (98)	21, 217, 366
97 (98):7	393
99 (100)	18, 20, 37, 92, 218
99 (100):4	326
101 (102):27	181
102 (103):1	59, 60
102 (103):2-3	50, 301
103 (104)	325, 363
103 (104):14-15	63
103 (104):27	196
106 (107)	111

(Psalms continued)
109 (110):1	354, 463
114 (116):8	59
115 (116b)	370
116 (117)	96, 223
117 (118)	373
117 (118):24-26	56, 419
118 (119):105	350
120 (121):4	103
122 (123):2	439
129 (130):4-5	31, 206
130 (131)	280
135 (136)	16, 233, 275
136 (137)	71
138 (139)	462
138 (139):1-2	74, 253
138(139):14	128
146 (147)	120
148	22, 23, 317, 345, 346
150	317, 370, 404
150:6	348, 349

SONGS OF SONGS
2:4	166
4:4	194
7:4	194
8:6	43

WISDOM
11:26	206
16:20	27, 151
18:14	203

ECCLESIASTICUS
24:20	207

ISAIAH
1:3	87, 433
2:1-5	93
5:1-4	315
6:1-3	174, 175, 177, 196, 373
6:8-9	186
7:14	46, 165, 213, 290
9:2-7	408
9:6	159, 165, 173, 244, 428, 448, 461
11:1-2	90, 101, 179, 290, 375, 436, 437
22:22	290
35:5-6	46
40:1-11	100, 292, 439
40:7-8	196, 254, 331, 431
40:9-11	141, 236, 345
40:31	426
43:1-4	109, 466

Index of Sunday and Feastday Themes

1st SUNDAY OF ADVENT

Year A   *Watch for his coming*
- 93   Come, let us go up to the Lord
- 302   O Jesus Christ, remember
- 440   Wake up, O people
- 469   Waken, O sleeper, wake and rise

Year B   *Wake up*
- 2   Abba, Abba, Father, you are the potter
- 156   Guide me, O thou great Redeemer
- 473   Return, Redeemer God
- 426   Though the mountains may fall

Year C   *Be prepared*
- 43   At the name of Jesus
- 164   Hark a herald voice is calling
- 477   Holy God, our great Redeemer
- 375   Songs of thankfulness and praise

2nd SUNDAY OF ADVENT

Year A   *The Kingdom is close*
- 470   Behold the Saviour
        of the nations
- 290   O come, O come, Emmanuel
- 331   On Jordan's bank
- 439   Wait for the Lord

Year B   *The Lord is coming*
- 100   Comfort, comfort my people
- 474   Hark, a voice is calling
- 236   Like a shepherd
- 292   O comfort my people
- 455   When is he coming

Year C   *Prepare the way*
- 478   Let all creation now rejoice
- 235   Like a sea without a shore
- 392   The coming of our God
- 399   The King of glory comes

3rd SUNDAY OF ADVENT

Year A   *The blind will see*
- 97   Come, thou long-expected Jesus
- 240   Lo, he comes with clouds descending
- 295   O for a thousand tongues
- 336   Open our eyes, Lord
- 471   The Saviour will come, resplendent in joy

Year B   *Good News for the poor*
- 105   Dear maker of the stars of night
- 144   God fills me with joy
- 152   God's Spirit is in my heart
- 475   Sing and rejoice, the Lord is near

Year C   *Rejoice*
- 479   As people of God, let us sing
        and rejoice
- 182   How lovely on the mountains
- 199   In the Lord I'll be ever thankful
- 352   Rejoice in the Lord always

4th SUNDAY OF ADVENT

Year A   *God with us*
- 164   Hark a herald voice is calling
- 290   O come, O come, Emmanuel
- 390   The angel Gabriel from heaven came
- 477   The sign of hope, creation's joy

Year B   *Annunciation*
- 180   Holy virgin, by God's decree
- 305   O Lady, full of God's own grace
- 390   The angel Gabriel from heaven came
- 476   The Saviour of the nations

Year C   *Visitation*
- 57   Bethlehem, of noblest cities
- 480   From the humblest of the cities
- 272   Mother of God's living Word
- 307   O little town of Bethlehem

CHRISTMAS

Midnight   *Light in the darkness*
- 36   Angels we have heard on high
- 229   Let all mortal flesh keep silence
- 365   Silent night
- 408   The race that long in darkness pined
- 481   Those who walked in deepest darkness

Dawn   *The manger*
- 83   Come and join the celebration
- 87   Come, come, come to the manger
- 165   Hark, the herald angels sing
- 458   While shepherds watched

Day   *Word made flesh*
- 182   How lovely on the mountains
- 482   Lovely feet upon the mountains
- 288   O come, all ye faithful
        (7 Adeste fideles)
- 327   Of the Father's love begotten
- 461   Word made flesh

HOLY FAMILY

The Presentation
- 483   Holy Jesus, in our likeness born
- 484   O God of Abraham
- 485   O God whose love for all we see
- 369   Sing of Mary, pure and lowly

MARY MOTHER OF GOD

Abba Father

2	Abba, Abba, Father, you are the potter
4	Abba, Father, send your Spirit
43	At the name of Jesus
141	Go, tell it on the mountain
486	O Christ, incarnate God
327	Of the Father's love begotten

2nd SUNDAY AFTER CHRISTMAS

He dwelt among us

327	Of the Father's love begotten
360	See him lying on a bed of straw
369	Sing of Mary, pure and lowly
487	Word made flesh, eternal Wisdom
461	Word made flesh

EPIPHANY

The nations come

488	Arise to greet the Lord of light
41	As with gladness men of old
326	O worship the Lord in the beauty of holiness
395	The first Nowell
447	We three kings

BAPTISM OF THE LORD

The beloved Son

491	All the glory of the heavens
489	Behold the Servant of the Lord
490	God whose thoughts and way exalted
308	O living water
379	Springs of water, bless the Lord

ASH WEDNESDAY

Out of the depths

145	God forgave my sin
492	Holy God, of righteous glory
214	Jesus, remember me
246	Lord, have mercy
273	My God, accept my heart this day

1st SUNDAY OF LENT

Year A *The second Adam*

2	Abba, Abba, Father, you are the potter
129	Forty days and forty nights
493	Lord of creation, forgive us we pray
347	Praise to the Holiest

Year B *Repent*

129	Forty days and forty nights
152	God's Spirit is in my heart
498	O God of truth, your dreadful might
324	O the word of my Lord

Year C *Trust in God*

109	Do not be afraid
503	God, we call upon you
256	Lord, who throughout these forty days
468	You who dwell in the shelter of the Lord

2nd SUNDAY OF LENT

Year A *Life beyond death*

494	Here in this holy time and place
646	Holy Christ in light transfigured
187	I watch the sunrise
444	We behold the splendour of God

Year B *The beloved Son*

192	If God is for us
499	Remember, O God
401	The light of Christ
444	We behold the splendour of God

Year C *Transfigured*

504	God of eternal light
185	I have made a covenant
273	My God, accept my heart this day
444	We behold the splendour of God

3rd SUNDAY OF LENT

Year A *Thirst for water*

291	O, come to the water
495	O God of all truth, our doubting forgive
308	O living water
435	Vaster far than any ocean

Year B *Jesus the new Temple*

1	A new commandment
126	For you are my God
290	O come, O come, Emmanuel (v. 5)
500	The wisdom of the living God

Year C *Jesus the new Moses*

38	As earth that is dry
186	I, the Lord of sea and sky
270	Moses, I know you're the man
505	The fire of grace and judgement

4th SUNDAY OF LENT

Year A *From darkness into light*

77	Christ is our King
79	Colours of day
166	He brings us into his banqueting table
496	Holy Shepherd, King divine

Year B *Saved*

31	Amazing grace
501	From death to life restored
145	God forgave my sin
148	God is love: his the care
256	Lord, who throughout these forty days

4th SUNDAY OF EASTER

Year A   *Healed by his wounds*
- 48   Battle is o'er, hell's armies flee
- 159   Hail, Redeemer, King divine
- 514   Let the world in concert name him
- 259   Loving shepherd of thy sheep

Year B   *The good Shepherd*
- 13   All glory to you, Redeemer and Lord
- 43   At the name of Jesus
- 54   Because the Lord is my shepherd
- 105   Dear maker of the stars of night
- 521   The power of God throughout the world

Year C   *The sheep brought to God*
- 205   Jerusalem the golden
- 259   Loving shepherd of thy sheep
- 528   Sing the gospel of salvation
- 387   Take our bread

5th SUNDAY OF EASTER

Year A   *The Way, Truth and Life*
- 183   I am the bread of life
- 216   Jesus, you are Lord
- 337   Open your ears, O Christian people
- 515   The temple of the living God

Year B   *The Vine*
- 84   Come and praise him
- 522   Sing a new and joyful song
- 417   This is my body
- 418   This is my will

Year C   *God lives among those who love*
- 1   A new commandment
- 33   And did those feet in ancient time
- 529   As I have loved you
- 205   Jerusalem the golden

6th SUNDAY OF EASTER

Year A   *I will not leave you*
- 27   Alleluia, sing to Jesus
- 49   Be still and know I am with you
- 88   Come down, O Love divine
- 181   How great is our God
- 516   Let all the world exultant sing

Year B   *Bear fruit by loving*
- 1   A new commandment
- 523   Come, let us live by love
- 147   God is love
- 417   This is my body
- 418   This is my will

Year C   *Peace*
- 4   Abba Father, send your Spirit
- 530   Holy Spirit, give us peace
- 262   Make me a channel of your peace
- 340   Peace I leave with you

ASCENSION
(See Index of Uses)

7th SUNDAY OF EASTER

Year A   *Eternal life is to know God in Christ*
- 49   Be still and know I am with you
- 518   Father, bless your people
- 202   Into one we all are gathered
- 244   Lord enthroned in heavenly splendour

Year B   *God is love*
- 147   God is love
- 148   God is love: his the care
- 525   Hear us, O God
- 432   Ubi caritas

Year C   *May they be one in us*
- 2   Abba, Abba, Father,
       you are the potter
- 58   Bind us together, Lord
- 152   God's Spirit is in my heart
- 532   Heaven is open wide
- 461   Word made flesh

PENTECOST SUNDAY
(See Index of Uses)

TRINITY SUNDAY
(See Index of Uses)

CORPUS CHRISTI

Year A   *Bread from Heaven*
- 80   Come and be filled
- 156   Guide me, O thou great Redeemer
- 539   Holy God, your pilgrim people
- 183   I am the bread of life
- 287   O bread of heaven

Year B   *Body and Blood*
- 540   God of the covenant
- 244   Lord, enthroned in heavenly splendour
- 258   Love is his word
- 348   Praise to the Lord, the Almighty
- 417   This is my body

Year C   *Plenty for all*
- 119   Feed us now, O Son of God
- 134   Gifts of bread and wine
- 151   Godhead here in hiding
- 541   See the holy table, spread for our healing

SACRED HEART

Year A   *I will give you rest*
- 24   All ye who seek a comfort sure
- 147   God is love
- 148   God is love: his the care
- 236   Like a shepherd

Year B *The love of Christ crucified*
109 Do not be afraid
376 Soul of my Saviour
423 This, then, is my prayer
429 To Jesus' heart all burning

Year C *The loving Shepherd*
236 Like a shepherd
322 O Sacred Heart
383 Sweet heart of Jesus
428 To Christ, the Prince of peace

SUNDAYS OF THE YEAR

1st SUNDAY See BAPTISM OF THE LORD above

2nd SUNDAY

Year A *Lamb of God*
33 And did those feet in ancient time
342 Peace is the gift
379 Springs of water, bless the Lord
542 Thus says the Lord of hosts

Year B *Called*
128 Forth in thy name, O Lord, I go
575 Let all creation worship you
238 Listen, let your heart keep seeking
270 Moses, I know you're the man

Year C *Bride and Groom*
113 Father and life-giver
202 Into one we all are gathered
338 Our hearts were made for you
375 Songs of thankfulness and praise
608 You we praise, O God most high

3rd SUNDAY

Year A *Light has dawned*
58 Bind us together Lord
104 Dear Lord and Father of mankind
543 Sing to God a song of gladness
408 The race that long in darkness pinned

Year B *Follow me*
104 Dear Lord and Father of mankind
122 Follow me, follow me
576 The voice of redemption
453 When Christ our Lord to Andrew cried

Year C *Good News*
77 Christ is our King
152 God's Spirit is in my heart
432 Ubi caritas
609 We have heard the prophet speaking

4th SUNDAY

Year A *Good News for the poor*
61 Blessed are my people
62 Blest are the pure in heart
64 Blest are you, O poor in spirit
544 O God of hope, your people save

Year B *The crowds stare*
49 Be still and know I am with you
578 Freedom! Freedom! let us cry
577 God has raised a prophet
311 O Lord, my God

Year C *Persecuted love*
74 Christ be beside me
610 Love's great endeavour
324 O the word of my Lord
388 Tell out, my soul

5th SUNDAY

Year A *Light*
545 Come, let us worship
410 The Spirit lives to set us free
422 This little light of mine
454 When I survey the wondrous cross

Year B *Healing the broken*
50 Be still and know that I am God
79 Colours of day
128 Forth in thy name, O Lord, I go
578 Freedom! Freedom! let us cry
234 Let's all join together

Year C *Called by the Holy God*
122 Follow me, follow me
174 Holy God, we praise thy name
186 I, the Lord of sea and sky
611 O God of grace, in glorious state

6th SUNDAY

Year A *What God demands*
98 Come to us, Lord of light
156 Guide me, O thou great Redeemer
209 Jesus Christ is waiting
546 O holy wisdom, gracious offer

Year B *Healing*
143 God be in my head
579 God of salvation
225 Lay your hands gently upon us
247 Lord Jesus Christ

Year C *Good News for the poor*
61 Blessed are my people
64 Blest are you, O poor in spirit
160 Hail the day that sees him rise
612 Happy are those who trust in you
466 You shall cross the barren desert

7th SUNDAY

Year A   *Love your enemies*
   1   A new commandment
   547   Holy God, eternal Father
   232   Let there be love
   309   O Lord, all the world belongs to you

Year B   *Forgiven and healed*
   31   Amazing grace
   77   Christ is our King
   145   God forgave my sin
   580   O holy God, our sins forgive
   466   You shall cross the barren desert

Year C   *Compassion*
   2   Abba, Abba, Father,
       you are the potter
   613   As you give to others, so you
       will receive
   262   Make me a channel of your peace
   452   Whatsoever you do

8th SUNDAY

Year A   *At rest in God*
   548   God is our strength from days of old
   189   I will never forget you
   245   Lord, for tomorrow and its needs
   362   Seek ye first
   426   Though the mountains may fall

Year B   *Wedded to God*
   58   Bind us together, Lord
   86   Come back to me
   581   In love, O God, you gently call us
   338   Our hearts were made for you
   375   Songs of thankfulness and praise

Year C   *Giving yourself away*
   74   Christ be beside me
   190   I will sing
   235   Like a sea without a shore
   614   O God, refine our faith

9th SUNDAY

Year A   *Building on rock*
   16   All my hope on God is founded
   248   Lord Jesus, think on me
   297   O God, our help in ages past
   549   O look upon us, Lord
   391   The Church's one foundation

Year B   *Freedom from slavery*
   578   Freedom! Freedom! let us cry
   582   God of redemptive power
   444   We behold the splendour of God
   446   We hold a treasure

Year C   *Outsiders are welcome*
   50   Be still and know that I am God*are*
   615   Christ, in every mortal language
   76   Christ is made the sure foundation
   109   Do not be afraid

10th SUNDAY

Year A   *I want love not ritual*
   550   Come, O God, like morning light
   128   Forth in my name, O Lord, I go
   186   I, the Lord of sea and sky
   258   Love is his word

Year B   *Adam and Satan*
   53   Be thou my vision
   583   O Source of goodness
   347   Praise to the Holiest
   463   Ye choirs of new Jerusalem

Year C   *The dead raised to life*
   77   Christ is our King
   96   Come, praise me Lord
   616   God of old, who sent the prophet
   183   I am the bread of life
   234   Let's all join together

11th SUNDAY

Year A   *Spread the Good News*
   84   Come and praise him
   142   Go, the Mass is ended
   148   God is love: his the care
   551   O God of the wilderness
   337   Open your ears, O Christian people

Year B   *Growth of the Kingdom*
   17   All over the world
   22   All the nations of the earth
   99   Come, ye thankful people, come
   124   For I'm building a people of power
   584   See the kingdom grow and flourish

Year C   *God forgives*
   31   Amazing grace
   617   Christ, at your table we present
   121   Firmly I believe
   145   God forgave my sin
   263   Many times I have turned

12th SUNDAY

Year A   *Do not be afraid*
   109   Do not be afraid
   187   I watch the sunrise
   347   Praise to the Holiest
   552   Sing to God, praise the Lord
   426   Though the mountains may fall

Year B   *The Conqueror of chaos*
52   Be still, my soul
585   God of love, whose voice we hear
227   Lead us, heavenly Father
391   The Church's one foundation
441   Walk with me, O my Lord

Year C   *Take up the cross*
122   Follow me, follow me
618   O the mystery of salvation
334   One bread, one body
453   When Christ our Lord to Andrew cried

13th SUNDAY

Year A   *Cups of water are rewarded*
26   Alleluia: give thanks to the risen Lord
122   Follow me, follow me
553   O come, all nations
443   We are the Easter people

Year B   *Victory over death*
586   God the source of life eternal
167   He is Lord
234   Let's all join together
247   Lord Jesus Christ

Year C   *Follow me*
122   Follow me, follow me
619   Holy God, we hear your call
270   Moses, I know you're the man
410   The Spirit lives to set us free

14th SUNDAY

Year A   *Humility*
24   All ye who seek a comfort sure
236   Like a shepherd
554   O let us rejoice and welcome our King
410   The Spirit lives to set us free

Year B   *Speak out*
74   Christ be beside me
109   Do not be afraid
152   God's Spirit is in my heart
169   He who would valiant be
587   The Spirit is upon us

Year C   *Make peace*
121   Firmly I believe
145   God forgave my sin
620   Holy God, give us peace
341   Peace is flowing like a river
454   When I survey the wondrous cross

15th SUNDAY

Year A   *The prodigal Sower*
38   As earth that is dry
238   Listen, let your heart keep seeking
386   Take my hands
555   The word of God, like seed, is sown

Year B   *Go preach and heal*
588   Called from safer pastures
142   Go, me Mass is ended
152   God's Spirit is in my heart
225   Lay your hands gently upon us

Year C   *God's Word is near you*
95   Come, Lord Jesus, come
621   Creator of all
197   In bread we bring you, Lord
244   Lord enthroned in heavenly splendour
452   Whatsoever you do

16th SUNDAY

Year A   *The lenient Judge*
99   Come, ye thankful people, come
234   Let's all join together
308   O living water
556   To you, O Lord. our only help

Year B   *The Shepherd*
54   Because the Lord is my shepherd
119   Feed us now, O Son of God
589   Listen to the voice of judgement
276   My shepherd is the Lord

Year C   *God in the midst*
49   Be still and know I am with you
74   Christ be beside me
622   Heal us, O God, our only help
323   O, the love of my Lord

17th SUNDAY

Year A   *Discernment*
2   Abba, Abba, Father,
     you are the potter
105   Dear maker of the stars of night
557   God is in his holy place
446   We hold a treasure

Year B   *The hungry are fed*
58   Bind us together, Lord
119   Feed us now, O Son of God
197   In bread we bring you, Lord
590   In hopeful trust, O God
427   Thy hand, O God, has guided

Year C   *Never stop asking*
81   Come and bless
145   God forgave my sin
623   O God, within this special place
362   Seek ye first

18th SUNDAY

Year A   *God's pity*
38   As earth that is dry
192   If God is for us
291   O, come to the water
558   O God of hope, your people hear

Year B   *Bread from Heaven*
    110   Eat this bread
    591   Holy manna, bread of heaven
    183   I am the bread of life
    287   O bread of heaven
    461   Word made flesh

Year C   *Rich before God*
    125   For the healing of the nations
    160   Hail the day that sees him rise
    296   O God of earth and altar
    624   Wisdom of the ages, help us
           and save us

19th SUNDAY

Year A   *Calm after the storm*
    104   Dear Lord and Father of mankind
    111   Eternal Father, strong to save
    188   I will be with you
    559   O God of truth and justice
    441   Walk with me, O my Lord

Year B   *The Bread of Life*
    110   Eat this bread
    183   I am the bread of life
    592   In every heart, O God
    287   O bread of heaven

Year C   *The virtuous saved*
    109   Do not be afraid
    625   God of liberation, let us hear your cry
    156   Guide me, O thou great Redeemer
    422   This little light of mine

20th SUNDAY

Year A   *God so loved the world*
    22   All the nations of the earth
    125   For the healing of the nations
    171   He's got the whole world in his hand
    560   Protector God, your people's strength
    402   The Lord hears the cry of the poor

Year B   *Come and eat*
    80   Come and be filled
    593   Here, upon a holy table
    183   I am the bread of life
    403   The Lord is alive

Year C   *Setting the world on fire*
    53   Be thou my vision
    169   He who would valiant be
    626   O God, renew our vision
    426   Though the mountains may fall

21st SUNDAY

Year A   *Built on rock*
    76   Christ is made the sure foundation
    561   Great Father of light, in glory above
    166   He brings us into his banqueting table
    391   The Church's one foundation
    427   Thy hand, O God, has guided

Year B   *To whom else would we go?*
    5   Abide with me
    27   Alleluia, sing to Jesus
    594   God of life and God of freedom
    188   I will be with you

Year C   *No east or west*
    14   All God's people, come together
    17   All over the world
    22   All the nations of the earth
    627   From east and west, from north and south
    171   He's got the whole world in his hand

22nd SUNDAY

Year A   *A living sacrifice*
    2   Abba, Abba, Father,
           you are the potter
    122   Follow me, follow me
    562   God of prophecy and promise
    454   When I survey the wondrous cross

Year B   *Submit to God's Word*
    595   Holy and unchanging
    209   Jesus Christ is waiting
    337   Open your ears, O Christian people
    402   The Lord hears the cry of the poor

Year C   *The heavenly Jerusalem for the humble*
    144   God fills me with joy
    628   God of true humility
    205   Jerusalem the golden
    322   O Sacred heart

23rd SUNDAY

Year A   *Responsibility for brothers and sisters*
    1   A new commandment
    262   Make me a channel of your peace
    563   O God of justice, righteous judge
    418   This is my will

Year B   *The deaf hear again*
    46   Awake, awake and greet the
           new morn
    596   Be not afraid, your God will come
    77   Christ is our King
    225   Lay your hands gently upon us

Year C   *Counting the cost*

  122   Follow me, follow me
  629   God eternal, cosmic wisdom
  386   Take my hands
  459   Will you come and follow me

24th SUNDAY

Year A   *As forgiving as God*

  145   God forgave my sin
  262   Make me a channel of your peace
  564   O all-forgiving God
  301   O, how good is the Lord

Year B   *What faith entails*

  122   Follow me, follow me
  192   If God is for us
  359   See, Christ was wounded
  597   The servant of the living God

Year C   *The prodigal Father*

   18   All people that on earth do dwell
   31   Amazing grace
  630   God of forgiveness, your people
        you freed
  149   God of mercy and compassion
  448   Welcome all ye noble saints of old

25th SUNDAY

Year A   *Generous to a fault*

   31   Amazing grace
  565   Look to the Lord of life
  301   O, how good is the Lord
  435   Vaster far than any ocean

Year B   *Servants of each other*

   62   Blest are the pure in heart
  598   Human wisdom has no measure
  262   Make me a channel of your peace
  452   Whatsoever you do

Year C   *The right use of money*

  125   For the healing of the nations
  145   God forgave my sin
  296   O God of earth and altar
  402   The Lord hears the cry of the poor
  631   The word of God rings harsh and clear

26th SUNDAY

Year A   *Humble repentance*

   43   At the name of Jesus
  566   God of truth and justice
  167   He is Lord
  216   Jesus, you are Lord
  263   Many times I have turned

Year B   *Whatsoever you do to the least*

  125   For the healing of the nations
  599   Help us, O God, to hear your word
  296   O God of earth and altar
  402   The Lord hears the cry of the poor
  452   Whatsoever you do

Year C   *Riches corrupt you*

   64   Blest are you, O poor in spirit
  209   Jesus Christ is waiting
  222   Kum ba yah
  632   The rich in splendid castle homes

27th SUNDAY

Year A   *Sour grapes*

  107   Deep peace of the running wave
        to you
  567   God, the great Creator
  315   O my people, what have I done to you
  340   Peace I leave with you

Year B   *Man and wife, one body*

   43   At the name of Jesus
   88   Come down, O Love divine
  600   God, who man and woman made
  257   Love divine, all loves excelling

Year C   *Increase our faith*

    9   Alabaré
   16   All my hope on God is founded
  633   How long, O God, the people cry
  426   Though the mountains may fall

28th SUNDAY

Year A   *Everyone is invited*

  568   God is longing to forgive
  274   My God, and is thy table spread
  405   The Lord's my shepherd
  427   Thy hand, O God, has guided

Year B   *The Kingdom is worth every sacrifice*

  122   Follow me, follow me
  386   Take my hands
  601   The spirit of wisdom is brighter
        than gold
  446   We hold a treasure

Year C   *Gratitude*

   77   Christ is our King
  634   God of creation, with what joy
  220   Keep in mind
  375   Songs of thankfulness and praise

29th SUNDAY

Year A   *God as Supreme King*

   16   All my hope on God is founded
   17   All over the world
  196   Immortal, invisible
  569   O God, through all the nations' life
  431   Turn to me

Year B   *Christ tested as we are*
    13   All glory to you, Redeemer
            and Lord
    244   Lord, enthroned in heavenly splendour
    309   O Lord, all the world belongs to you
    347   Praise to the Holiest
    602   The Servant, crushed with pain

Year C   *Unrelenting prayer*
    635   Eternal God, you cry for justice
    125   For the healing of the nations
    388   Tell out, my soul
    402   The Lord hears the cry of the poor

30th SUNDAY

Year A   *Loving neighbours is like loving God*
      1   A new commandment
    184   I give my hands
    570   Let us rejoice in God our strength
    402   The Lord hears the cry of the poor
    452   Whatsoever you do
    455   When is he coming

Year B   *Lord that I may see*
    31   Amazing grace
    77   Christ is our King
    244   Lord, enthroned in heavenly splendour
    348   Praise to the Lord the Almighty
    603   Sing for joy, all the earth

Year C   *God prefers sinners*
      5   Abide with me
    636   Come, holy God, our spirit cleanse
    214   Jesus, remember me
    402   The Lord hears the cry of the poor

31st SUNDAY

Year A   *A warning for priests*
      3   Abba, Father, let me be
    62   Blest are the pure in heart
    571   Great Father of us all
    378   Spread, O spread, thou mighty word

Year B   *Loving God and neighbour*
      1   A new commandment
    16   All my hope on God is founded
    348   Praise to the Lord the Almighty
    604   The great command we would obey
    452   Whatsoever you do

Year C   *God saves the lost*
    31   Amazing grace
    77   Christ is our King
    98   Come to us, Lord of light
    148   God is love: his the care
    637   God of salvation, loving and longing
    348   Praise to the Lord the Almighty

32nd SUNDAY

Year A   *Keep watch*
    135   Give me joy in my heart
    581   In love, O God, you gently call us
    440   Wake up, O people
    572   Wisdom is ever bright

Year B   *Giving one's all*
    95   Come, Lord Jesus, come
    145   God forgave my sin
    605   Lord, from the greatness of our wealth
    386   Take my hands
    396   The head that once was crowned with thorns

Year C   *Always alive before God*
    96   Come, praise the Lord
    183   I am the bread of life
    638   O listen to our prayer
    393   The day of resurrection
    403   The Lord is alive

33rd SUNDAY

Year A   *Using our talents*
    573   God of peace and order
    386   Take my hands
    440   Wake up, O people
    452   Whatsoever you do

Year B   *Saved from disaster*
    145   God forgave my sin
    606   In fear and in hope
    302   O Jesus Christ, remember
    375   Songs of thankfulness and praise

Year C   *Don't give in*
    105   Dear maker of the stars of night
    152   God's Spirit is in my heart
    639   The dreaded day will surely dawn
    466   You shall cross the barren desert

34th SUNDAY (CHRIST THE KING.)

Year A   *Bandaging the wounded*
    160   Hail the day that sees him rise
    209   Jesus Christ is waiting
    574   Lord Christ, triumphant
    259   Loving shepherd of thy sheep
    452   Whatsoever you do

Year B   *Christ Supreme*
    21   All the ends of the earth
    607   Christ, come in glory
    101   Crown him with many crowns
    176   Holy, holy, holy is the Lord
    261   Majesty, worship his majesty

Year C   *A place for us in the Kingdom*
    640   Christ reigns triumphant
    162   Hail to the Lord's anointed
    214   Jesus, remember me
    217   Joy to the world
    244   Lord, enthroned in heavenly splendour
    396   The head that once was crowned with thorns

Index of First Lines

Acknowledgements

The publishers wish to express their gratitude to the following for permission to use copyright material in this book:

Alba House Communications, PO Box 595, Canfield, Ohio 44406, USA for *What can we offer you* © 1971.

Mike Anderson, 11A Rampit Close, Penny Lane, Haydock, Merseyside, WA11 OYH for *The Clapping Gloria* © 1983.

Karen Barrie, 511 Maple, Wilmette, IL 60091, USA for *I have made a covenant* © 1973.

The Benedictine Foundation of the State of Vermont, Inc., Weston Priory, Weston, Vermont 05161, USA for *Hosea (Come back to me)* © 1972 from the recording 'Listen'.

Birdwing Music/BMG Songs, Inc./Cherry Lane Music/Ears to Hear Music, Bedford House, 69-79 Fulham High Street, London, SW6 3JW for *There is a Redeemer*.

Fred Bock Music Company, PO Box 570567, Tarzana, California 91357, USA for *Thou art worthy* © 1963, 1975, renewed 1991. All rights reserved. Used by permission.

The Rev'd E Burns, Christ Church Vicarage, 19 Vicarage Close, Fulwood, Preston, PR2 4EG for *We have a gospel to proclaim* (words).

Burns & Oats Ltd, Wellwood, North Farm Road, Tunbridge Wells, Kent, TN2 3DR for *Battle is o'er, New praises be given, O Sacred Head ill-used*, and *Star of Ocean* (translations).

Geoffrey Chapman, a division of Cassell plc, Villiers House, 41/47 Strand, London WC2N 5JE for the words of *Blest are you, O poor in spirit, Christ be beside me, Come, adore this wondrous place, Come, praise the Lord, Day is done, Forth in the peace of Christ, This day God gives* and *This is my will* © 1969 James Quinn S. J.

CopyCare Ltd, PO Box 77, Hailsham, East Sussex, BN27 3EF, for *Father we adore you* © 1972 Maranatha! Music, *Glorify thy name (Father we love you)* © 1976 Maranatha! Music, *Open our eyes* © 1976 Maranatha! Music, *Seek ye first* © 1972 Maranatha! Music, *Jesus, name above all names* © 1974 Scripture in Song, *This is the day* © 1967 Scripture in Song, *Welcome all ye noble saints* © 1977 Dawn Treader Music, *Freely, freely* © 1972 Bud John Songs Inc., *Holy, holy* © 1972 Bud John Songs Inc., *The Old Rugged Cross* © 1913 The Rodeheaver Co/Word Music Inc./Word Music (UK) and *This is my body* © 1978 Bud John Songs Inc. All administered by CopyCare Ltd and used by permission.

The Church of the Messiah, 231 East Grand Blvd, Detroit, Michigan 48207, USA for *The Lord is present* © 1975.

Collins Litugical, an imprint of HarperCollins Religious, 77-85 Fulham Palace Road, London, W6 8JB for *Adoramus Te, Bless the Lord, Eat this bread, In the Lord I'll be ever thankful, Jesus, remember me, Laudate Dominum, O Lord, hear my prayer, Stay with me, Ubi Caritas, Veni, Sancte Spiritus, Wait for the Lord, Within our darkest night, Kyrie, Gloria* © Les Presses de Taize from 'Music from Taize'.

The Abbot of Downside Abbey, Stratton on the Fosse, Bath, BA3 4RH for *O King of might and splendour, O Salutaris, Salve, Regina,* and *Adoremus in aeternum.*

The Rt Rev'd Timothy Dudley-Smith, 9 Ashlands, Ford, Salisbury, Wilts, SP4 6DY for the words of *Fill your hearts with joy* and *Tell out, my soul* © Timothy Dudley-Smith.

Faber Music Ltd, 3 Queen Square, London, WC1N 3AU for the words of *See, Christ was wounded for our sake, Lord, as I wake* and *Holy Spirit, come confirm us* ©1971 by Faber Music Ltd, reproduced from 'New Catholic Hymnal'.

Franciscan Communications, 1229 South Santee Street, Los Angeles, CA 90015-2566, USA for *Make me a channel of your peace* © 1967, *Take my hands* © 1966 and *All that I am* © 1966. All rights reserved. Reprinted with permission.

GIA Publications, 7404 S. Mason Avenue, Chicago, Illinois 60638, USA for *Awake, awake* © 1983, *Here in this place* © 1982, *I am the bread* © 1971, *Take our bread, we ask you* © 1966, *Christ has died* (Wise) © 1970 and *Kyrie* (Haugen) © 1984. All rights reserved. Used by permission.

David Highams Associates Ltd, 5-8 Lower John Street, Golden Square, London, W1R 4HA for *Morning has broken* (words) © Eleanor Farjeon.

Michael Hodgetts for *God fills me with joy* (translation).

Hope Publishing Company, Carol Stream, Illinois 60188, USA for *Great is thy faithfulness* © 1923. Renewal 1951 by Hope Publishing Co. All rights reserved. Used by permission.

High-Fye Music Ltd, 8-9 Frith Street, London, W1V 5TZ for *Come and join the celebration* © 1972. All rights reserved. Used by permission.

The Iona Community, Community House, Pearce Institute, Govan, Glasgow, GS1 3UU for *Jesus Christ is waiting,* and *Will you come and follow me* © 1990 Iona Community/Wild Goose Publications.

Rev. Willard F Jabusch, Calvert House, 5735 S. University Avenue, Chicago, IL 60637, USA for the words of *He is risen, Many times I have turned, Open your ears, The King of glory comes* and *Whatsoever you do.* Used by permission.

Jubilate Hymns, 61 Chessel Avenue, Southampton, 502 4DY for *See him lying on a bed of straw* © Michael Perry/Jubilate Hymns.

Kingsway's Thankyou Music, PO Box 75, Eastbourne, East Sussex, BN23 6NW for *Abba, Father, let me be* © 1977 Kingsway's Thankyou Music, *All over the world* © 1984 Kingway's Thankyou Music, *Be still for the presence of the Lord* © 1986 Kingsway's Thankyou Music, *Bind us together, Lord* © 1977 Kingsway's Thankyou Music, *Colours of day* © 1974 Kingsway's Thankyou Music, *Come and bless, come and*